George Herbert and the Business of Practical Piety

George Herbert and the Business of Practical Piety

Nudging Towards God

CERI SULLIVAN

OXFORD
UNIVERSITY PRESS

Great Clarendon Street, Oxford, OX2 6DP,
United Kingdom

Oxford University Press is a department of the University of Oxford.
It furthers the University's objective of excellence in research, scholarship,
and education by publishing worldwide. Oxford is a registered trade mark of
Oxford University Press in the UK and in certain other countries

© Ceri Sullivan 2024

The moral rights of the author have been asserted

All rights reserved. No part of this publication may be reproduced, stored in
a retrieval system, or transmitted, in any form or by any means, without the
prior permission in writing of Oxford University Press, or as expressly permitted
by law, by licence or under terms agreed with the appropriate reprographics
rights organization. Enquiries concerning reproduction outside the scope of the
above should be sent to the Rights Department, Oxford University Press, at the
address above

You must not circulate this work in any other form
and you must impose this same condition on any acquirer

Published in the United States of America by Oxford University Press
198 Madison Avenue, New York, NY 10016, United States of America

British Library Cataloguing in Publication Data
Data available

Library of Congress Control Number: 2024931863

ISBN 9780198906810

DOI: 10.1093/9780198906841.001.0001

Printed and bound by
CPI Group (UK) Ltd, Croydon, CR0 4YY

Cover image: John Parkinson, *Paradisi in sole paradisus terrestris.*
A Garden of all Sorts of Pleasant Flowers … with
A Kitchen garden … and An Orchard (1656),
Bodleian Library, University of Oxford, R2.10 Med, title page.

Links to third party websites are provided by Oxford in good faith and
for information only. Oxford disclaims any responsibility for the materials
contained in any third party website referenced in this work.

The book is dedicated to Ian Gregson, with respect.

Acknowledgements

The book's main premise—that the doleful conclusions of predestinarian theology are challenged by the advice in practical divinity to adopt modest, tactical, and even irrational nudges to overcome despair—is based on my experience of teaching under covid. Most students oscillated between the roles of Bartleby and Pollyanna, thus forcing me into the part of Mary Poppins. Briskly, we created cognitive niches out of cheerful, concrete, and definite activities, to combat the chaos of the world outside lockdown. We might be enduring a pandemic, we told ourselves, but that should be no reason to misplace a comma or misread a sonnet.

Lockdown makes this the shortest acknowledgements page I've ever written. Derek Dunne, Lloyd Bowen, Jenny Richards, Liz Foyster, Tony Claydon, Mary Morrissey, and Andrew Hadfield kindly shared leads to sources. Helpful responses to material from the book came from participants at a Society for Renaissance Studies event on bureaucracy (organized by Derek Dunne), the University of Reading early modern seminar series (run by Mary Morrissey, Michelle O'Callaghan, and Alanna Skuse), and the Renaissance Society of America 2022 conference. I am particularly grateful to Mark Llewelyn and to the two anonymous readers for the Press, who were most generously attentive in following the intricacies of argument, and made incisive, scholarly, and helpful suggestions, which substantially improved what I was saying. The Press handled the manuscript with rapid and expert care, and I would especially like to thank Rachel Addison, Henry Clarke, Ellie Collins, and Priyan Gopathy for this.

Shorter, earlier versions of Chapters 3 and 5 have been previously published, and my thanks go to the journals' editors for their comments on the material, and permission to reproduce it here:

'George Herbert's Building Works', *Essays in Criticism*, 66 (2016), 168–197, https://doi.org/10.1093/escrit/cgw007;

'Early Modern Protestant Listicles: God's "Done" and George Herbert's "To Do" Lists', *The Review of English Studies*, 72 (2021), 85–103, https://doi.org/10.1093/res/hgaa035.

Contents

List of Figures	viii
Note on the Text and Abbreviations	ix

1. Introduction: Contracting   1
    1 Nudging the Self into Godliness   1
    2 Things Think Too   7
    3 Contracts for Godly Actions   16
    4 Herbert Gets Going   28

2. Cleaning   36
    1 Enjoying Housework   36
    2 Heart Housework   46
    3 Herbert's Housework   57

3. Building   67
    1 Ideal Spaces for Worship   67
    2 The Reality   69
    3 Obdurate Monuments   83
    4 Playing with Glass   91

4. Conversing   100
    1 Conversational Prowess at Little Gidding and Bemerton   100
    2 Advice on Amiable Conversation   107
    3 Dialogues of Reproof and Refutation   114
    4 Conversation in *The Temple*   121

5. Listing   131
    1 Lists and Cognitive Niches   131
    2 Devotional Lists to Reason with, to Delight, and to Move   136
    3 Herbert's 'Done' and 'To Do' Lists   152

6. Working to a Conclusion   162
    1 The Duty to Endure Work   162
    2 A Duty to Enjoy Work?   165
    3 Herbert Keeps Busy   177
    4 Conclusion: Reasons to be Cheerful   189

Bibliography   190
Index   206

List of Figures

2.1. Anonymous, *The Description of a Bad Housewife* (1699), Bodleian Library, University of Oxford, Ashmolean Museum Douce Prints W.1.2 (27).   42

3.1. Pierre Le Muet, *The Art of Fair Building* (1623), trans. R. Pricke (1670), Bodleian Library, University of Oxford, Vet. A3 b.35, H8r.   74

5.1. Nicholas Byfield, *The Signes, or An Essay Concerning the Assurance of Gods Love, and Mans Salvation* (1617), Bodleian Library, University of Oxford, Vet A2 f413 (1), 18.   148

6.1. John Parkinson, *Paradisi in sole paradisus terrestris. A Garden of all Sorts of Pleasant Flowers ... with A Kitchen garden ... and An Orchard* (1656), Bodleian Library, University of Oxford, R2.10 Med, title page.   167

Note on the Text and Abbreviations

All Herbert's poems have been taken from George Herbert, *The English Poems*, ed. Helen Wilcox (Cambridge: Cambridge University Press, 2007), and references to this edition are made in the text in parentheses.

References to the *George Herbert Journal* have been abbreviated to *GHJ*.

1

Introduction: Contracting

1 Nudging the Self into Godliness

This book contends that early modern devotional writing, fearing that entropy will threaten zeal, recommends self-conscious, practical, environmental nudges, which can pull a self together to make the right decisions. George Herbert's poetry is a prime site to test whether erecting cognitive niches, formed of these nudges, can help with the paralysing emotional effects of believing that divine grace alone can make works good. More widely, the book takes literary criticism's current interest in extended mind theory into a new area of behavioural economics, that of choice architecture. As payment in return, the literature studied here can help show how it feels to be nudged into action, one way or another.

Behavioural economists are fascinated by how humans so often make irrational choices. The ideal decision-maker would be one who is paying full attention, and has complete information, iron self-control, and massive cognitive ability. Real people, however, have limited time, energy, intelligence, and expertise to devote to complex decisions, especially those about unfamiliar situations or where outcomes will occur much later than the decision. Accordingly, we develop shortcuts to limit the mental resources needed to make a choice—leaving us open to being nudged subtly down a particular line by the way in which options are presented. Prospect theory studies how small changes in the environment in which a decision is made (whether physical, social, or verbal) can influence the outcome.

The early modern godly—those expert depth psychologists—were valuing nudges long before behavioural economists! Suggestions about how to frame choices to produce desired results are studied here in three early modern groups of texts: advice books (both religious and secular) about doing practical tasks, documents left by the religious community at Little Gidding founded by Herbert's friend, Nicholas Ferrar (particularly useful because the group explicitly debate how to influence their own decisions and actions), and Herbert's *The Temple* (1633), which can be read as a compendium of the techniques of choice architecture. All three groups relish the humour emerging from a life of

George Herbert and the Business of Practical Piety. Ceri Sullivan, Oxford University Press.
© Ceri Sullivan (2024). DOI: 10.1093/9780198906841.003.0001

2   INTRODUCTION: CONTRACTING

faith which is willing to guard high ideals by low cunning, stooping to use the least little things to change a self.

First, to sketch the basis of prospect theory: how do humans decide how to act? From 1969 two cognitive psychologists, Daniel Kahneman and Amos Tversky, began identifying common rules of thumb which produce predictable trends in the way people assess probable outcomes.[1] Their research was notable for relying on experiments which offered participants choices about situations and then analysed what lay behind their decisions, rather than assuming that choices were made through conscious and explicit reasoning by a *homo economicus* (the model which had dominated choice theory until then). Such empirical work showed that errors in decision-making tend to be caused by systemic biases in cognition (such as relying on implicit associations, seeking out coherent narratives, and thinking with metaphors), used to give a rapid (albeit rough) sense of reality. Kahneman and Tversky initially focused on three such heuristics as the basis of what they called prospect theory. The first is our tendency to start from, or be primed with, a known fact, and then adjust for a new situation based on this, even if the initial piece of information is not relevant: the 'anchor and adjust' heuristic. The second bias is our tendency to place undue reliance on information or examples which come easily to mind in selecting an option. The more recent, more vivid, or more personally experienced that information, the more salience it has for the chooser, who thus relies on the 'availability' heuristic. The third heuristic is our preference for options which appear to mirror what is already known or understood, such as deciding on the basis of stereotypes: the 'representativeness' heuristic. In this case, decisions are made regardless of base line probabilities, or the relative sample sizes of the two comparators, or the reliability of any prior knowledge. Those who doubt the insidious power of such nudges might glance at an unused gadget near them, and remember the internal monologue which prompted them to buy it: 'half-price—must be worth it! And I've seen the great X use one. Anyway, I always think those sorts of things come in handy when doing Y'.

---

[1] D. Kahneman, *Thinking, Fast and Slow* (2011; London: Penguin, 2012); D. Kahneman and A. Tversky, eds., *Choices, Values, and Frames* (Cambridge: Cambridge University Press, 2000); A. Tversky and D. Kahneman, 'Availability: A Heuristic for Judging Frequency and Probability', *Cognitive Psychology*, 5 (1973), 207–232; A. Tversky and D. Kahneman, 'Judgment Under Uncertainty: Heuristics and Biases', *Science*, 185 (1974), 1124–1131; A. Tversky and D. Kahneman, 'The Framing of Decisions and the Psychology of Choice', *Science*, 211 (1981), 453–458; D. Kahneman, 'New Challenges to the Rationality Assumption', *Journal of Institutional and Theoretical Economics*, 150 (1994), 18–36; D. Kahneman, J. L. Knetsch, and R. H. Thaler, 'Anomalies: the Endowment Effect, Loss Aversion, and Status Quo Bias', *Journal of Economic Perspectives*, 5 (1991), 193–206.

1 NUDGING THE SELF INTO GODLINESS 3

Over the succeeding decades, economists developed a long and horribly knowing list of other problematic biases. 'Unreasonable optimism' haunts our plans. We suffer 'loss aversion', making us twice as miserable about losing something as happy about gaining its equivalent. We go along with the status quo. We make different decisions when in an aroused emotional state than when calm. We put more weight on certain or improbable events than on events of moderate probability. We pay more attention to items ranked first and last than those in the middle. We have a herd instinct that causes us to follow others' views, partly because we think they know more than us, and partly from peer pressure. We are over-impressed with confident presentation. We internalize group decisions as our own. We make choices which we think people like us would make, regardless of what we really think (especially when we are not given anonymity).

But can anything be done about such tendencies? Nudges (for good, at least) can try to move the chooser back in the direction of accurately and helpfully assessing probabilities. In 2008 the economist Richard Thaler and jurist Cass Sunstein put forwards a theory of choice architecture, on how to use heuristics to prompt people to select options which they, in the long run, would agree were best for them. Thaler and Sunstein compiled an influential catalogue of apparently insignificant designs which policy-makers might use, focusing on techniques which affect the general public, and on techniques which the latter might use on themselves, as a form of self-help.[2] These included commitment strategies (such as publicizing plans), care over the settings for defaults, anonymizing other choosers, giving realistic anchors for a decision, mental accounting (giving attention in planned ways to different activities), setting up checklist rituals, translating alternatives into relevant terms for the choosers, structuring and reducing options to manageable numbers, giving incentives to choose well, curating the options offered, and the like. These humble and pragmatic strategies direct the decision-maker's attention meaningfully.

Although not hitherto drawn on by literary criticism, such theories have gained rapid traction in a variety of other disciplines, including medical ethics, peace negotiation studies, consumer economics, legal analysis, and wellbeing schemes. Policy-makers are attracted to them: despite worries about a lack of transparency, the techniques of choice architecture can be demonstrated to work because they involve their target audience, and they are, moreover, cheaper to use to change the attitudes (and hence actions) of citizens than are

---

[2] R. H. Thaler and C. R. Sunstein, *Nudge: Improving Decisions about Health, Wealth, and Happiness* (2008; New York: Penguin, 2009), 1–102.

4 INTRODUCTION: CONTRACTING

state mandates or central provision.[3] In 2010, for instance, the UK government set up a Behavioural Analysis Team to solve social and economic problems by nudges from the bottom rather than directives from the top. Now a part-owned government think tank, the Team's website lists a wide range of situations in which nudges are being used, from increasing disclosure of management fees on investments, to reducing plastic pollution in the Pacific, to promoting diversity in the police.[4] In 2020 the World Health Organization appointed Cass Sunstein as chair of its technical advisory group on Behavioural Insights and Sciences for Health; he had already served under the Obama administration from 2009 to 2012 in the White House Office of Information and Regulatory Affairs.

Calling on today's cognitive theory to read early modern texts involves recognizing that the mind is an historical artefact, John Sutton argues. Since distributed cognition is coupled with external resources at moments in time, then it has to be understood in its historical setting. The 'unique historical and cultural features' of the human mind are 'not accidental extras added to a basic biologically given mind', so one should 'look at activities of remembering and reasoning, imagining and decision-making, acting and feeling, in the light of cognitive artefacts of their period which have been designed to facilitate these'.[5]

Discerning the cognitive strategies in early modern godly texts sharpens our sense of just how psychologically acute and concrete were the suggestions coming from seventeenth-century practical theologians. Our own period's findings about how rarely calculation comes into human decisions pose a challenge to the Weberian argument that the Protestant ethic is a highly rational one.[6] There are, Thaler and Sunstein note, particular problems in making a good decision when feedback on it will be delayed. For a Christian, the personal costs of a godly lifestyle are front-end loaded, while the consequences of deciding to live in this way are a long way off—after death. The seventeenth-century's divines can be said to be calculating only in so far as they assume that they are dealing with the unregenerate heart, which, when faced with the clearest of choices between obedience or disobedience to God, will haver about

---

[3] P. John et al., *Nudge, Nudge, Think, Think. Experimenting with Ways to Change Civic Behaviour* (2011; London: Bloomsbury Academic, 2013), especially v–ix, 9–20.

[4] https://www.gov.uk/government/organisations/behavioural-insights-team.

[5] J. Sutton, 'Material Agency, Skills and History: Distributed Cognition and the Archaeology of Memory', in C. Knappett and L. Malafouris, eds., *Material Agency: Towards a Non-Anthropocentric Approach* (Berlin: Springer, 2008), 37–38, 44–47.

[6] M. Weber, *The Protestant Ethic and the Spirit of Capitalism*, trans. T. Parsons (1930; London: Allen & Unwin, 1985), 160–164, 174, 180 ff.

actually making that choice, or about acting on it, once made. Thus, these writers rationally propose modest and irrational means to tempt the reader to make what will turn out to be the right decision in the long run.

The other advantage of using nudge theory on seventeenth-century godly advice texts is to bring out the humour, common sense, and good will of their perspicacious authors. The latter are fully aware of the absurdity, as well as the effectiveness, of the self-conscious tricks which humans play on themselves to get those selves into line. The 'on themselves' point is important. Nudgers are sometimes accused of reducing free choice. Their defences are twofold: that all options should remain open (even if not equally easy to take), and that the aims of the nudger should be clear. These points hold in the case of early modern practical divinity, which works hard to make the way to salvation seem attractive but never blinks from looking at the other option available. Moreover, the books register the knowledge that it is not merely dangerous but also frankly absurd not to choose the good. When a 1656 chamber pot can baldly declare that 'Eart I Am Et Tes Most Tru Des Dan Me Not For So Ear You', nudging its user to laugh in solidarity with its bathetic union of the numinous and the concrete, so can more extended texts.[7]

In other words, it might be possible to trace a different tone in practical divinity—and in Herbert's poetry—to the rational, disciplined, and terrifying one which is often attributed to zealous Protestantism. From the latter angle, Peter Iver Kaufman and John Stachniewksi, for instance, demonstrate how texts can present the self as recreated by being broken apart by self-loathing, before being recast into a godly shape. Therapeutic despair was a staple of advice texts, bringing submission to God's will; feeling oneself near hell was necessary to avoiding being sent there.[8] Similarly, David Leverenz argues that Puritans had to develop psychological defences against a fear of damnation by creating an internalized superior to sternly discipline and amend a weakly sinful self. They show 'a preoccupation with should, a compulsive patterning, fear of dirt and impurity, pleasure in rigid and repetitive order, ... [and] calls for achieving self-esteem through dedicated work'.[9]

---

[7] T. Hamling, 'Old Robert's Girdle: Visual and Material Props for Protestant Piety in Post-Reformation England', in J. Martin and A. Ryrie, eds., *Private and Domestic Devotion in Early Modern Britain* (Farnham: Ashgate, 2012), 161–162.

[8] P. I. Kaufman, *Prayer, Despair, and Drama: Elizabethan Introspection* (Urbana: University of Illinois Press, 1996), 24–26, 41–71; J. Stachniewski, *The Persecutory Imagination: English Puritanism and the Literature of Religious Despair* (Oxford: Clarendon Press, 1991), 27–61.

[9] D. Leverenz, *The Language of Puritan Feeling: an Exploration in Literature, Psychology, and Social History* (New Brunswick: Rutgers University Press, 1980), 3–4, 5, 113 ff.

6   INTRODUCTION: CONTRACTING

And yet ... the tone of many books of practical divinity does not always sound so absolute. Spiritual journals do indeed have entries about how their authors have ripped up their hearts to expose their sin, in descriptions which are so powerful that it can be difficult to look beyond the extreme soteriological fear. Writers also express moments of overwhelming joy, as Alec Ryrie shows, when they feel they are in communion with God.[10] But there is a middle way between the agony and the ecstasy: a homely, part-willed cheerfulness, arising from keeping busy in the faith. Kaufman acknowledges, but does not explore, how the godly find humble ways to fulfil their obligation to live well.[11] He cites Thomas Playfere's argument that self-castigation can take away energy needed for acting well: 'We may looke back a little, and remember both what we have done ill, to amend it, and also what wee have done well to continue it. Otherwise, the remembrance eyther of vices or vertues, is so farre from putting us any whit forward, that it casteth us quite backward.'[12] Nigel Voak sketches the orthodox position voiced by Richard Hooker: the elect are 'saved on the condition of "beleving fearing and obedientlye serving", rather than absolutely without regard to their behavior ... Predestination presupposes the means of salvation ... and God wills to save the elect through the conditional means of a sanctified life'.[13] Among moderate Puritans, by contrast, Leif Dixon finds an 'emergent trend' of preparationism:

> the idea that the pre-converted believer could ready themselves for the reception of grace through prayer, repentance and godly living. They could, in other words, participate—if not, strictly speaking, in the imputation of saving faith (which must always be passively received) then in the phase of spiritual growth which led up to that point. The line between full preparation and formal conversion was potentially so finely drawn that the two could be made to collapse into each other in practice, with the effect that saving faith could more or less be self-willed.[14]

However, the advice in both cases was the same: believers could and should ignore angst and focus on living in a godly way, tending their faith to allow them to wait with patience for the arrival of grace.

---

[10] A. Ryrie, *Being Protestant in Reformation Britain* (Oxford: Oxford University Press, 2013), 80–81, 84–87.

[11] Kaufman, *Prayer, Despair, and Drama*, 24.

[12] T. Playfere, *The Pathway to Perfection* (1593), 13.

[13] N. Voak, 'English Molinism in the Late 1590s: Richard Hooker on Free Will, Predestination, and Divine Foreknowledge', *Journal of Theological Studies*, 60/1 (2009), 144 ff.; W. David Neelands, 'Predestination', in W. J. T. Kirby, ed., *A Companion to Richard Hooker* (Leiden: Brill, 2008), 187 ff.

[14] L. Dixon, *Practical Predestinarians in England, c.1590–1640* (Farnham: Ashgate, 2014), 184–196.

My argument similarly focuses not on the subtleties of who is saved or not, but on how to act, regardless. Early modern divinity instructs its readers to create cognitive niches to support cheerful, godly thought and action, in a way which is very far from being compulsive. This chapter, calling on theories of the extended mind, first asks what sort of minor physical and social structures could be put in place to scaffold decisions. The discussion then moves on to a subset of these structures: contracts with the self, written or spoken, which keep their maker acting consistently in daily life with the published self-image of the contract. Succeeding chapters look at how the everyday activities of building, cleaning, conversing, listing, and working are likewise used to influence choices.

2 Things Think Too

From 1631 the Ferrar family at Little Gidding agreed to meet regularly to discuss how to live a godly life from first principles, in the light of reason and the scriptures. Each took on an allegorical persona to speak through (either a function of the debate or a virtue they hoped to develop). Material was based on historical events, sometimes great, sometimes small, to allow everyone to consider parallels in their own lives.[15] Nicholas Ferrar acted as the secretary to the meetings (he was expert at shorthand), made occasional contributions to the discussions, and wrote them up afterwards (in texts which became known as the Little Gidding Story Books).[16] Herbert knew of these, and asked for a copy of some of the 'Storyes' in October 1631; his messenger, Arthur Woodnoth (a cousin of the Ferrars), thought Herbert would receive them 'with very great acceptation'.[17] A copy of the first of the Story Books was in the Bemerton Rectory at the time of Herbert's death, in March 1633. Woodnoth told Ferrar that in Herbert's 'first letter after the receipt of it he told me he liked it exceeding well'.[18]

---

[15] A. M. Williams, ed., *Conversations at Little Gidding ... Dialogues by Members of the Ferrar Family* (Cambridge: Cambridge University Press, 1970), xix ff. For the identity of the speakers, see xxxiii.

[16] Contrary to assertions by his early biographers, Nicholas did not script the debates. If he had, his brother John would have mentioned it in his recollections, given how meticulous he was over other details. L. R. Muir and J. A. White, eds., *Materials for the Life of Nicholas Ferrar. A Reconstruction of John Ferrar's Account of his Brother's Life, Based on All the Surviving Copies* (Leeds: Leeds Philosophical and Literary Society, 1996), 18.

[17] B. Blackstone, ed., *The Ferrar Papers* (Cambridge: Cambridge University Press, 1938), 269.

[18] A. M. Charles, *A Life of George Herbert* (Ithaca: Cornell University Press, 1977), 125.

8 INTRODUCTION: CONTRACTING

Members of the Little Academy, as they called the group, are urged by its Chief (Mary Collett) to turn to quotidian objects or events to express their ideas:

> Dimme eies see better in a shady Light then in the brightness of the Sunne, and midling Examples and arguments more prevaile with weake and feeble minds then those that are more excellent in all other kinds, so especially in Matters of Vertue. That which must strongly move to imitation must not bee too farre removed from hope of matching in some good proportion. Wonder not, therefore, if now and then you heare that which may seeme but ordinary.[19]

Framing choices by translating the options into terms most relevant for the decision-maker becomes a principle of action as well as expression among them.[20] Examining the virtues of an austere life, the Cheerful (Hester Collett) asks the Academy if they should be 'recommending good examples every day, I may say, almost all the day long, & never goe about to follow them. Why should wee not even from this Houre proportionally sett in hand with the performance of that, which we so magnifie'. The Mother (a role assumed by Mary Collett from October 1632) argues that even women can

> preach by our Actions ... Let us not blame either our sex or condition, as disabled for the advancement of Gods Kingdome. Wee have a Talent & a great one committed to us, if wee bee carefull to imploy it, Not in the Tongue, No, that belongs to the Ministry but in the hands & in the feet, that's common to all Christians. Wee may tread out the way to heaven & wee may lead on by good works.[21]

Little Academy stories developed this principle, as in their tale of a bishop who was trying to get his mother to give alms during her lifetime rather than doing so in her will. 'Her good son perceiving that by solid Arguments he was not able to perswade her, bethought himself by a more plaine & material kind of proof to convince her'. He told her he would send torches after her to light her over a dangerous bridge, rather than sending them before her.[22]

---

[19] E. Cruwys Sharland, ed., *The Story Books of Little Gidding. Being the Religious Dialogues Recited in the Great Room, 1631–2* (London: Seely and Co., 1899), 21.

[20] Thaler and Sunstein, *Nudge*, 25, 100–101.

[21] Williams, ed., *Conversations*, 171–172.

[22] Williams, ed., *Conversations*, 11.

The debaters (like the bishop) use an object or action as a metaphor to explicate an opinion. Recently, however, religious historians have pointed out how the physical world plays a more central role in devotion, basing their arguments on millennial research into cognitive anthropology and philosophy.

In the mid-1990s the anthropologist Edwin Hutchins influentially argued that systems of cultural activity have cognitive properties of their own which are different from those of the individuals who work in those systems. He brought ethnographic skills to studying how decision-making structures worked in a goal-oriented setting (a US Navy ship, which had lost power and needed to navigate into deep water to coast to a stop). Hutchins found that the cognitive processes used to do so were not internal, but partially and provisionally internalized from physical artefacts, learned concepts and skills, and social relations, both institutional (between ranks and roles held by the navigation team and officers) and personal. 'Humans create their cognitive powers by creating the environments in which they exercise those powers', he concluded.[23] Language may be the agent in such environments which is most readily recognized by literary critics, but it is not the only feature of a cognitive niche.

Around the same time, philosophers Andy Clark and David Chalmers devised a much-discussed thought experiment involving the amnesiac 'Otto' and his notebook, in which are written directions to get to places in New York. Clark and Chalmers argue, like Hutchins, that in the limit case of Otto—but also more widely—the environment takes an active role in driving cognition. Cognition is not a brain-bound activity, but unevenly distributed across social, technological, physical, and biological realms. The human mind is born a cyborg, in this functionalist approach; indeed, Clark and Chalmers claim, since both the human mind and its environment cause cognitive processing, they should have parity of status.[24]

Religious historians have taken up these lines of argument to investigate how domestic objects or practices could be coupled into a cognitive system of devotion. The issue of using external ceremonies to create a feeling of reverence was fought out in the early modern period in the field of liturgical theology.

---

[23] E. Hutchins, *Cognition in the Wild* (Cambridge, MA: M. I. T. Press, 1995), xvi.

[24] A. Clark and D. Chalmers, 'The Extended Mind', *Analysis*, 58/1 (1998), 7–19; A. Clark, *Supersizing the Mind: Embodiment, Action and Cognitive Extension* (Oxford: Oxford University Press, 2011), 44–59, 220–232; R. Menary, 'Introduction: the Extended Mind in Focus', in R. Menary, ed., *The Extended Mind* (Cambridge, MA: M. I. T. Press, 2010), 1–26.

10   INTRODUCTION: CONTRACTING

As urged by Hooker (at the time, vicar of Bishopsborne, Kent), the use of ceremonies makes an observer

> stirred vp vnto ... reuerence, deuotion, attention & due regard ... Unto this purpose not only speech, but sundry sensible means besides haue alwaies bin thought necessary, & especially those means which being obiect to the eye, the liueliest & the most apprehensiue sense of all other, haue in that respect seemed the fittest to make a deepe and strong impression; from hence haue risen not onely a number of praiers, readings, questionings, exhortings, but euen of visible signes also.[25]

Now this practice was brought home by the radical godly—literally: homely cognitive niches were created to transform a domestic space into a place which inspired zeal. This was not a case of second-generation reformers dolefully retreating indoors to reform themselves, having failed to bring the national church into line. The godly were thinking of Protestantism as a communal and dynamic force to reach its members at the most personal and local of levels.

Jill Stevenson, Tara Hamling, Joe Moshenka, and Matthew Milner have shown how conceptual blending, in which various mental and physical inputs are combined by the mind, turns devotional objects and gestures into material anchors for spiritual experience. Such things hover between the physical and the metaphorical. These commentators call for a study of religious items in action and use, not as static devotional objects. Grasping an object, such as a girdle prayer book, or developing a habit of making a devout gesture when doing a daily task, such as uttering an ejaculatory prayer when lighting a bedroom candle, can bring godly feelings from the past to mind and reignite them in the present.[26] For instance, Herbert, 'to testifie his independencie upon all others, and to quicken his diligence ... used in his ordinarie speech, whenever he made mention of the blessed name of our Lord and Saviour Jesus Christ, to adde, *My Master*' (as Ferrar's preface to *The Temple* explains).[27] Moreover, he speaks about how he writes the phrase '*Lesse then the least/ Of all thy mercies*' 'on my ring,/ ... by my picture, in my book' ('The Poesie'). In both instances,

---

[25] R. Hooker, *Of the Lawes of Ecclesiasticall Politie* (1593), 168.

[26] J. Stevenson, *Performance, Cognitive Theory, and Devotional Culture: Sensual Piety in Late Medieval York* (New York: Palgrave Macmillan, 2010), 87–89, 104–113; Hamling, 'Visual and Material Props', 145–148; M. Milner, *The Senses and the English Reformation* (Farnham: Ashgate, 2011), 132–134, 186–199; J. Moshenka, '"A Sensible Touching, Feeling and Groping": Metaphor and Sensory Experience in the English Reformation', in B. Cummings and F. Sierhuis, eds., *Passions and Subjectivity in Early Modern Culture* (Farnham: Ashgate, 2013), 190–198.

[27] H. Wilcox, ed., *The English Poems of George Herbert* (Cambridge: Cambridge University Press, 2007). All citations of Herbert's poems will be taken from this edition.

he consciously shapes a verbal or physical environment in order to set up his future mental state.

Texts as well as objects were part of this environment. Mary Patterson argues that popular godly books told 'their readers and hearers that it is in the most prosaic challenges of daily realities ... that the deepest opportunities lie for experiencing the divine', through small, portable texts 'supplying the word of encouragement before a difficult conversation, or in a moment of temptation, or a sudden stab of grief'.[28] Andrew Cambers, showing how often godly books were read out aloud in many households, points out that although in doctrinal and ecclesiological terms early modern Protestantism appears to be a religion of isolated interiority, its devotional practices were often communal and sociable.[29]

Take the example of Nehemiah Wallington, a London turner, whose copious journals and private papers give insight into the life of a zealous Protestant (his editors talk of him as typical in attitude, if not in the volume of his writings). Like Herbert, Wallington used practical external means to inspire internal exhortation and reproof. The sin of anger, for instance, he tried to curb by removing himself from its occasion: leaving the room or the house altogether, or going to bed until the feeling had passed (and then 'I have rose and put one my cloes and have bine frends againe'). The sin of feeling dull at church services he dealt with by pinching himself or stabbing himself with a pin. However, since he did not always do this hard enough to rouse himself ('nature wil favour itselfe in these things', he noted sagely), he took instead to biting into pepper, ginger, or cloves when he felt sleepy (the sounds and smells from the Wallington family pew must have been unusual!)[30] Wallington also turned to books and religious artefacts to help him keep his word. His failure to keep the godly resolutions he had made when he got married, for instance, made him so unhappy that he began to dwell on thoughts of death. He turned these thoughts to good account by surrounding himself with appropriate props, in a touchingly thorough way: buying Christopher Sutton's best-selling *Disce Mori: Learn How to Die*, a range of funeral sermons, some pictures about death, and his most cherished piece of kitsch, an 'Anotime [anatomy] of Death, and litel black coffin to put it in, and upon it written Meemento Mory' (which he moved

---

[28] M. Patterson, *Domesticating the Reformation: Protestant Best Sellers, Private Devotion, and the Revolution of English Piety* (Cranbury: Fairleigh Dickinson Press, 2007), 37, 53.

[29] A. Cambers, *Godly Reading: Print, Manuscript and Puritanism in England, 1580–1720* (Cambridge: Cambridge University Press, 2011), 7–10, 31–33.

[30] N. Wallington, *The Notebooks of Nehemiah Wallington, 1618–1654. A Selection*, ed. D. Booy (Aldershot: Ashgate, 2007), 46–47.

12 INTRODUCTION: CONTRACTING

around with him over the course of the day, from bedside to dining table and back).[31]

The early modern godly also took up the opportunities of socially extending acts of devotion. Sometimes, this was mere cognitive thrift, which off-loaded activity onto the environment.[32] For instance, in 1605 Samuel Page (chaplain to the Earl of Nottingham) described how the latter's dying son-in-law, Sir Richard Loveson, used him as part of Loveson's extended mind. Loveson felt his memory and understanding becoming so weakened that he was not able to lay his heart open to scrutiny or find fit words to pray. Thus he 'earnestly desired [Page] to conceive a form of confession of his sins to God, and a prayer for those mercies which I might leave with him when I should depart from him'. Page considered that he 'soone satisfied him, for I had more use herein of my memory of that which he had delivered to me [before, in conference] than of my invention for that which I was to deliver to him'. After Loveson had used Page's words, he asked Page to supply 'the weakness of his memory' in finding further fit thoughts for a dying man.[33] Effectively, Page starts as Loveson's external memory, giving back to him what Page had heard Loveson confess before, then turns into a storehouse of other material to be investigated.

Sometimes shared worship is used to amplify a spirit of grace. Foulke Robarts (prebendary of Norwich) notes 'how doth the visible and expressive devotion of one Christian, beget and encrease the same in an other'. By marking and copying others' demeanour, the believer's own feelings are amplified, for 'there is such correspondency, and sympathy between the Soule and the body; as maketh to accord with one an other, like those Creatures and wheels' (referring to Ezekiel 1.20–21, where spirits power God's chariot).

> Every man findeth in his owne experience, that his Soule doth sympathise with the temper of his body. For, if the body be tired with labour, the mind becometh heavy and dull. And do wee not perceive plainely, that when we betake our selves to our knees for prayer, the Soule is humbled within us, by this very gesture? And when wee lift up our hands and our eyes towards God, wee feel an elevation of the Soule also towards the throne of grace.[34]

John Swan (curate of Duxford St Peter, Cambridgeshire) likewise speaks of how, 'by outward ceremonies, and sensible signes, our mind is incited to tend

---

[31] Wallington, *Notebooks*, ed. Booy, 270–271.
[32] W. Fitzgerald, *Spiritual Modalities: Prayer as Rhetoric and Performance* (University Park, P. A.: Penn State University Press, 2012), 111, 113–114.
[33] S. Page, *A Sermon Preached at the Funerall of ... S. Richard Loveson* (1605), B4r, C2v–C3r.
[34] F. Robarts, *Gods Holy House and Service* (1639), *3r, 61–62.

towards the Lord'; 'let so cheerefall and so good a light shine forth before men, that thereby the forwardnesse and alacrity of one, may stir up the dull drooping soule of another'.[35]

Robarts and Swan are describing what today's theologians Warren Brown and Brad Strawn (drawing on Clark's term) call a 'super sizing' of a believer's awareness of God's presence, which may occur when worshippers come together in person. Brown and Strawn argue that the soul is not disembodied, apart from the rest of creation, but formed by its interactions with the world. Communal worship offers experiences of spirituality which are not accessible to individual worshippers, based on shared attention and an unconscious imitation of others' gestures, expressions, and tones of voice, all of which create empathy with others' underlying emotions and thoughts. Like Otto's notebook, for a church member 'the church *holds* my beliefs ... is the place where I go to be *reminded* of what I believe, even believes *for* me when I can't believe myself. And these beliefs are held, repeated, and referenced over and over via elements such as liturgical readings, creeds, songs, sermons, and the like'.[36]

This approach does not assert that such actions create a conduit of grace: my argument skirts the current vigorous debate among Herbert critics about his position on ceremonies, especially the sacraments. Achsah Guibbory argues that his poems express the period's tussle between a ceremonial integration of spiritual and corporeal experience and a puritan ideology which wishes to separate the two. The challenge which Herbert faces in his poetry, of 'how to create a non-idolatrous devotion', is settled, she concludes, by him valuing objects for their ability to prompt meditation.[37] Robert Whalen coins the term 'sacramental Puritanism' for Calvinist interiorized ceremony, which is sufficient 'to penetrate and to articulate the innermost workings of the soul', particularly through its use of eucharistic topoi (such as water, wine, grapes, bread, eating, and the altar) to express how divinity suffuses creation. 'If anyone created a devotional space susceptible to predestinarian anxiety and doubt' it was Herbert, Whalen argues, but 'it is precisely his stubborn fondness for sacrament and ceremony that allowed [him] to avoid the potentially

---

[35] J. Swan, *Profano-mastix. Or, a Briefe and Necessarie Direction Concerning the Respects which Wee Owe to God, and His House* (1639), 46, 55.

[36] W. S. Brown and B. D. Strawn, *The Physical Nature of Christian Life: Neuroscience, Psychology, and the Church* (Cambridge: Cambridge University Press, 2012), 2–8, 121–139; W. S. Brown and B. D. Strawn, 'Beyond the Isolated Self: Extended Mind and Spirituality', *Theology and Science*, 15/4 (2017), 411–423.

[37] A. Guibbory, *Ceremony and Community from Herbert to Milton: Literature, Religion, and Cultural Conflict in Seventeen-century England* (Cambridge: Cambridge University Press, 1998), 45, 69.

14 INTRODUCTION: CONTRACTING

paralyzing syndromes of an otherwise puritan psyche.'[38] Ryan Netzley argues that Herbert's poems attempt to preserve desire for Christ's presence, even while worshipping it as a grace already obtained: 'the eucharist enjoins an affective, intensive attachment to an immanent divinity, but does not imagine the ceremony as overcoming a dialectical division between inner and outer, immanent and transcendent realms, or human and divine spheres.'[39] Kimberly Johnson is interested not so much in the sacramental theology of the poems as in the way poetic language, claiming to embody meaning, works when dealing with the eucharist. She concludes that, in Herbert, poetic forms, anagrams, and graphic confusion make present what appears to be absent: Christ's grace. Thus, the poems are a 'ritual of material immanence.'[40]

Whalen emphasizes that this communion is both 'psychological and ceremonial'. However, my own approach focuses on the former element, and does not engage with eucharistic topoi. Instead, it asks how the godly, including Herbert, arrange the quotidian material of their lives—their buildings, households, conversations, texts, and occupations—*prior* to receiving grace, and irrespective of how confident they are that it will be granted as a result of their actions. They see preparation as a godly duty, regardless of its results.

In looking at the physical and social conditions which help fulfil this duty, my argument comes close to existing studies which recognize how Herbert thinks through metaphors of an ailing body, in which his images of poor digestion, ill health, infection, and disability are seen as dynamic responses to his spiritual crises.[41] However, my perspective is closer still to recent studies into the devotional implications of extended mind theory. Brent Dawson argues that the meditative strain in Herbert's poetry offers a materialist account of distributed cognition. Since God is in all his creatures, Herbert recognizes an existence in common with them, even as he celebrates their infinite variety in such poems as 'Providence.'[42] David Glimp goes further: 'more than a

---

[38] R. Whalen, *The Poetry of Immanence: Sacrament in Donne and Herbert* (Toronto: University of Toronto Press, 2002), xii–xvii, 112, 126.

[39] R. Netzley, *Reading, Desire, and the Eucharist in Early Modern Religious Poetry* (Toronto: University of Toronto Press, 2011), 23–25, 33.

[40] K. Johnson, *Made Flesh: Sacrament and Poetics in Post-Reformation England* (Philadelphia: University of Pennsylvania Press, 2014), 30, 43–52.

[41] For instance, M. Schoenfeldt, *Bodies and Selves in Early Modern England* (Cambridge: Cambridge University Press, 1999), 96–130; D. Thorley, '"In All a Weak Disabled Thing": Herbert's Ill-Health and its Poetic Treatments', *GHJ*, 34/1–2 (2010–2011), 1–33; Y. Yan, 'George Herbert and Plague', *GHJ*, 36/1 (2012), 77–98; S. Skwise, 'George Herbert, Sin, and the Ague', *GHJ*, 28 (2004–2005), 1–27; C. Chenovick, '"A Balsome for Both the Hemispheres": Tears as Medicine in Herbert's *Temple* and Seventeenth-Century Preaching', *ELH*, 84/3 (2017), 559–590.

[42] B. Dawson, 'The Life of the Mind: George Herbert, Early Modern Meditation, and Materialist Cognition', *ELH*, 86/4 (2019), 895–918.

collection of objects upon which one might meditate, the creature was also understood to possess a devotional agency all its own'. Glimp draws parallels with such biblical passages as Psalm 148, where a vast network of human and non-human creatures worship God. The latter demonstrate a mode of belief not rooted in consciousness, and so are able through their mode of being to register God's presence without distraction, inconsistency, or hypocrisy, problems which trouble the humans trying to praise him.[43]

An influential theorist of distributed cognition in early modern literary studies, Miranda Anderson, offers a fascinating hint of how Glimp's position might be taken further still. She argues that early modern divines thought of 'man as a decentred and synecdochal subject because he was both a creation and an extension of God'. Individuals are extended through their bodies, through other people, and through the world. All these are creations of—extensions of—God, but also, since the Fall, separated from the divine.[44] Such extended subjectivity has ethical implications, Anderson points out, since if a self is thought to be mutable, and formed by multiple elements, then there is a collective responsibility for its actions. Anderson's concern is with Renaissance humanist and scientific models of the soul, so she does not take this line of thought into the private devotional practice of the period. This leaves room for me to consider the opportunities and challenges the concept of the extended mind poses when meeting the extreme logic of predestination, under which humanity does not own its own thoughts and actions (expressed by Herbert in the entwined pronouns of 'Clasping of Hands', where 'thou are mine, and I am thine,/ If mine I am: and thine much more'). I will argue that one of the affordances of words, objects, and activities for Herbert is their potential to adopt him as part of a self that is God's. They have agency, even if he does not. In 'The H. Scriptures II', for instance, God's 'words do finde me out, & parallels bring,/ And in another make me understood' and, in 'Affliction' 3, 'My heart did heave, and there came forth, *O God!*' His own heart is only part of the whole environment through which God's will is manifested. In fact, taking Clark and Chalmer's Otto as the model, Herbert might be said to become God's notebook!

---

[43] D. Glimp, 'Figuring Belief: George Herbert's Devotional Creatures', in J. H. Anderson and J. Pong Linton, eds., *Go Figure: Energies, Forms, and Institutions in the Early Modern World* (New York: Fordham University Press, 2011), 113–114, 122–127.

[44] M. Anderson, *The Renaissance Extended Mind* (Basingstoke: Palgrave Macmillan, 2015), 60–62, 81, 155.

16   INTRODUCTION: CONTRACTING

3 Contracts for Godly Actions

Contracts, resolutions, and commitments are a subset of environmental nudges, in which an individual potentially puts herself into an embarrassing situation, should she not live up to her publicized plan. Charles Lloyd Cohn shows how the word 'covenant' in the early seventeenth century had two contrasting connotations: the bargain and the alliance. The first covenant with God was held to be that of works, which humanity was able to perform because Adam had been created sufficient to have fulfilled the terms of his bargain with God. However, a covenant of grace, an alliance between God and humanity, was needed after the Fall, under which aid was freely transferred from the former to the latter.[45] An increasingly contractual vocabulary was used by early seventeenth-century conformist divines, including William Perkins, Richard Sibbes, and John Preston, and studies of covenant theology in Herbert's poems tend to draw on these writers to argue about whether Herbert viewed covenants made between God and humanity as undertakings by the two parties which were bilateral (a bargain) or unilateral (an alliance).[46] Richard Strier, for instance, argues that Herbert rejects the idea that God's grace can be resisted or bargained for, taking a 'grandly condescending attitude' to any worry that God will not save those who believe in him.[47] Other Herbert scholars, such as Clarissa Chenovick and Kristine Wolberg, lean more on Herbert's insistence that the soul could cooperate with God by preparing itself to receive grace, hence fulfilling its side of a covenant.[48]

The following discussion differs from these commentators by concentrating not on the theology of the covenant, but on the psychology behind agreeing with oneself, or with a group, over ways to live in the future. How does a covenant prompt one to behave?

Like many other families, the Little Gidding community used writing to scaffold a godly environment. 'Advises in a written Book', drawn up by Ferrar, cover how the household was to behave in a variety of situations, from running its pharmacy, to praying during the night watches, to relaxing with appropriate pastimes.[49] Collections of godly sayings to guide conduct were pinned up on

---

[45] C. Lloyd Cohen, *God's Caress: The Psychology of Puritan Religious Experience* (New York: Oxford University Press, 1986), 48–72.

[46] R. Strier, *Love Known: Theology and Experience in George Herbert's Poetry* (Chicago: University of Chicago Press, 1983), 84–113. See also L. Gordis, 'The Experience of Covenant Theology in George Herbert's *The Temple*', *Journal of Religion*, 76/3 (1996), 383–401.

[47] Strier, *Love Known*, 112.

[48] Chenovick, 'Tears', 261–267; K. Wolberg, 'Posture and Spiritual Formation: Sanctification in George Herbert's *The Country Parson* and *The Temple*', *Christianity and Literature*, 66/1 (2016), 57–72.

[49] Blackstone, ed., *Ferrar Papers*, 21.

3 CONTRACTS FOR GODLY ACTIONS   17

the walls of Little Gidding, and the dining room even had blank tablets to be inscribed with useful points as they came to mind. Such writing on domestic walls and furnishings was widespread, and served the same two functions as a godly conduct book, Hamling observes, of regulating habits of thought and behaviour, and of advertising how spiritual concerns were at the heart of home life.[50]

More unusual was Little Gidding's solemn habit of writing out a decision which had been made, then reading the document out aloud, then handing over the script, then noting down the circumstances in which it had been delivered. In 1626, on the night after Nicholas Ferrar had been ordained deacon, he 'came home to his Mother, & prayed her to hear him read what he had to shew her written in Vellome, which he drew forth from his breast, which read was the Solemn [vow to take orders] he had therein made to God, written and signed with his own hand.'[51] In 1631 Anna Collett gave her sister a letter to deliver to Ferrar, asking him to support her decision to stay unmarried. Even then, Ferrar insisted on a cooling-off period, requiring Anna to 'keepe it by her' for a day, before he read it 'in the Afternoone' in her sister's presence.[52] When Woodnoth consulted Herbert about whether to change career path, Herbert heard him out and reserved judgement overnight. When they met the next day, Woodnoth found that Herbert 'for better satisfaction of mee had sett down his opinion in writing that I might the better consider of itt which hee first read [out] & then delivered mee.'[53] When John Ferrar was in dispute with his wife Bathsheba, he affirmed that 'often in writing' he had confirmed he wanted to content her, and added that 'what Ever yeat there was that troubled her in this or any other thing lett her give me notise of it in writing', and he would act on it.[54] Nicholas took the same path with Bathsheba on another occasion. His diary notes how, on 'Saterd: morning the 22 may 1636— my sister [in-law] came to me and after much discours on her parte to which I made noe aunswere at all I wrote the ensuing paper which I reade to her in her husbands presence and afterwards offered it to her but shee went away'. He later reflected on how the meeting had gone:

> my sister having heard this paper after Shee had Interrupted it with many undue speeches which God I humbly beseech him to Cancell That they

[50] T. Hamling, *Decorating the 'Godly' Household: Religious Art in Post-Reformation Britain* (New Haven: Yale University Press, 2010), 23.
[51] Blackstone, ed., *Ferrar Papers*, 26.
[52] Blackstone, ed., *Ferrar Papers*, 264–266.
[53] Blackstone, ed., *Ferrar Papers*, 267.
[54] Blackstone, ed., *Ferrar Papers*, 280.

18 INTRODUCTION: CONTRACTING

> rise not upp agaynst her departed away—not accepting the writing which I reached forth unto her but without saying any one word for in truth my hearte [warns] mee not to dare to speake in these like occasions.[55]

Even on his deathbed, Ferrar remembered to confirm in writing that he had verbally ordered that his hampers of secular books be burned.[56]

Joyce Ransome is 'surprised' and 'curious' about the family's habit of making covenants, writing out solemn promises, and sending letters to coinhabitants. She thinks it arises from Ferrar's aim to make the community an example for other groups to follow. The increasing size of the household permitted a 'more elaborate programme of devotions', which had, accordingly, to be ordered carefully and which were more likely to continue if members felt a voluntary commitment to their aims. Hence, Ferrar stressed gaining explicit assent to specific proposals by all would-be participants. Ransome also suggests that Ferrar's leadership style was more persuasive than commanding; putting issues into writing rather than discussing them face to face might minimize personal conflict and emotional confrontation.[57]

These explanations, which take account of Ferrar's point of view, might be supplemented by a third: the way people use peer pressure and publicized plans to nudge themselves. For instance, the Little Academy was set up by members entering

> into a joynt Covenant between themselves & some others of Neerest Bloud ... for the performance of divers Religious Exercizes, Least as sweet Liquours are oftentimes corrupted by the sowreness of the vessels wherein they are infused, there should arise in their hearts a Distaste or Abuse of those Excellent things, which they proposed.

Such a commitment strategy tries to pre-empt any future falling off by being definite about the activities to be undertaken, such as agreeing 'every day at a sett houre to conferre together of some such subject' that would aid a better 'Course of Life'.[58] Moreover, the confident presentation of such a promise by one of the group influences its take-up by the others.[59] When the Guardian (John Ferrar) makes a vow, the Chief says that 'this Resolution is not now to be

---

[55] Blackstone, ed., *Ferrar Papers*, 292, 294.

[56] Blackstone, ed., *Ferrar Papers*, 62–63.

[57] J. Ransome, *The Web of Friendship: Nicholas Ferrar and Little Gidding* (Cambridge: James Clarke and Co., 2011), 14, 20, 67, 74–77, 110, 195.

[58] Williams, *Conversations*, 3, 5. On planning ahead, see Thaler and Sunstein, *Nudge*, 44–49.

[59] On the confidence heuristic, see Thaler and Sunstein, *Nudge*, 58.

made on your part, though it now to bee published. Not for the Confirmation of your own purposes, which are enrolled in a higher Court, but for our Invitation to the like'.[60] Deciding whether to celebrate Christmas in a solely spiritual way (no feasting or secular entertainments), the Moderator (Susannah Ferrar Collett) wants the issue to be settled by it being

> personally voted, whether the Encrease in Gods grace be the cheif of our desires & ends. Not that I feare any Bodies dissent, but that I hold it Necessarie, that every one, whom it concernes, should actually express their Agreements in the Foundation, before wee goe forward with the Building.

In other words, the vote is not to inform the decision about cancelling Christmas festivities, but to bind the voters by a public repetition of what they have previously committed to.[61] The Patient (Anna Collett) sees the sense in this: 'you say very well. An Explicite assent will in this case be needfull like the subscription of hands in publick attempts to bind men the firmer to the performance of what they undertake. I for my part make profession'. This confident assertion precipitates a cascade of agreements by the Affectionate (Margaret or Elizabeth Collett) and the Guardian ('therein I joyn with you' and 'I give my Ball to the advancement of this self same end').[62] These then allow the Patient to go further still: the aim is not merely to get a 'particular declaration like these, that have now beene made, from the rest of our Familie in this way', but also 'a profession on their behalf, that cannot doe it themselves by those, that have the Cheif interest in them'.[63]

Debora Shuger argues that, 'given that the Ferrar uncles had been senior members of the Virginia Company', they knew of, and deliberately chose, forms based on equality for religious self-dedication, using 'voting and covenanting' as 'a group formulating its own rules', with 'members freely binding themselves to obey them'.[64] Night watches in the chapel, for instance, were supposed only to be done by those 'who should of their own free will and choice approve of the thing for none should be enforced or the less well thought of that did not only like of it, or would not be ready to take a part in it', according to John Ferrar.[65]

---

[60] Williams, *Conversations*, 60.
[61] On the consistency bias, see Thaler and Sunstein, *Nudge*, 7–8, 71–72.
[62] On informational cascades, see Thaler and Sunstein, *Nudge*, 53–57.
[63] Williams, *Conversations*, 76–79.
[64] D. Shuger, 'Laudian Feminism: The Household Republic of Little Gidding', *Journal of Medieval and Early Modern Studies*, 44/1 (2014), 85.
[65] Muir and White, eds., *Ferrar*, 92.

20 INTRODUCTION: CONTRACTING

However, as the existence of such commitment strategies suggests, there were implicit limits on this apparent freedom. The Little Gidding community was encouraged to remember it was always being observed by God (the Submisse, Joyce Collett, sings a hymn in one session about how you are 'alone less never are/ Then when alone you seeme').[66] Members applauded a story about such unavoidable scrutiny, in which a holy man in disguise comes to see Lais, a famous courtesan of Alexandria. She leads her apparent client into a 'stately roome'; 'not secret enough', he objects. She takes him into an inner room; 'not sure enough', he says, 'is there yet no more private Chamber?' Lais replies that her 'Cabbinet is more remote, and altogether fitt for your shamefast heart. With that she unlocks the dore, and smilingly tells him, Now you may be bold, for but God in heaven, none can see nor know what is done here'. The holy man then springs his trap: God is watching them, right now![67]

Moreover, as Joyce Ransome observes, backsliders had the family to deal with, though she warns that the degree of peer pressure which was exerted is 'challenging to evaluate in retrospect' (and, she notes shrewdly, would have varied depending on an individual's position in the family hierarchy).[68] Nicholas Ferrar's own room was in the middle of the building, in order that he could 'hear and see good order observed'.[69] The Mother nudges acceptance of the Christmas proposal by an appeal to group observation:

because the matter is so weighty & ought to be altogether voluntarie, I shall advize the deferring of it for the present. & that in the end the performance may bee made in writing, which were [to] more solemly oblige them, who agree & more seriously & plainly represent their true condition and Estate to them, who shall refuse this subscription.[70]

Ferrar Collett, though, does not stop there, asking the Moderator (his mother) to

impose on him by way of her Motherly Command the perpetual Observancie of this good Counsell ... & by Doubling of the Obligation to bind himself the

---

[66] Sharland, ed., *Little Gidding*, 72.
[67] Sharland, ed., *Little Gidding*, 195.
[68] J. Ransome, 'George Herbert, Nicholas Ferrar, and the "Pious Works" of Little Gidding', *GHJ*, 31/1–2 (2007), 3; Ransome, *Web of Friendship*, 14, 114–115, 148–153.
[69] Sharland, ed., *Little Gidding*, xxv.
[70] Williams, *Conversations*, 179; on peer pressure, see Thaler and Sunstein, *Nudge*, 54–60, 66–72.

3 CONTRACTS FOR GODLY ACTIONS 21

more firmly in his inward Affections & to provide a safe & ready ward against all outward Assaults either of violence or intreatie … [which] would be cleane deaded by the opposal of this solemne injunction.

Effectively, he edits down his future options to choose how to act in the future, at any time of the year. The Moderator

gladly accorded ye grant of her sons Petition & so by an absolute Command makes it an undefeazable Obligation by a Tripartite Covenant between God, Himself, & his Freinds. That he should never goe into Tavern or Ale-house to drink wine or any strong Liquor of what kind soever for his own or any others Pleasure whosoever.[71]

The group find eliminating or curating possible choices an effective nudge. By 1634 meetings of the Academy had been halted for nearly two years, despite the wishes of Mary Ferrar. However,

finding that the intimation of her desires by word of mouth did not prevail for the renewing and prosecution of this intermitted work, she preceeded to the expressing of them by writing with such Lowlines of intreaty where she had the right of Command … [as was] found upon Record signed with her own hand.

After her death, the others agree to restart the dialogues, but decide 'to make shew of the matter as a Practize of Dutie rather then of voluntary choice, representing it with the stamp of her injunction upon it to any, that should call it into question'. This group decision to declare to others that they have no power of choice safely locates that power in a post-dated resolution by another, on their behalf. The newly reformed group allow different participants to join them in the debates as long as the invitees will say 'Conditionally, that they would be subject to the main Laws of the Busines'. Thus, an 'offer of Admission into Copacinery' (a joint share in an inheritance) is made to Susanna Mapletoft, provided she 'would Conform her self to the Common Agreements & Resolutions of the Societie'.

---

[71] Blackstone, ed., *Ferrar Papers*, 100–102; on reducing choices, see Thaler and Sunstein, *Nudge*, 97–98.

22 INTRODUCTION: CONTRACTING

The Resolved (John Collett) suggests, moreover, that the Academicians should move from discussion to action:

> every one should be bound to the performance of what they spake, Making their practizes keep equall pace to their Discourses. That is, Every one ratably and respectively to doe that, which they particularly undertook for themselves, or imposed as necessarie on others of like disposition & Quality to themselves.
>
> This Condition, however it did at first proposal somewhat startle the rest, yet being upon serious thought & solemne Discussion found every way reasonable, as including Justice, Benefitt, & Necessitie, was formally ratifyed by particular subscription of every one of their Hands.

Once again, peer pressure is brought into play:

> it was adjudged absolutely necessary, that it should be distended in writing for the clearer Expression of their present intents, & for their surer Obligation to the Constant Practize of them. Whilest they should by this meanes become lyable not only to the secret remorse of their own Consciences, but to the smart & shame of open reproof & Tax from the world, remayning Prevaricators upon Record, If they should doe lesse or otherwise then they had thus bound themselves unto by deed indented and Enrolled.

The resulting document is signed by all members, with a 'sincere and irrevocable Protestation of Putting in Execution' its resolutions.[72] Such a contract becomes a self-conscious, self-fulfilling prophecy: the Academicians are thinking about how (rather than about what) they currently think and how this may change in the future, so determining an appropriate social structure to influence this.

Little Gidding was not the only household whose legalistic approach nudged its members into compliance with resolutions they had made earlier. Ryrie notes that early reformers distrusted covenants, as showing a sinful reliance either on their maker's own willpower or in the power of the vow itself. By the 1590s, however, the godly acknowledged that since vows were used by biblical figures they could still be made, provided certain conditions were observed: subject matter was not to be immoral or trifling, and vowers had to have the power to bind themselves (so married women, for instance, could not make vows about subjects on which they owed obedience to their husbands). Collective covenants, where the participants undertook to help keep one another to

---

[72] Blackstone, ed., *Ferrar Papers*, 108–111.

their promises, were encouraged.[73] For instance, on 6 August 1629, thirty godly inhabitants of Salem, Massachusetts, agreed to enter into a 'solemn Covenant with God, and one another'. Copies were written out for each person of a 'Confession of Faith and Covenant in Scripture-language', which was agreed as an overall 'direction'. To ensure that it was the spirit not the form of words which was being sworn to, 'no man was confined unto that form of words, but onely to the Substance, End, and Scope of the matter contained therein'. Future members of the group would have to give written consent to the covenant, or to offer written or publicly spoken witness to their belief and conversion.[74]

Confidence in the power of self-contracting produced lists of articles to reform home life, such as the ones which Wallington repeatedly drew up for himself and his household. He went one better than popular domestic handbooks, such as *Of Domesticall Duties* (1622) by William Gouge (a celebrated preacher at Blackfriars, London), which frames the duties of each role in a household (husbands, wives, children, masters, and servants) as a matter of maintaining suitable attitudes in relationships. The articles which Wallington's household eventually signed up to are more pragmatic: they focus on actions rather than attitudes, and impose a cash fine if a fault is committed. Thus, where Gouge speaks movingly of how husbands and wives should pray together as a 'mutuall dutie which one oweth to the other', giving each other every blessing and help they can, and being always 'mindfull of one another', Wallington's list says baldly and briskly:

First, that we pray all together every morning & evening if we can convenient, or else by our selves. If not to pay to the poors box a penny ...

4. That they that lie till six o'clock upon the Lords' Day, then they pay a farthing ...

8. If any counsel [conceal] the faults of the ware, or use words of deceit, or take more for the ware than it is worth, then to pay to the poors' box a half-penny.

9. If any tell a lie, then to pay one penny ...

To these laws we all set our hands: NW [Nehemiah Wallington], GW [Grace Wallington], James Wells, Obediah Sely, Theophilus Ward, Susan Patie.[75]

---

[73] Ryrie, *Being Protestant*, 131–140.
[74] Cited in E. S. Morgan, *Visible Saints: The History of a Puritan Idea* (Ithaca: Cornell University Press, 1965), 83. Women might testify in private.
[75] W. Gouge, *Of Domesticall Duties* (1622), 235; 'Writing Book' of Nehemiah Wallington (1654), in L. Cowen Orlin, ed., *Elizabethan Households: An Anthology* (Washington, D.C.: Folger Shakespeare Library, 1995), 31–32. On spiritual covenants in diaries, see A. Cambers, 'Reading, the Godly, and Self-Writing in England, circa 1580–1720', *Journal of British Studies*, 46 (2007), 806.

24 INTRODUCTION: CONTRACTING

After Gouge's transcendent approach to the love which should structure a family, Wallington's rules might sound bathetic. From another angle, however, the young household seems laudable in trying to frame itself by thinking up concrete (and potentially endless) lists of ways to bring God into the minutiae of life.[76] Such resolutions provide the enchanting prospect of people being seriously playful, just as the Little Academy becomes, when it tries to live up to the stories it tells.

Contracting was a practice, Wallington says ruefully, which 'made some conformity of the life of Grace in me, although it were painful and some what chargeable unto me'.[77] In making his system so detailed, and by levying a different fine for each broken resolution (ranging from a farthing for each time he was idle at work to 2d for failing to take an opportunity to teach godly ways to members of his household), Wallington was nudging himself: definite, near-at-hand results from a choice of action are more likely to be appreciated than those which are unclear and far off.

A mental budget made during a period of zeal may help to allocate time and energy properly, when more quotidian moments arise.[78] Fantasizing about how one might become godly, and drawing up the rules to make oneself so, is pleasant and easy. However, judging whether they have been kept is a more mortifying and exacting activity. It is not the summary in itself, but the nudge given by the prospect of an upcoming summary which directs its maker's time, during the day, towards proper objects. Richard Rogers (lecturer at Wethersfield, Essex) speaks of how

> as the Steward of some Noble mans house doth not make a generall reckoning and account of much money laid out, but writeth the particulars, daily and hourely, as he giveth out and receiveth ... so and much more ... doth the wise man looke daily to his waies, and through the day ... So will hee even set downe many parts of his life in writing also, such as are principally to be kept in record (as Gods benefits and his own sinnes) as he is able, and all to help him to be better directed in it.[79]

Wallington 'found it a hard worke to Examin al my thought, words and Actions of the day and if for one day how much harder is it to examin a weeke or a

---

[76] Oaths are a common feature of group formation in youth. See J. Kerrigan, *Shakespeare's Binding Language* (Oxford: Oxford University Press, 2016), 68, 78.

[77] Wallington, *Notebooks*, ed. Booy, 48.

[78] On mental budgeting, see Thaler and Sunstein, *Nudge*, 41–42, 49–52.

[79] R. Rogers, *Seven Treatises, Containing Such Direction as is Gathered Out of the Holie Scriptures* (1603), 308–309.

monthe.[80] His diaries show him trying and failing, again and again, to keep his own rules: 'I find it by woful experience that I am intangled and have laid to heavie a burden on myselfe that I am not able to beare', 'I did draw out Artickles and tied myselfe with many penelties which I was never able to perform', there is a 'breach of my covenants … made unto God', 'my heart smote me (as it doth many times) for breaking promise or vows which I have made', and 'I brooke all my porposes: promises and covenantes with my God', on occasions varying from eating a pear without saying grace beforehand (against his 'promise') to mourning the death of his daughter.[81] There is no concern for perspective because he is concentrating not on the damage done by the failing in itself, but on the damage done by breaking faith with God. Since such self-reflexive thinking is exhausting, any attempt at it can produce further failure, in a contagion of insufficiency: 'I would have Examined my Examinations but it was to hard a worke for mee'.[82]

Writing out the terms of a resolution allows performance to be measured. The spiritual diary of the Suffolk non-Conformist Owen Stockton sets out lists of rules to regulate his behaviour, and promises himself that he will repeatedly 'ey', 'ponder upon', and 'apply' these lists.[83] Rogers gives an example from 1588, when nearly twenty 'well minded persons' (that is, ministers) met together to dine and discuss how to reform their lives more strictly than their previous 'cold' and 'negligent' attempts to do so. They asked one of those present to sum up 'their conference and communication together, for the better putting of them in rememberance of it to practise it, as also that they might see what the summe of their conference was: which, seeing they agreed unto, they called a Covenant'.[84] Rogers's diary shows how the group were already practiced in second-order thinking about how to inflame devotion. Late in 1587, for instance, they were 'bethinckinge of our selves how we might rouze upp our selves to a further case of beseeminge the gospel'; '12 of us mett to the stirreing up of or selves'; 'we fasted betwixt our selves … to the stirring upp of our selves, … and then we determined to bring into writing a direction for our lives'.[85] Rogers regularly checks how he is doing against the contract (at

---

[80] Wallington, *Notebooks*, ed. Booy, 16.
[81] Wallington, *Notebooks*, ed. Booy, 22, 23, 27, 48, 49, 270.
[82] Wallington, *Notebooks*, ed. Booy, 23.
[83] J. Schildt, '"In My Private Reading of the Scriptures": Protestant Bible-Reading in England, c.1580–1720', in A. Ryrie and J. Martin, eds., *Private and Domestic Devotion in Early Modern Britain* (Aldershot: Ashgate, 2012), 199.
[84] Rogers, *Seven Treatises*, 477–478.
[85] M. M. Knappen, ed., *Two Elizabethan Puritan Diaries, by Richard Rogers and Samuel Ward* (Chicago: American Society of Church History, 1933), 69.

26 INTRODUCTION: CONTRACTING

monthly intervals, by the end of 1588), to clarify his progress and encourage himself to further efforts. He notes how,

> reading the writeings of an other brother about his estat an houre and longuer, I was moved to write, and to bring my hart into a better frame, which in the beginning was impos[sible] to me, but, I thanck god, I feel a sensibl chaung of that, and will set downe after how myne heart groweth better seasoned.

Rogers favourably compares this decision to 'vew my life continually, with the former wherin I did it by fits and thus was oft unsettled, out of order ... sometimes dumpish and too heavy, sometimes loose'.[86] He speaks of how he 'read my Writeinges [of six years before], whereby I perceived how daungerously I am broken from the holy league which there I finde that most faithfully I entered into with the Lord', an autobiography which stretches from drafting an ideal self to auditing its current state.[87]

Such contracts have been examined as speech acts, their swearers stating that, as they speak or sign a document, they create an obligation to God and to each other.[88] Nudge theory would suggest that the latter addressee might be as psychologically persuasive a factor as the former. The knowledge that others are making the same decision persuades each group member that they are doing the right thing in itself, that they have the support of the group in doing so, and that the group's knowledge of their commitment will help them keep it, for sheer shame's sake.

However, even when contracts are made with the self alone, as vows, they create a third party: a verbal object which is a check on compliance.[89] A desire to be consistent with one's own resolutions, a desire for self-approval, becomes a motivating factor.[90] Gouge speaks of how a vow 'doth as it were set a tutor over us, to call upon us to perform our duty, to check us when we are slack therein, and to keepe us within that compasse that we have set unto our selves'. William Crashaw (vicar of St Mary Whitechapel, London) recommends making vows audible, at least to the self: the heart is to 'command the ... tongue and lips to utter and publish the same promise, the better to bind it selfe to obedience'.[91] Daniel Dyke (chaplain to Lord Harington of Exton) likewise advises that his readers 'register, and record in thy accountes-booke this thy covenant,

---

[86] Knappen, *Elizabethan Puritan Diaries*, 70, 81, 84.
[87] Knappen, *Elizabethan Puritan Diaries*, 81.
[88] Kerrigan, *Binding Language*, 9–15.
[89] W. Gouge, *The Whole-armor of God* (1619), 465.
[90] On the bias towards consistency with a self-image, see Thaler and Sunstein, *Nudge*, 57–58, 71–72.
[91] W. Crashaw, *Londons Lamentation for her Sinnes* (1625), C8r.

that so when thy deceitfull heart shalbe offering to start aside, and give thee the slippe, thou maist presently recall it, and keep it in with putting it in mind of this covenant.'[92]

Mostly, these contracts to combat sin and reform life are explicit and encouraging, offering promises of transformation. Through them, believers can come to understand that some spiritual problems are common to all and can be overcome by clear definitions and step-change programmes, which seem achievable because they are presented as reasonable and incremental. Rogers gives practical directions on how, 'every day in the best manner', his parishioners can be 'mery in the Lord, and yet without lightnes; sad and heavie in heart for their owne sins, and the abhominations of the land, and yet without discouragement or dumpishnes'. The key is to target low-hanging fruit from the start, setting moderate targets in

> a daily direction to guide us, and whiles we doe every day with conscience set our selves to honour and obey God, as in our callings, and by other occasions offered, we shall be able, and not wanderingly and uncertainly, as we have been wont to doe.[93]

Rogers ran a group experiment on these lines (possibly while a curate of Radwinter in Essex or possibly at Wethersfield). Formal instruction should come first, such as reading 'some one or two well penned [books], either of the whole Christian religion, or any particular argument, & matter, and them often, rather then a leafe of one and a chapter of another, as idle readers use to doe for novelties sake'. But then comes the really important stage: getting 'proofe of this knowledge'.

> Experimentall knowledge in all trades and sciences, what a difference there is betwixt it, and bare and naked skill in the same without experience ... He that hath been trained up in an occupation, it may be, hee hath got knowledge and skill in his science or trade: but he is not able to use it to the best advantage and his owne greatest profit, neither how, where, and when, to buy and to sell ... all for want of experience ... Even so it is in the spirituall trade.

---

[92] D. Dyke, *The Mystery of Selfe-deceiving* (1614), 351.

[93] Rogers, *Seven Treatises*, A5v, B2v, 289, 279, 338–341. See also C. Sullivan, *The Rhetoric of the Conscience in Donne, Herbert, and Vaughan* (Oxford: Oxford University Press, 2008), 58–59. Stephen Egerton and Ezekiel Culverwell, in prefatory letters, talk of the work as a necessary reformed version of the rules of life set out in the Jesuit Robert Persons's *Christian Directory ... Appertayning to Resolution* (1582), whose specificity had proved popular with readers of all denominations.

28 INTRODUCTION: CONTRACTING

Laying out what today's performance managers would term specific, measurable, assignable, and realistic targets, Rogers particularized a daily regime of spiritual and secular activities:

> how to keepe company, how to be solitarie, how to be occupied in their labours, how to cease from them, how to rise and how to lye downe ... not discouraged at night though they did not all duties, (which in one day cannot be) but quiet and chearfull, seeing they did those which by good direction they saw most necessary.

His parishioners doubted that the plan would work, and worried that such 'order' was going in the direction of papist ritual; Rogers answered that he had taken all his directions from scripture. Reassured, the group agreed to give the scheme a month's trial (later extended to three months), and to note 'faithfully, how they felt it to helpe them forward in well passing the day, more then when they walked without it in the world', but also to say where it proved hard, and even where it failed. Each participant in the trial was to do their homework, following its directions privately, then discuss the results with the group. Such a mode of operation allowed for user-generated content, which could be assessed publicly. It was an engaging approach which proved (according to Rogers, at least) a resounding success: participants told him 'they were able with chearfulnes and without tediousnesse to passe the day in their calling, and in the performance of other necessarie duties either at home or abroad as occasion was offered, which they could never do before, for any long time together'.

4 Herbert Gets Going

Herbert's Country Parson never lets the best be the enemy of the good. He is 'a diligent observer, and tracker of Gods wayes, [so] sets up as many encouragements to goodnesse as he can, both in honour, and profit, and fame; that he may, if not the best way, yet any way, make his Parish good'. He is, for example, frank about the 'any way' of bribery. The minister, before giving charity, makes the recipients 'say their Prayers first, or the Creed and ten Commandments, and as he finds them perfect, rewards them the more'.[94] However, the minister

---

[94] G. Herbert, *A Priest to the Temple, or, The Country Parson* (1652), in F. E. Hutchinson, ed., *The Works of George Herbert* (Oxford: Clarendon Press, 1941), 244, 245.

gives no set pension to any, for this in time will lose the name and effect of charity with the poor people … But the Parson … causeth them still to depend on him; and so by continuall and fresh bounties, unexpected to them, but resolved to himself, hee wins them to praise God more, to live more religiously, and to take more paines in their vocation, as not knowing when they shal be relieved; which otherwise they would reckon upon, and turn idlenesse.[95]

As Chauncey Wood remarks, turning pensions into rewards is a matter of social control.[96] The parson refuses to publicize his resolution because intermittent reinforcement of incentives tends to inspire more obedience than those which are expected to be given.

It is not surprising, therefore, that Herbert's poetry is amused at the canny way the self can nudge the self by contracts. Sometimes, he starts by praising or suggesting an enduring written resolution, shows how it is superseded or fails, then waits for God to step in. In 'Nature' the speaker pleads with God to 'smooth my rugged heart, and there/ Engrave thy rev'rend law, and fear'. Yet by the next line this should-be enduring record is found wanting: 'Or make a new one, since the old/ Is sapless grown' and cannot now 'hold' Christ. Similarly, the tiny words 'so' and 'as' in 'Sepulchre' point to a previous, failed covenant:

> as of old, the law by heav'nly art
> Was writ in stone; so thou, which also art
> The letter of the word, find'st no fit heart
> To hold thee.

In both poems, the speaker acknowledges that all he can do is ask Christ humbly to sign a new contract of love, on behalf of both parties.

But there are other poems in which the speaker takes a more active contractual role. Helen Wilcox points out that 'Good Friday' refers to the Epistle reading for that day of Hebrews 10.16 ('I will put my laws into their hearts, and in their minds will I write them'), and notes that Paul is citing Jeremiah 31.33.[97] This can be taken further: Jeremiah is referring to God's 'new covenant with the House of Israel' (31.31), which will not fail (unlike previous attempts

---

[95] Herbert, *Priest*, 244–245. On incentives, see Thaler and Sunstein, *Nudge*, 99–102.

[96] C. Wood, 'George Herbert and the Widow Bagges: Poverty, Charity, and the Law', in C. Hodgkins, ed., *George Herbert's Pastoral: New Essays on the Poet and Priest of Bemerton* (Newark: University of Delaware Press, 2010), 177.

[97] Wilcox turns to a more contemporary context, the emblem book tradition of depicting hearts as books. See Herbert, *Poems*, ed. Wilcox, 125–129.

30 INTRODUCTION: CONTRACTING

at covenant renewal, noted in Exodus 34, Joshua 23–24, 1 Samuel 12) because it is founded solely in God's grace. Hebrews and Jeremiah start with the fact that 'This is the covenant I will make with them'. In the poem, Herbert stands by God's elbow and all but writes the contract for the Almighty, providing paper, ink, place to write, content to refer to, and words to use. God is asked to 'write there' (right there, Strier reads) on Herbert's heart, with Herbert's 'bloud', his 'sorrows … and bloudie fight'.[98] Herbert—now God's notebook—outlines a checklist of what will oppose Sinne: 'Thy whips, thy nails, thy wounds, thy woes'. Then follows a further stipulation about storing the resolution safely: God should 'keep possession', so Sinne might not 'all the writings blot or burn'. This is God's document, formally, but Herbert gives him little freedom over whether to sign it or not.

Some expectation on the speaker's side hardens into impudence in 'Judgement', where God is expected to 'call/ For ev'ry mans peculiar book'. This will be confidently handed over by those who rely on their own 'merit'. Herbert, however, impatiently declines, declaring that he intends to 'thrust' God's own 'peculiar book' into God's hand: the 'Testament' of God's previous resolution. Here, 'thou shalt finde my faults are thine'. This is theologically correct, of course: Christ's sacrifice atoned once for all sins. But remembering a contractual context revives the impertinence in the tone of this last clause. It would be quite different if the word was 'virtues', but only a barrack-room lawyer would voice the doctrine of the atonement in such a bald way. To try to embarrass God by citing his own writings against him, as proof that he once agreed to save 'poore wretches', is a form of peer pressure worthy of Little Gidding.

A three-part self-contract is successively developed in 'Obedience'. The poem is often read through its legal terminology of purchase and sale, but it might also be thought about in terms of the feelings aroused when making resolutions. Herbert's opening position sounds correct but self-regarding: he offers a simple '*gift* or *donation*' of himself to God, binding himself by a 'poore paper'. The tone is uninspired, noting how his heart 'doth bleed/ As many lines, as there doth need', but no more. Having written out his resolution, Herbert formally delivers it out loud: 'To which I do agree,/ And here present it as my speciall deed', then adds some small print about how there is no small print or 'reservation,/ Or some such words in fashion', which might undermine future performance. His is an ungracious gift, anticipating a breakdown even as it is made. Then Herbert pauses, suddenly remembering how God has already offered him a gift of grace which is both unilateral and irresistible, 'no faint

---

[98] Strier, *Love Known*, 53.

proffer,/ Or superficiall offer/ Of what we might not take, or be withstood'. Herbert finds he can only recover some standing by turning his gift into a *'purchase'*, and doubling up on what he can offer (albeit this is still an infinitely unequal bundle of good, at least from the divine point of view). Thus *some* reader (Herbert ostentatiously avoids directly addressing *the* present reader, and thus pressurizing them) is nudged to 'thrust his heart/ Into these lines'. As *the* reader goes down the last two stanzas of the poem, however, it starts to dawn on her that she is indeed the one whose response is being solicited, to deliver 'both our goods'. Herbert's breezy, act-on-reading tone is the opposite of the close and suspicious consideration which legal documents demand. The reader is apparently free to choose: she is encouraged (not exhorted, nor required) through a series of courteously indirect and conditional suggestions ('He that will', 'may set his hand', 'if he to it will stand'), ending with a wistful fancy about the speaker's own position ('How happie were my part,/ If some kinde man would'), and an airy promise of final triumph for both, if the offer is accepted ('till in heav'ns court of rolls/ They were by winged souls/ Entred'). A U-shaped self-help narrative appears: first, insufficiency is created in the reader; then, a recovery programme is laid out, with authorial examples; finally, a happy end is promised. Such heavy-handed hinting is more disturbing than a frank direct address, since enforcing the proper response is left to the reader's conscience, thus doubling her feeling of guilt if she does not act.

Despite the anticipated failure of godly resolutions, some of Herbert's seventeenth-century admirers kept on making them. In 'Vows Broken and Rewarded', Herbert's imitator, Christopher Harvey (vicar of Clifton-on-Dunsmore, Warwickshire), robustly looks forwards to renewing his vows, despite admitting they will not bind him for long: 'What shall I doe? Make vows and break them still?'[99] His principal objection is over wasting time, not over being hypocritical: it will be 'labour lost', as 'The businesse will be crost'. His reasons for continuing to do so are voiced with similar calculation: 'thou canst not tell, what strength/ Thy God may give thee', 'thou may/ Perhaps perform it when thou thinkest least', and at least God 'permits thee but to call'. This is a 'why not' nudge to keep going: what has Harvey got to lose? At the other end of the scale, Henry Vaughan answers Herbert's 'Obedience' in a moment of hot zeal, promising to 'thrust my stubborn heart/ Into

---

[99] C. Harvey, *The Synagogue, or, the Shadow of The Temple* (1640), 11–12. Francis Cockin also responds to Herbert's image of the contract, in *Divine Blossomes: A Prospect or Looking-Glass for Youth* (1657), in R. H. Ray, ed., 'The Herbert Allusion Book: Allusions to George Herbert in the Seventeenth Century', *Studies in Philology*, 83/4 (1986), 59–60.

32 INTRODUCTION: CONTRACTING

thy *Deed*', and barring reservations, 'there from no *Duties* to be freed' ('The Match').[100] But, as his ardour cools, he can scarcely credit that this was his own resolution:

> I wrote it down. But one that saw
> And envyed that Record, did since
> Such a mist over my minde draw,
> It quite forgot that purpos'd glimpse.
> I read it sadly oft, but still
> Simply believed, 'twas not my Quill ('The Agreement').[101]

It takes divine grace to put the situation right.

One might ask why these writers fling themselves into agreements which all assume, even as they are made, will not stand. Why would anyone keep going? Coming at this question from a soteriological angle, Kate Narveson argues that believers felt that they were still being sincere, not hypocritical, in consciously adopting ideas and attitudes they knew would fade from view because they thought of their selves as pieces of work in the making, never as final products. Failure could be anticipated and compensated for on the 'two steps forwards, one back' principle, without justifying accusations of shallowness.[102]

Nudge theory highlights the implicit element of cheerfulness in this sober approach. Discussions of today's self-help books can bring out the comfort and pleasure of repeatedly making a new start by making vigorous small changes to the local environment. Beth Blum has said of self-help books that their suggestions on how to live a better life are enjoyable fantasies in themselves, in defining situations which were inchoate before, and providing action plans which seem practical, if only a little willpower and reason can be applied. Blum points out, however, that such bibliotherapy is not necessarily successful because the reader believes exaggerated promises of secrets to happiness, but because of the way the texts ask to be read and applied in any way their reader finds useful. The books have an open-ended aesthetic which encourages observation and playtesting of the rules offered, giving the user power to do some first-hand experimentation.[103]

---

[100] H. Vaughan, *Silex scintillans: Sacred Poems and Private Ejaculations* (1655), first page series, 53.
[101] Vaughan, *Silex scintillans*, second page series, 64.
[102] K. Narveson, *Bible Readers and Lay Writers in Early Modern England: Gender and Self-Definition in an Emergent Writing Culture* (2012; London: Routledge, 2016), 79 ff.
[103] B. Blum, *The Self-Help Compulsion: Searching for Advice in Modern Literature* (New York: Columbia University Press, 2020), 4–8, 92, 173.

Just so with some of the preparation in the early modern period for a godly life. Ransome points out Ferrar's suggestion to Woodnoth that the pair 'follow a systematic programme of practical steps':

> Lett us ... begin to live indeed—every hower otherwise bestowed is Lost if not worse.—Lett it bee thefore yf you will an agreement to this purpose between you and mee thus [,] since the whole frame of what wee intend is to much to bee sett doune at once and requires much Length of tyme perhaps, that wee will at least every weeke present each other with some piece that wee have finished.[104]

Readers of practical divinity are willing to experiment, to try out regimes to see if their zeal can be increased. The pleasure of achievement in, say, working down a list of the signs that one is saved can encourage a user to consider and apply the content of the list to her own life. There is nothing numinous about this process: it is a technique, perhaps even a trick, not a transfer of grace—but it works!

People make good choices over issues where they have had past experience of similar decisions, where there is reliable, substantial, and relevant information about the situation, and where they will get prompt feedback about the effect of continuing along a certain line. None of these are true about the most vital of all decisions facing the early modern godly: *A Case of Conscience the Greatest Taht* [sic] *There Ever Was, How a Man May Know, Whether He Be the Son of God or No* (the eye-catching title of the bestseller by a fellow of Christ's College, Cambridge, William Perkins). Prospect theory's guiding principle is that people evaluate options by their expectation of the subjective value to them of a change. The effective carrier of such value is not the final position, but changes in the ongoing experience.[105] In other words, people tend to make choices based on how they can affect the margin in the present, rather than considering the eventual whole. The principle is borne out by the way the godly work to find a home for grace in them, even though the fate of their souls has already been finalized. Nudge theory can supplement studies of the theology of the period to show how practical predestinarians (in Dixon's term) focus on the small gestures which help bracket off the final and absolute end of the soul to focus on what must be done here and now.

The following five chapters study how the godly nudge a self into godliness, both physically (in building, cleaning, and working) and verbally (in

---

[104] Ransome, *Web of Friendship*, 140–141.
[105] Kahneman, *Thinking*, 433–448.

34 INTRODUCTION: CONTRACTING

conversing and listing). Chapter 2 observes how early modern soteriology often uses the vocabulary of clean and dirty. Behavioural psychology suggests an emotional association between cleanliness and morality, which explains how Herbert's specific references to domestic chores see the most grubby and unglamorous of actions as a significant help to developing a godly disposition. Chapter 3 discusses the emotional aim of the substantial investment in church renovation of the 1620s, undertaken by Herbert and others. It argues that physical objects in Herbert's poems about buildings are approached as things to pray with, as much as analogies for the activity of praying. Such things, more or less successfully, can be repaired and rearranged to create cognitive niches. Chapter 4 looks at the period's advice on face-saving and adversarial devices in conversation. In Herbert's poems, would-be egalitarian discussion is recast as an impertinent nudge to get God to join in. The speaker's exquisite tact in asking for God's help is met by God's blunt rebuttal of any inappropriate concern for the divine's feelings. Chapter 5 discusses how different sorts of lists are created in devotional writing: to reason with, move, and prompt to action. Speakers in many of Herbert's poems compile lists of actions to remove doubt about their situation. Only when these turn out to be pointless, though, do these figures realize that being troubled is a distinguishing mark of salvation, not damnation. Chapter 6 looks at how occupational manuals and practical theology recast work as a pleasure, not a duty, side-stepping the problem of *sola fide*. In Herbert's poems on the vocation, it concludes, the speakers seem happiest when busiest.

This book tries to find in early modern practical divinity some of what Richard Strier has provocatively (and unrepentantly) celebrated in the wider culture of the period: a Renaissance which values passion, worldliness, and pride, as well as a Reformation which values self-restraint, reason, and repentance. However, Strier makes Herbert an exception, thinking that while he allows unfettered expressions of emotion, he is also wary of physical pleasures. In a much earlier article, Strier also found Herbert to show 'anxious moderation' at best towards the natural world, and actual negativity towards the social world, concluding that the poet did not endorse civic humanism.[106] Given that Herbert was always amused at the way base realities may win out over abstractions, perhaps he may now be admitted to the fun group? In one Cambridge oration, for instance, he invites his audience to take part in a thought experiment. They are to imagine how,

---

[106] R. Strier, *The Unrepentant Renaissance: From Petrarch to Shakespeare to Milton* (Chicago: University of Chicago Press, 2011), 20, 54–56; R. Strier, 'George Herbert and the World', *Journal of Medieval and Renaissance Studies*, 11 (1981), 211–236.

while you, there, dedicating yourself to Philosophy, are in the midst of arguing that the chain linking body and soul hinders contemplation, a Soldier rushes into your room set aside for the Muses and frees you with his sword. And while you, over there, exploring the stars, are handling imaginary spheres and heavens, the commanding officer breaks in and hurls you together with your heavens down to hell.[107]

Practical divinity may not always state openly that individualism, or even self-assertion, are expressions of God's creativity, but the advice these texts give—to start, right now, preparing to receive grace—does call on these qualities. Early modern godly advice can be *cheerful*. I hope that the tone of Herbert's poems as he registers this, as much as the theological positions he ends on, may encourage readers to let him back into the Renaissance, after all.

---

[107] 'Tu, qui Philosophiae incumbis, cùm corporis cum animâ vinculum impedimento esse ad contemplandum causaris, irruit Miles in Musaeum tuum, & gladio te liberat. Tu, qui astra scrutaris, dum globos tractas & coelos fictitios, perrumpit primipilus, & te cum coelis tuis ad inferos deturbat', G. Herbert, 'Oration ... [at the] Return from Spain of ... Prince Charles' (1623), trans. G. Miller and C. Freis, *GHJ*, 41/1–2 (2017–2018), 18–19.

2

Cleaning

1 Enjoying Housework

Housework, Kathleen Brown points out, is not a grim repetition, over the centuries, of the same dreary activities to service a household. Rather, it engages with a society's current standards for spiritual and social purity, manners, and decency.[1] On dealing with dirt, there are two camps. Those who follow Mary Douglas focus on categorization: dirt is matter out of place, and so the dirty can be (at least potentially) reordered into cleanliness.[2] Those who follow William Miller find that some sorts of dirt are viscerally disgusting, so are reluctant to believe that these can ever be redesignated.[3] Early modern practical divinity uses these as complementary concepts: acknowledging that the soul is inherently depraved, yet hoping that God may be enticed to recategorize it.

Cleaning is a behavioural nudge. Psychologists have asked whether the physical action of cleaning, as also the state of cleanliness, can influence decisions. Their findings are based, in part, on imaginatively devised empirical experiments along the lines of how often people who have been induced to tell or type a lie then use mouthwash or hand-sanitizer, or how their judgements on moral defects tend to vary when foul or fair smells are blown through a room. In experiment after experiment, cleaning (especially of the self, but also of other people and things) has been found to reduce the impact of past experiences (the 'clean slate' effect, where physical cleaning is an embodied procedure of psychological separation from previous states of mind), to increase motivation to act on a decision (physical clarity affecting mental clarity), and to encourage pro-social behaviour.[4] Moreover, cleaning tends

---

[1] K. Brown, *Foul Bodies: Cleanliness in Early America* (New Haven: Yale University Press, 2009), 4.

[2] M. Douglas, *Purity and Danger: An Analysis of the Concept of Pollution and Taboo* (1966; London: Routledge, 2002), 43–50, 197–199.

[3] W. I. Miller, *The Anatomy of Disgust* (Cambridge, MA: Harvard University Press, 1997), 5–18, 38–59.

[4] S. W. S. Lee and N. Schwarz, 'Clean-Moral Effects and Clean-Slate Effects: Physical Cleansing as an Embodied Procedure of Separation', in R. Duschinsky, S. Schnall, and D. Weiss, eds., *Purity and Danger Now: New Perspectives* (London: Routledge, 2016), 148–173; A. Körner and F. Strack, 'Conditions for the Clean Slate Effect after Success or Failure', *Journal of Social Psychology*, 159 (2019), 95–105; S.

George Herbert and the Business of Practical Piety. Ceri Sullivan, Oxford University Press.
© Ceri Sullivan (2024). DOI: 10.1093/9780198906841.003.0002

to reinstate a sense of moral integrity (behavioural psychologists call this the 'Macbeth effect'). Cleaning also appears to affect judgements about wrongdoing: it attenuates feelings of guilt over one's own misdeeds, and one's moral assessment of other transgressors may depend, in part, on whether they are more or less clean.[5] There may be physiological reasons for this: moral and emotional disgust share overlapping regions of the brain, which are activated in similar ways. There may also be an evolutionary advantage to the response of disgust. For an individual to behave in a dirty way threatens the health of the group physically, so once a norm of cleanliness is established any deviation from it tends to be responded to as a problem of social cohesion.[6]

Environmental psychologists also discuss how cleaning the space around a person can help form identity, since it can maintain both a coherent conceptual system and self-esteem. People project themselves onto their physical surroundings, which can mirror their preferred self-image back to them, and out to others. Moreover, any psychic work to deal with disturbances in a sense of self tends to be done best in places which are felt to be most restorative when they have an internal coherence.[7] Eliminating dirt from the environment, Douglas finds, is not a negative activity, but a positive effort to improve the environment, 'a creative movement, an attempt to relate form to function, to make unity of experience'.[8] Homes as well as the body may be tidied and cleaned to create cognitive niches.

This chapter looks first at the approving register in which domestic work is handled by housekeeping manuals and at Little Gidding. The discussion next turns to the surprisingly concrete way in which devotional texts go beyond images of scrubbing the heart to using housework as a nudge to further godliness. Finally, it points out how unusual Herbert is among early modern poets in the density and specificity of his references to domestic chores. He talks about tasks bent on removing traces of organic life (scrubbing, tidying up, dumping refuse, sweeping, bed-making, airing, and physicking), and about activities aimed at creating a comfortable life (heating, cooking, furnishing,

---

Schnall, 'Clean, Proper, and Tidy are More than the Absence of Dirty, Disgusting, and Wrong', *Emotion Review*, 3/3 (2011), 264–266.

[5] C-B. Zhong and K. Liljenquist, 'Washing Away Your Sins: Threatened Morality and Physical Cleansing', *Science*, 313/5792 (2006), 1451–1452; J. L. Preston and R.S. Ritter, 'Cleanliness and Godliness: Mutual Association Between Two Kinds of Personal Purity', *Journal of Experimental Social Psychology*, 48/6 (2012), 1365–1368.

[6] R. Giner-Sorolla and J. Sabo, 'Disgust in the Moral Realm: Do All Roads Lead to Character?', in Duschinsky, Schnall, and Weiss, eds., *Purity and Danger Now*, 87–102.

[7] K. M. Korpela, 'Place Identity as a Product of Environmental Self-regulation', *Journal of Environmental Psychology*, 9/3 (1989), 245; H. M. Proshansky, A. K. Fabian, and R. Kaminoff, 'Place-Identity: Physical World Socialisation of the Self', *Journal of Environmental Psychology*, 3 (1983), 57–83.

[8] Douglas, *Purity and Danger*, 3.

38   CLEANING

spinning, clothes-making, gardening, and hosting a dinner). Though most of these tasks (and cleaning in particular) were generally seen as work for servants and women, Herbert recasts the most grubby and unmentionable chores as constant nudges in a life of faith, used by all ranks and both sexes. The chapter's conclusion argues that, in his poems, doubt about his state of grace is experienced as a form of stinking thinking, one which productively irritates him into a frenzy of further cleaning.

Housework is not now generally valued. Its first sociologist, Ann Oakley, influentially argued that those who do such chores experience them as unremitting tasks with no durable result; they are felt to be monotonous, isolating, and thankless. To make things worse, domestic workers often devise high standards of work to hold themselves to, thus harshly internalizing their own oppression.[9] Carol Wolkowitz is critical of how social theory about dirt, such as that by Douglas and Miller, tends to glide over the low social status and pay given to those who deal with physical grunge.[10] Literary criticism is rarely more positive. Katie Kadue thinks that housework ('boring', 'menial, ceaseless, and poorly compensated') is a metaphor reached for by Renaissance poets when they reflect on the arduous and ill-appreciated process of gathering, ordering, and preserving literary material.[11] Wendy Wall considers that when housework appears on stage it expresses anxiety about how dependent a family could be on the work of its women.[12] From the perspective of economic history, Susan Cahn argues that the decline of the subsistence household during the seventeenth century tended to mean that the housewife was increasingly spoken of as a purchaser and consumer rather than a producer, ignoring the value created by her housework.[13] The feminist historian Olwen Hufton draws a picture of a 'makeshift economy' in which early modern housewives were engaged, moving to and fro between cleaning, childcare, cooking, shopping, nursing, outwork, and servicing workshops attached to the household.[14]

But Hufton's model of an 'economy of expedients' tends to underplay the thorough executive ability demanded to order the different tasks involved in

---

[9] A. Oakley, *The Sociology of Housework* (1974; Bristol: Policy Press, 2018), 74–94.

[10] C. Wolkowitz, 'Linguistic Leakiness or Really Dirty? Dirt in Social Theory', in B. Campkin and R. Cox, eds., *Dirt: New Geographies of Cleanliness and Contamination* (London: I. B. Taurus, 2007), 15–24.

[11] K. Kadue, *Domestic Georgic: Labors of Preservation from Rabelais to Milton* (Chicago: University of Chicago Press, 2020), 5–8, 13, 19–20.

[12] W. Wall, *Staging Domesticity: Household Work and English Identity in Early Modern Drama* (Cambridge: Cambridge University Press, 2002), 114–126.

[13] S. Cahn, *Industry of Devotion. The Transformation of Women's Work in England, 1500–1660* (New York: Columbia University Press, 1987), 4–5, 33–50, 124.

[14] O. Hufton, *The Prospect Before Her: A History of Women in Western Europe... 1500–1800* (London: Harper Collins, 1995), 152–172.

running a house. Housework is praised in the period as a complex activity, which draws on bureaucratic, physical, and emotional skills to put in hand a wide range of overlapping tasks. In his commemorative verse collection *Memoriae matris sacrum* ('A Sacred Gift in Memory of my Mother'), Herbert remembers his mother's managerial skills in keeping her household in order: after morning prayer, 'then she surveys her household, and carefully distributes the tasks:/ Of meals, the garden, and the day's spinning./ To each its proper time and place is given'.[15] Lower down the social scale, the chapters on the wife's work in estate manager John Fitzherbert's best-selling advice to farmers open with her in a furore of ordered and ordering activity:

> first in the morning when thou awakest, and purposest to rise, give prayse to God for all his benefits past which he hath bestowed upon thee, and when thou art uppe and readie, see that thy house bee cleane swept, and all things in the same placed in very comely and decent order: then milke thy kine, suckle thy Calves, and take up thy chyldren and make them ready. Provide also for their breakefast, thy husbands, and thy servants, and likewise for their dinner and supper that day. Ordaine corne for the Mill to bake, and Malt to brewe withal.

After all that, the woman starts her farming jobs: dairy work, poultry keeping, tending the kitchen garden, growing flax and hemp, spinning linen and wool, cloth-making, hay-making, marketing, and so on. It suddenly strikes Fitzgerald that this is a well-nigh impossible schedule, for he thoughtfully mentions that 'it may fortune many times, that thou shalt have so many things to do, that thou shalt not verie well know where is best to beginne, then looke what it is that would bring greatest losse if it bee not donne, and in what time it may be done, and beginne with that first'.[16] When Richard Rogers thinks his wife may die in childbirth it is the loss of her domestic management which is foremost in his mind. Losing 'so fitt a companion for religion, huswifry, and other comf[ort]s' will mean, he anticipates, having to take on or manage a great deal of extra housework and childcare—and he does not think he will do it very well. There is likely to be 'losse and decay in subst[ance]', and 'the care of household matters cast on' him will prevent him from giving time to the study expected of a minister.[17]

---

[15] '*Dein familiam lustrat, & res prandij,/ Horti, colíque distributim pensitat./ Suum cuique tempus & locus datur*', G. Herbert, *The Complete Poetry*, ed. J. Drury and V. Moul, trans. V. Moul (London: Penguin, 2015), 304–305.

[16] J. Fitzherbert, *Booke of Husbandrie* (1523; 1598), 175, 177.

[17] Knappen, ed., *Elizabethan Puritan Diaries*, 74.

40 CLEANING

Cleaning is the task which underpins all the others. Gervase Markham (nine years a tenant farmer) pauses during his prescriptions about dairy work to note that 'cleanliness be such an ornament to a Hus-wife, that if she want any part thereof, she loseth both that and all good names else', especially in the dairy, where 'not the least moat of any filth may by any meanes appeare, but all things either to the eye or nose [be] so void of sowernesse or sluttishnesse, that a Princes bed chamber must not exceed it'.[18] Conduct literature, associating cleanliness with social status, emphasized the importance of removing the hidden dirt (which might otherwise be revealed by smell), as well as the surface dirt (evident to the sight).[19] But the frequent collocation of 'clean and sweet' in texts of the period, referring to sight and smell, is also based on the assumption that infection could be transmitted by bad air. Sweeping, wiping down, and airing are matters of health as much as rank or pleasure.[20] In advice on how to order great households, nearly every office holder is repeatedly instructed to keep their spaces, products, clothes, and utensils 'fynne and neatlie', 'sweete and cleanlie', 'well and cleanlie', 'sweet and neatlie', whether they be gentleman ushers of the Great Hall or the estate's slaughtermen.[21]

Such cleaning takes technical know-how as well as managerial and physical effort.[22] The yeoman of the wardrobe, for instance, must 'see as occasion serveth, that all his beddes, bolesters, and pillowes, with all the rest of furniture for beddinge, be airede, and beaten, and that there bee noe duste in them, neither any mothes bredde, which both is a greate spolie to stuffe, but in that case dried wormewoode is very good, and ofte turninge and airinge'.[23] One of the earliest printed compilations of advice on practical household management, that by Hannah Woolley, is divided by the roles which women servants might take. All, from scullery maid to lady's maid, must keep things orderly, all day, every day. The scullery maid is to 'keep sweet and clean' the lower offices (kitchen, pantry, and wash house), to 'wash and scour' the kitchen and

---

[18] G. Markham, *Countrey Contentments: or, the English Huswife* (1623), 178, 179.
[19] S. North, *Sweet and Clean? Bodies and Clothes in Early Modern England* (Oxford: Oxford University Press, 2020), 19–20.
[20] On civic regulation of dirt as a health issue, see M. Jenner, 'Early Modern English Conceptions of "Cleanliness" and "Dirt" as Reflected in the Environmental Regulation of London, *c.*1530–1700', D. Phil Oxford (1992), 143–158.
[21] 'A Breviate Touching the Order and Government of a Nobleman's House (1605)', in *Archaeologia ... the Society of Antiquaries of London*, 13 (1807), 321–340. See also R. B. [misattributed to Richard Brathwait], *Some Rules and Orders of the Government of the House of an Earle* (MS *c.*1605) (London: R. Triphook, 1821), 8–9, 11, 15, 20, 26–34, 38.
[22] North, *Sweet and Clean?*, 209–258; C. Hole, *The English Housewife in the Seventeenth Century* (London: Chatto and Windus, 1953), 76–78, 109–112; C. Davidson, *A Woman's Work is Never Done: A History of Housework in the British Isles, 1650–1950* (London: Chatto and Windus, 1982), 115–163.
[23] 'Order and Government of a Nobleman's House', 335.

chamber utensils, and then to wash her own clothes. The house maid is to 'make clean the greatest part of the house, and ... suffer no room to lie foul, ... look well to all the stuff, and see that [the rooms] be often brushed, and the Beds frequently turned'. No items are to be moved between rooms, for 'that is the way to have them lost'. Additional duties for the house maid run from emptying and scouring a guest's chamber pot to helping the laundry maid on washing day. 'Under-cook maids' are told that 'though your employment be greasie and smutty, yet if you please you may keep your self from being nasty, therefore be it in your care to keep yourself clean'. Cooks are to be 'cleanly about every thing', both surfaces and food (left-over scraps will 'spoil and stink'). There are occasional details about the techniques (bed curtains, for instance, are to be 'often beaten in the sun, and well brushed').[24] Given such arduous tasks, housekeepers might have felt envy underneath any disapproval in looking at a contemporary print of a badly run kitchen (Figure 2.1): one maid asleep over her spinning wheel, another cleaning a dish with a dog's tail as it licks out a pot, utensils everywhere, a rat after the tallow candle, a huge cobweb in the corner, and a cat swimming in the cauldron![25]

At Little Gidding, the Ferrar sisters gained personal experience in such housewifely arts as making bread, needlework, cooking, and minor first aid. They also took turns, month on month, to run the household: directing the servants and noting household expenses (which were balanced at the month's end for the next incumbent, 'whereby they became perfect accountants and book-keepers').[26] The Little Academy pondered on the place of housework in the godly home. A poorly run household becomes an image of how

> Cares and desires touching reputation, like flys and lesser Vermin, in ... sluttish houses, keepe mens mynds and bodys in a restless Vexation, every buzzing in their Eares, ever biting on their Flesh ..., in Bed & at Board, in our pleasures & in our businesses, they put us to a restlesse shrugging, a Continual Fencing, & an endlesse watchfull Carking ..., all the day, I ... and greatest part of the Night too.[27]

Even so, the value of housework is not assured. While thanking her daughters for a copy of the first Story Book, Mary Ferrar comments that it was

---

[24] H. Woolley, *The Gentlewomans Companion* (1673), 207–217, 112.

[25] 'The Description of a Bad Housewife' (1699), a later version of an Elizabethan woodcut; M. Jones, *The Print in Early Modern England. An Historical Oversight* (New Haven: Yale University Press, 2010), 321–328.

[26] Muir and White, eds., *Ferrar*, 86–87.

[27] Williams, ed., *Conversations*, 132.

42 CLEANING

Figure 2.1 Anonymous, *The Description of a Bad Housewife* (1699), Bodleian Library, University of Oxford, Ashmolean Museum Douce Prints W.1.2 (27).

more significant to spend time producing the volume than on domestic chores:

> as for matters of Huswifery, when God puts them upon you it would bee sin either to refuse them or to perform them negligently, and therefore the

ignorance of them is a great shame and Danger for women that intend Marriage. But to seek these kinds of Businesses for pleasure, and to make them your delights, and to pride yourselves for your care and curiositie in them, is a great vanitie and Folly at the best, and to neglect better things and more necessarie by pretence of being imployed in these things is surely, though a common Practize, yet a peice of sinfull Hypocrisie. Doe them therefore, when God puts them upon you, and doe them carefully and well, and God shall reward you, however the things themselves bee but mean, accepting them at your hands as if they were greater matters, when they are done and undergone out of Obedience to his Command. But let your Delight bee onely in the better part.[28]

However, the other women put up a spirited defence of the virtues and pleasures of housework. In a dialogue from Christmas 1631, the Affectionate (a Collett sister) initially argues that 'all the high prized Follies in the world' come from impatience with one's lot, including that of being house proud:

What (sayd the Guardian smilingly) will you perswade us that all your womanly Niceties of rubbing floores till you may see your Faces shine in them, of whiting Linning till it passe the driven snow, of conserving, preserving, and all those other busy Curiosities for which you soe magnify yourselves, have their Creditt cheifly for the better Inducement and support of Impatiency?

I, verily (sayd shee), and all those other more boisterous and more pernicious vanities you Men ar carried with, of building, of hunting, of keeping Company, and the like.

The Guardian (John Ferrar) insists that it is 'utterly unworthy the Dignity of Mans Nature to take any pleasure or delight' in housework, and wrong to use the will and reason 'in the Love and prosecution of such abject Matters'. Stung by this, the Affectionate extends her argument: housework employs 'exercize of Invention, of Composition, of Order, and of all the other excellent operations of the Soule, and the Beauty, and Pleasure, and other good effects that arise from these Imployments. And herein lies our delight, not in the things themselves'.[29]

---

[28] Sharland, ed., *Little Gidding*, liii. The first thing Mary Ferrar did on arriving at Little Gidding was to arrange for the chapel (previously housing cattle and pigs) to be cleaned. See Sharland, ed., *Little Gidding*, xxii.

[29] Sharland, ed., *Little Gidding*, 133–134. See also 169–170.

44 CLEANING

The results of all this skill and toil are enjoyed greatly: as Barbara Ehrenreich says, 'to be cleaned up after is to achieve a certain magical weightlessness and immateriality'.[30] One foreign traveller to England was delighted to meet there with 'the neate cleanlines, the exquisite finenesse, the pleasaunte and delightfull furniture in every poynt for household ... chambers and parlours strawed over with sweete herbes ... nosegayes finely entermingled wyth sundry sortes of fragraunte floures in their bed chambers and privy roomes'.[31] A translation of a work by the Italian humanist Torquato Tasso echoes Xenophon's praise of order in the household, down to how mundane stores of clothes, blankets, and utensils become beautiful when stored tidily.[32] It describes building and housekeeping as necessary complements to each other: 'the forme of a house is the order, and the reformation of the house or familie, none other than a second setting it in order'. Tidying up is good management.

> As things preserued, may the better be disposed, if they be carefully prouided for, and ordered, the good Huswife ought aboue all things to be dilligent heerein. For if she reserue not things confusedly but seperat, and placd in sonder, according to their quallitie, and the opportunitie of vsing them, she shall alwaies haue them ready and at hand, and euermore know, what she hath, and what shee wants.

Thus,

> the carefull Steward or surueighor of the house, should ... haue a speciall care, that in the house, Cortes, Tables or Coffers, be no vncleanes, filth or Rubbishe, but that the very walles and pauements, lofts and sellers, Harnes and implements of houshold, maie bee pollished and kept so cleane, that (as we terme it) it may shine like Siluer, or looke as bright as Christall.

Such cleaning is positively creative:

> for cleanlines is not onelie pleasing or delightfull to beholde, but adioyneth worth, and bettereth things by Nature base and filthie, as continuallie beastlines and filth, corrupt, disgrace and spoile, thinges otherwise of value and account: besides, Cleanlines increaseth and preserueth the health, as much

---

[30] B. Ehrenreich, 'Maid to Order', *The Guardian*, 20 August 2000 (https://www.theguardian.com/theobserver/2000/aug/20/features.magazine37).

[31] L. Lemnius, 'A Dutch Physician', in W. B. Rye, trans. and ed., *England as Seen by Foreigners ... The Journals of the Two Dukes of Wirtemberg in 1592 and 1610* (London: John Russell Smith, 1865), 78.

[32] *Xenophons Treatise of House Hold*, trans. G. Hervet (1532; 1573), ff. 30r–32v.

as sluttishnes annoyeth and impay[r]eth it. Nay what more is, euery seruant should perticulerlie haue such care of scowring and keeping cleane those tooles and instruments he works withall, and that belong vnto his office, as the Souldiour hath to see his weapons to be bright, for such are, is, or shold be, euery toole to him that hath the exercise thereof, as are the weapons which the Souldiour vseth.

In fact, ordered domestic space is like a form of exterior (that is, artificial) memory:

if there can be no similitude inferd to this purpose worthie of consideration, most notable is that of Memory, which laying vp, preseruing and imprinting in it selfe al the Images and formes of visible & intelligible things, could not vtter them in time conuenient and dispose them to the tongue and penne, vnlesse it had so ordered, and oftentimes recounted them, as without that the memory it selfe coulde scarce containe them, of so great efficacye and force is order, but it hath also no lesse grace and comlines, in beautifying and adorning things ... as he that doe acquaint his study with the use of poetry very easilie perceiveth.[33]

Composing a room is like composing verse.

Such enjoyment in noticing and dealing with disorder and dirt does not sit well with the advice found in courtesy manuals. The latter insist that civilized people should never call attention to what may disgust others. An immensely popular courtesy manual by the papal secretary of state Archbishop Giovanni Della Casa says that in the sight of others 'we must not only refrain from such thinges as be fowle, filthy, lothsome, and nastie: but we must not so much as name them ... [or] by any act or signe ... put a man in minde of them'. Washing one's hands in the company of others, for instance, 'puts them in minde of some filthy matter that hath bene done aparte'. Even hands themselves can become such a sign, without any such overt action of cleaning, so servants are not to hide them behind their backs or in their clothes, 'but beare them abroade without any suspicion and keep them (in any case) washt & clean without any spot of durt upon them'. Della Casa has a lengthy list of disgusting habits which involve excretions: urinating in public, sneezing or coughing loudly, spitting when speaking, gazing into a used handkerchief, offering a friend a bit from

---

[33] T. Tasso, *The Householders Philosophie ... The True Oeconomia and Forme of Housekeeping*, trans. T. Kyd (1588), 16v, 21v–22r.

46 CLEANING

one's half-eaten fruit, head-scratching, breathing into someone's face, blowing ashes off toasted food, and so on.

The specificity of Della Casa's examples does exactly what he warns against: his vignettes are embarrassing (readers silently recognizing that they have, at one time or another, committed some such *faux pas*), and hence both fascinating and funny. He is particularly interested in how dirt entices the imagination, even stretching to potential ooze. For instance,

> it is ... an vnmanerly parte, for a man to lay his nose vppon the cup where another must drinke: or vppon the meate yt another must eate, to the end to smell vnto it: But rather, I would wish he should not smell at all, no not to that which he himselfe should eate and drinke: because it may chaunce there might fall some droppe from his nose, that would make a man to loath it: although there fall nothing at all in deede.

One should not draw attention to such matter:

> it is no good maner, when a man chaunceth to see, as he passeth the waye (as many times it happeneth) a lothesome thing, that wil make a man to cast his stomacke, to tourne vnto the company, & shewe it them. And much worse I like it, to reache some stynking thing vnto a man to smell vnto it: as it is many a mans fashion to do ... yea, thrusting it vnto their nose, saying: Foh, feele I pray you, hovv this doth stink: vvhere they should rather say, smell not vnto it: for it hath an yll sent.[34]

Such advice is needed because dirt has a strange fascination: the passer-by feels called on to observe it. It is precisely the energy created by this contradictory set of feelings—being impelled to notice what disgusts one—from which devotional texts profit.

2 Heart Housework

Tara Hamling and Catherine Richardson argue that a drive by popular divines to connect theological concepts to everyday practice, in order to anchor them in comprehensible reality, helps give housework a simultaneously low and central status. Given the early modern household was a primary model of good

---

[34] G. Della Casa, *Galateo ... a Treatise of the Manners and Behaviours, it Behoveth a Man to Use and Eschewe, in his Familiar Conversation*, trans. R. Peterson (1576), 6, 9, 14.

governance, a principal locus of production and consumption for both family and church, housework's 'pragmatic, quotidian tasks, especially those that stretched out over long periods of time, become the site of metaphorical interest'.[35] Proverbs used in the early modern period, for instance, find physical cleanliness a pointed metaphor for moral cleanliness: wrapping up problems in clean linen, washing one's hands of them, not being able to wash them away (or vice versa), and so on.[36]

Godly texts are enthusiastic about the image of heart housework. John Downame (formerly rector of St Margaret Lothbury, London) uses the notion to explore the process of preparing a heart to receive grace. Christ's blood is needed to wash out sin's 'skarlet dye' to leave a 'snowy whiteness'; without this, the heart remains in 'naturall filthinesse'. After that, ceaseless work is needed to preserve this state ('as the cleanest house will gather soyle, if it bee not sometime swept'), preventing the likely appearance of major sins by zero tolerance of minor ones ('as when the house is already somewhat fouled, men care not greatly though it be fouled more, whereas when they see it cleane, they more carefully keepe it so from all annoyance'). The standard of cleanliness is set according to the greatness of the guest, 'As we are extraordinarily carefull to have our houses cleansed from all filth, when we prepare them to give entertainment to an honourable and respected friend, who hating all sluttishnesse, will curiously looke into every corner'. If God is going to run a white-gloved finger over obscure surfaces, it is fortunate that Christ is prepared to step in beforehand, as a tolerant and friendly daily char,

> to make [hearts] more cleane, when we have cleansed them as well as we can. For he is not a curious carper at our infirmities, but a cheerfull helper to reform and amend them ... [giving] assistance for the purging of the filth and guilt of sinne, which lurketh in such secret corners, that it was not subject to [our] own view.

Christ declutters the heart, casting 'out of those storehouses the rubbish and trash of sinful vanities'.[37] Perkins similarly recommends close inspection of the household of the conscience: the property owner entering 'into his house at midnight, he findes or sees nothing out of order: but let him come in the

---

[35] T. Hamling and C. Richardson, *A Day at Home in Early Modern England. Material Culture and Domestic Life, 1500–1700* (New Haven: Yale University Press, 2017), 7–9, 69–70.

[36] M. P. Tilley, ed., *A Dictionary of the Proverbs in England in the Sixteenth and Seventeenth Centuries* (Ann Arbor: University of Michigan Press, 1950), for instance, H122, L306, W85, W91.

[37] J. Downame, *A Guide to Godlynesse* (1622; 1629), 57, 62, 63, 64, 186; Kaufman, *Prayer, Despair, and Drama*, 43.

48   CLEANING

day time, when the sun shineth, and he shall then perceive many faults in the house, and the very motes that fly up and down.[38] The preacher at Batcombe, Somerset, Richard Bernard, speaks of how,

> as some spots and sprincklings wil not off with light brushing; but need more forcible meanes, and therefore thou wilt vse rubbing, yea and washing too; if otherwise the dirt will not out, euen so, some sinnes will not off with easie meanes, but wee must vse rubbing & washing, that is, ardent prayer, and much fasting, & wash them with abundant teares of a penitent heart: yea and bring our selues vnto the fountaine of grace, & desire of God to rinse vs throughly in the blood of Christ ... That as washed clothes need wringing, and also the warme Sunne to drie them againe, so needeth the penitent spirit, sory for sinne, and wrung with contrition, the comfortable promises, of the warm Sun beames of the Gospell, to drie vp his deepe sorrow.[39]

An adaptation of Psalm 51 by the master of the children of the Chapel Royal, William Hunnis, expands on two verses ('Wash me thoroughly from mine iniquity, and cleanse me from my sin', and 'Purge me with hyssop, and I shall be clean: wash me, and I shall be whiter than snow', verses 2, 7) with engaging specificity. His faults are

> More noisome, and more odious,
> more fowler to be tride,
> Than euer was the lothsome swine,
> or menstruall cloth beeraid ...
>
> Polluted cloths with filth distaind
> doo manic washings craue,
> Ere that the Launder can obteine
> the thing that he would haue.
>
> My soule likewise (alas) dooth need
> thy manie dewes of grace,
> Ere it be cleane; for cankred sinne
> so deepe hath taken place ...
>
> But, Lord, thy mercie is the Sope,
> and washing lee also,

---

[38] W. Perkins, *A Discourse of Conscience* (1596), 159–160.
[39] R. Bernard, *A Weekes Worke, and a Worke for Every Weeke* (1616), 52–54.

That shall both scowre & clense the filth
which in my soule doo grow.[40]

Christopher Harvey's sinner is equally as vigorous in scrubbing his heart. A reference to Jeremiah 2:22 ('For though thou wash thee with nitre, and take thee much soap, yet thine iniquity is marked before me, saith the Lord') is brought up to date by specifying the type of soap:

> O endlesse misery!
> I labour still, but still in vaine
> The staines of sinne I see
> Are oaded all, or di'd in graine.
> There's not a blot
> Will stirre a jot
> For all that I can doe:
> There is no hope
> In Fullers sope,
> Though I adde nitre too.
>
> I many wayes have tri'd,
> Have often soakt it in cold feares,
> And, when a time I spi'd,
> Powred upon it scalding teares,
> Have rins'd, and rub'd,
> And scrap't and scrub'd,
>
> And turn'd it up, and downe:
> Yet can I not
> Wash out one spot,
> It's rather fouler growne.

(It serves the sinner right: he is using 'hands that are defil'd'; at least Herbert, in 'Love Unknown', meets with an expert in laundry).[41]

It is notable that these texts fantasize about washing clothes, not the body, even though they are talking about a heart to be cleaned, and even though bathing was a more accessible and applicable image open to them. Following Georges Vigarello's research, until recently it was assumed that dry washing

---

[40] W. Hunnis, *Seven Sobs of a Sorrowfull Soule for Sinne* (1583), 37–39. See also T. Playfere, *The Sicke-mans Couch* (1604), 45.
[41] C. Harvey, *Schola Cordis, or, the Heart of It Selfe, Gone Away from God* (1647), 69–70.

50 CLEANING

was the norm, where people would rub themselves down and change their under linen.[42] However, Susan North has shown how wet washing was the more usual (not least because it is quicker and easier to wash the body than to wash cloth fouled by that body).[43] Unlike other cleaning work, laundry was always a task for women.[44] *The Country Parson*, for instance, recommends that though the unmarried minister may have 'men servants at home', he always gets 'his linnen washed abroad'.[45] Yet these devotional writers eschew images of washing themselves to give fair descriptions of the arduous activities of wash day, when linen would be sorted, the soap lathered up into suds, hot water added, the linen batted in soapy water, then rinsed, then bucked (soaked in lye to whiten it), then rinsed again, then starched, then wrung, then dried, then smoothed.[46] Imagining doing their own washing is a deliberately inappropriate fantasy, used in a mood of asceticism in which unpleasant activities, foreign to these men's normal life, are embraced.[47]

There are even closer links made in the period between spiritual and physical cleanliness. Michelle M. Dowd has shown how the mistresses of two large households interspersed supervision of the household with extended periods in private in which they reviewed and managed their souls, just as systematically and competently. Spiritual practice and household chores, she concludes, could be equally valued and mutually dependent.[48] Such arguments could be extended to those of both sexes in the lower ranks who were engaged in domestic chores throughout the day, and who relied on practical divinity's assurance that diligent work in one's vocation was a form of worship. Perkins speaks of the particular calling (to work in a specific estate or occupation, appointed by God) as a matter of proper order: 'As in a campe the generall appointeth to every man his place & standing; one place for the horseman, and another for

---

[42] G. Vigarello, *Concepts of Cleanliness: Changing Attitudes in France Since the Middle Ages* (1985), trans. J. Birrell (Cambridge: Cambridge University Press, 1988), 1–10; K. Ashenburg, *Clean: An Unsanitized History of Washing* (2007; London: Profile Books, 2008), 97–124.

[43] North, *Sweet and Clean*, 1–7.

[44] R. B., 'Breviate', 45; Powell, *Tom of All Trades*, G3r. See also K. Mertes, *The English Noble Household, 1250–1600. Good Governance and Politic Rule* (Oxford: Basil Blackwell, 1988), 57–59; J. Whittle, 'The House as a Place of Work in Early Modern Rural England', *Home Cultures*, 8/2 (2011), 138.

[45] Herbert, *The Country Parson*, 237.

[46] *A Profitable Booke Declaring Dyvers Approved Remedies, to Take Out Spottes and Staines, in Silkes, Velvets, Linnnen [sic] and Woollen Clothes*, trans. L. Mascall (1583); G. Ruscelli, *The Seconde Part of the Secretes of Master Alexis of Piemont*, trans. W. Warde (1560), 94 ff.; D. Leed, '"Ye shall have it cleane": Textile Cleaning Techniques in Renaissance Europe', *Medieval Clothing and Textiles*, 2 (2006), 101–120.

[47] E. Durkheim, *The Elementary Forms of the Religious Life* (1912), trans. J. W. Swain (1915; London: George Allen and Unwin, 1976), 308–321.

[48] M. M. Dowd, *Women's Work in Early Modern English Literature and Culture* (Basingstoke: Palgrave Macmillan, 2009), 95–132. See also C. Richardson, *Domestic Life and Domestic Tragedy in Early Modern England: The Material Life of the Household* (Manchester: Manchester University Press, 2006), 46–47.

the footman, ... [and] no souldier can depart his standing, without the leave of the general', and 'in a clocke made by the arte and hand worke of man, there be many wheeles, & every one hath his severall motion, some turne this way, some that way, some go softly, some apace', but all are needed where they are. Even housework is blessed, and 'thus may we reape marvellous contentation in any kind of calling, though it be but to sweepe the house, or keepe sheepe'. Contrariwise, not acting in this order is sinful: 'the sea if it moved not could not but putrifie ... the idle and slouthful person is a sea of corruption'.[49]

Collections of printed prayers often include texts for both male and female servants which see housework and holiness as mutually dependent. Private prayers for maid-servants, written by Thomas Bentley (a London citizen), Johann Habermann (professor at Wittenberg), and Thomas Sorocold (rector of St Mildred Poultry, London), ask God to make her 'so faithful and trustie in all my busines, that nothing be at anie time either marred or lost of those things committed to my charge, either through my negligence or unthriftines', and to 'neither waste, spoile, or destroy any thing. Let fire or other casualities (through my negligence) no way harme my Maisters house'. She prays to be made 'faithfull and trusty, wise and warie in the ordering of such goods as are committed to my custody by my Master or Mistresse'.[50] Handbooks to order a family, such as those which Wallington consulted, suggest that disorder encourages the accumulation of physical dirt, and can give the occasion for such sins as sloth, theft, and malicious gossip. Robert Cleaver advises the housewife to

be a stirrer in every place ... sometimes gently teaching [the servants], sometimes commending, ... Sometimes friendly putting them in mind, how by slouth, forgetfulnesse, or sluttishnesse, they shall get an ill name for their service, and so become turne-awaies from every good house. She must lay a diligent eye to her household-stuffe in every Roome, that nothing be embezeled away, nothing spoyled or lost for want of looking to, nothing mard by ill usage, nor nothing worne out by more using then is needeful, nothing out of place, for things cast aside, are deemed to be stolen, and then there followeth uncharitable suspitions.[51]

---

[49] W. Perkins, *A Treatise of the Vocations, or, Callings of Men* (1603), 3, 12–13, 34. Bishop Joseph Hall uses the same image for the slothful (a 'standing pool' of 'uncleanliness') in his popular collection of *Characters of Virtues and Vices* (1606), cited by J. Powers-Beck, *Writing the Flesh: The Herbert Family Dialogue* (Pittsburgh: Duquesne University Press, 1998), 80.

[50] T. Bentley, *The Fift Lampe of Virginitie* (1582), 171; J. Habermann, *The Princes Prayers*, trans. anon (1610), 371; T. Sorocold, *Supplications of Saints: A Booke of Prayers* (1612), mispaginated [344–345].

[51] R. Cleaver, *A Godlie Forme of Householde Government* (1598), 93.

52 CLEANING

The 'pious prentice' depicted by Abraham Jackson (prebendary of Peterborough) gets even quantities of advice on his religious conduct and his domestic work: 'be carefull that nothing be spoiled or lost or miscarry by your negligence', and do not 'repine' at being allocated a chore but 'accept it cheerefully' (with the eye-catching injunction not to run pins into a baby to make it cry, so as to dodge more childcare!)[52]

Walter Darell, describing a serving man's duties, argues that godliness underlies the servant's three principal virtues of cleanliness, confidence, and diligence, for 'nothing can prosper which we taken in hand, or goe about, unless we applie our minde to the service of God'. Religious and domestic service are mingled, as when, arriving at night at an inn, the servant attends to his

> maister, that his lodging may in any wise be sweete and cleanly, his sheetes white washed, and very well ayred, his boots see forthwith made cleane and stuffed with strawe in time of foule wether, and bring them up to his chamber: see nothing be wanting when he riseth the next morning ... Be not negligent: but at night, when thou goest to bed, and quietly art laide, call to minde what things thou hast done all the whole daye, as also what weightie affairs have been committed to thy charge, and thou shalt with continuall use bring thy selfe to a moste quicke and perfect memorie, and shalt not onely by this means have a good remembraunce, but besides ... thou maist with a repentant heart call thine own conscience to reckoning.[53]

Likewise, linking the two forms of accounting clears both a 'to do' list and a conscience in the penultimate stanza of 'The Church-porch'. The reader is urged to use the necessary daily chores of dressing (both putting on clothes and, more generally, making oneself clean and decent) and winding one's watch as nudges to examining the soul, in a methodical, low-key way:

> Summe up at night, what thou hast done by day; / And in the morning, what thou hast to do. / Dresse and undresse thy soul: mark the decay / And growth of it: if with thy watch, that too / Be down, then winde up both.[54]

Ferrar's sets of rules for the children at Little Gidding urge creating the same mental link each morning: 'dressing and composing your inward man' by

---

[52] A. Jackson, *The Pious Prentice* (1640), 67–68, 76.

[53] W. Darell, *A Short Discourse of the Life of Servingmen* (1578), B2r, C3r.

[54] Nicholas Ferrar spoke of how 'the best minds are like clocks which to goe right need daily winding upp'. See Ransome, *Web of Friendship*, 13, 64, 221.

'Winding up your Watch of your mind', a state expressed by a decent personal appearance.[55]

The Country Parson draws the minister's attention to seemingly trivial details of housekeeping in his home and church. At home, 'the furniture of [the minister's] house is very plain, but clean, whole, and sweet, as sweet as his garden can make'. It is kept so by servants demonstrating their 'Neatnesse, or Cleanlinesse', one of the three principal qualities their employer looks for.[56]

As to his church, Herbert goes beyond the requirements of the 1604 Canons of the Church of England, which simply ask that the space be in 'orderly and decent sort, without dust, or anything that may be either noisome or unseemly'.[57] Visitation articles of the two dioceses in which he was employed (Lincoln and Salisbury) are fairly general about good order in the physical church. The books which it was mandatory to keep in the church are to be 'all well and fairly bound', the church is to be 'decently and comely kept', 'cleanly kept', and 'decent'. There was, however, increasing desire to go further. J. F. Merritt finds in sermons of the 1630s 'an obsessive, almost prurient concern with the possible pollution of the church building, church utensils, and the service', as church buildings came to be seen as consecrated spaces in themselves, and not sacred because people met there to do holy things.[58] The 1619 articles for Norwich (on which those of Salisbury were based) add phrases not appearing in the Salisbury version, requiring that 'all things [be kept] in orderly and decent sort, without dust', forbidding 'any thing that may be either noysome or unseemely for the house of God', and asking visitors to enquire if any have 'annoyed your churchyard or the fence thereof, by putting in of cattell, by hanging of cloathes, or by laying there any dust, dung, or other filthines'.[59]

The Country Parson cites 1 Corinthians 14.40 ('Let all things be done decently and in order') to insist that the church be 'swept, and kept clean, without dust, or Cobwebs, and at great festivalls strawed, and stuck with boughs, and perfumed with incense' (thus, soft to walk on, beautiful to look at, and delightful to smell). The books appointed to be kept in it must not be 'torne, or fouled, but whole and clean, and well bound'.[60] Herbert thinks a clean church

---

[55] J. Ransome, '"Courtesy" at Little Gidding', *The Seventeenth Century*, 30/4 (2015), 418.

[56] Herbert, *Country Parson*, 240.

[57] J. V. Bullard, ed., *Constitutions and Canons Ecclesiastical, 1604, Latin and English* (London: Faith Press, 1934), 88.

[58] J. F. Merritt, 'Puritans, Laudians, and the Phenomenon of Church-Building in Jacobean London', *The Historical Journal*, 41/4 (1998), 957.

[59] K. Fincham, ed., *Visitation Articles and Injunctions of the Early Stuart Church*, 2 vols. (Woodbridge: Church of England Record Society and Boydell Press, 1994–1998), 1.70, 80–82, 159–160, 173–176.

[60] Herbert, *Country Parson*, 246.

54   CLEANING

so important that, Kristine Wolberg points out, he widens the application of the biblical verse (which in the original refers to how worship should be conducted 'decently and in order') to include physical cleaning and repairs, for 'right appearances serve to edify'.[61] Here, externals are valued because they affect the worshipper's internal disposition, but the influence can also go in the opposite direction: 'The Parsons yea is yea, and nay nay; and his apparrell plaine, but reverend, and clean, without spots, or dust, or smell; the purity of his mind breaking out, and dilating it selfe even to his body, cloaths, and habitation'.[62] The same advice appears in 'The Church-porch':

> Affect in things about thee cleanlinesse,
> That all may gladly board thee, as a flower.
> Slovens take up their stock of noisomnesse
> Beforehand, and anticipate their last houre.
> Let thy mindes sweetnesse have his operation
> Upon thy body, clothes, and habitation.

Wilcox comments that here spiritual purity and personal hygiene are signs of each other.[63] The mind operates on the concentric circles of body, clothes, and home, and this, in turn, encourages the virtue of sociability from others.

Moreover, elsewhere in *The Temple*, there is a hint that this works the other way too, since 'Slovens' are unlikely to find their 'last houre' pleasing, given that the experience of God's presence is usually felt as 'fresh ... sweet and clean' ('The Flower'). Thomas Churchyard states this outright: cleanliness promotes self-respect and hence virtue. 'The comely cleane attire, doth carrie mind aloft,/ Makes man think scorne to stoup to Vice, and loke to Vertue oft'.[64] Practical divines are quick to take advantage of this link, anticipating John Wesley's epigram that 'cleanliness is next to godliness'.[65] Keith Thomas points out how personal cleanliness was recommended both as good stewardship of God's gift of the body and as a sign of respect to God (one was always in his presence, so should always be decent).[66] John Angier, minister at Denton, Lancashire, describes how,

---

[61] K. Wolberg, *'All Possible Art': George Herbert's The Country Parson* (Madison: Fairleigh Dickinson Press, 2008), 126.

[62] Herbert, *Country Parson*, 228, 241.

[63] Herbert, *Poems*, ed. Wilcox, 79, 367. For other examples of sweetness, see xlv.

[64] T. Churchyard, *A Discourse of the Queenes Majesties Entertainment in Suffolk and Norfolk* (1578), E2v.

[65] For Wesley's use of this phrase, see Mugglestone, 'Cleanliness', 322.

[66] K. Thomas, 'Cleanliness and Godliness in Early Modern England', in A. Fletcher and P. Roberts, eds., *Religion, Culture, and Society in Early Modern Britain: Essays in Honour of Patrick Collinson* (Cambridge: Cambridge University Press, 1994), 56–83.

when we are to come to the house of God, we prepare our bodies, in regard of the company we come unto, we wash ourselves, and change our apparell, and see that it be clean, we put on some clothes that were not worne since they were washed, but are prepared in the week for that day, and we should condemn a man of uncomliness & rudeness, of rashness & indiscretion that should come unprepared in body.

Angier cites Genesis 35.2, in which Jacob tells all the members of his household to clean themselves before making an altar to God (the Geneva Bible's marginal note is that 'by this outward act they should shewe their inwarde repentence').[67] Bernard cites Ruth 2.3 to speak of how 'outward civill cleanliness ... is praiseworthy', 'healthfull to us, delightsome to others, and commendable'; it befits the 'good report' of a Christian, and it is 'sluttish, nasty, and beastlike' to be 'uncivill' (though it is sinful, also, to spend too much time on cleaning oneself).[68] The popular conduct book by the Bishop of Geneva, Francis de Sales, asks that

touching cleanliness ... [of] our apparel, upon which as near as may be, we should not permitt anie kind of uncomely, foulnes or slovenrie. Exterior neatness ordinarilie signifieth the inward cleanlinesse of the soul. God him self requireth corporall cleanlynesse, in those that approache nigh his altar, and have the principall charge and care of devotion.[69]

Collections of prayers and meditations recommend that their readers couple the daily acts of personal hygiene and devotion. On waking, Lewis Bayly (Bishop of Bangor) recommends, 'having washed thy selfe, and adorned thy body with apparell which beseemeth thy calling, and the image of God, which thou bearest, shut thy chamber doore, and kneele downe at thy bedside, or some other convenient place', and pray.[70] Bernard speaks of how, 'in brushing and making cleane thy garments; thinke that as thy rayment is subiect to dust, and other vncleannesse, in the vse, or to mothes in lying still: euen so art thou

---

[67] J. Angier, *An Helpe to Better Hearts for Better Times* (1647), 220, mentioned in Thomas, 'Cleanliness', 61; *The Holy Bible* (1560), Gen. 35.2.

[68] R. Bernard, *Ruths Recompence* (1628), 255, mentioned in Thomas, 'Cleanliness', 63.

[69] F. de Sales, *An Introduction to a Devout Life* (1609), trans. J. Yakesley (1613), 390. In 1636 the Ferrars bound a copy of this text for a client. See H. Kelliher, 'Crashaw at Cambridge', in J. R. Roberts, ed., *New Perspectives on the Life and Art of Richard Crashaw* (Columbia: University of Missouri Press, 1990), 186–187.

[70] L. Bayly, *The Practise of Pietie* (1613), 319.

56 CLEANING

thy selfe subiect to corruptions'.[71] Bentley advises his reader to, when 'Washing your hands, praie thus',

> Wash my soule, O God, with the water of thy diuine grace, from all the filth and pollusion of sinne, wherewith it is altogither defiled in thy sight. Sprinkle it, Lord, with the hyssope of true repentance, and sorowfull contrition; that being clensed in the most cleere fountaine of thy grace, I may be whiter than snowe.

The reader is to kneel again at family morning prayers, in some 'sweete, cleane, and convenient place'. At night, 'when you wash your feete, pray thus',

> with Peter I humblie beseech thee, vouchsafe now to wash me in the sweet bath of thy pretious bloud, from all the filth and pollusions of my sinnes, that I may be whiter than snowe. Wash thou, I saie, not my feet onelie, O Lord, but my hands and head: yea my verie hart, soule, and conscience also. For if thou wash me not, I shall haue no part with thee; but if thou wash me, I shall be cleane euerie whit in all parts, yea cleaner than the glasse.[72]

Such a tradition lies behind Herbert's reflection on how

> Sometimes, when as I wash, I say
> And shrodely, as I think, Lord wash my soul
> More spotted then my flesh can be. ('Love', Williams manuscript only)[73]

The moment is quickly followed by a recollection of how baptism has already cleansed him, and Paul Gaston criticizes the poem for allowing doctrine to overtake experience.[74] However, the adverb 'shrewdly' (pointed up by the pretend-humble reference to 'as I think') has the connotations of mischievous, cunning, and keen, so alters the tone in which this pious gesture is done. During this mundane and repeated ('Sometimes', not once) daily moment, Herbert is deliberately and delightedly nudging God, in the comfortable knowledge that he will get the response he always gets when doing this: a memory of baptism.

---

[71] Bernard, *Weekes Worke*, 51–52.
[72] Bentley, *Monument of Matrones*, 376, 378, 989.
[73] Herbert, *Poems*, ed. Wilcox, 12.
[74] P. Gaston, 'The Excluded Poems: Steps to *The Temple*', in E. Miller and R. DiYanni, eds., *Like Season'd Timber: New Essays on George Herbert* (New York: Peter Lang, 1987), 154.

3 Herbert's Housework

Cleaning both place and person, then, may be part of a particular vocation, act as a nudge, and express a godly state of mind, so domestic work is one of the principal occupations which Herbert notices in his poems. He sometimes admires the end result: 'I looked on thy furniture so fine, .../ Thy glorious household-stuffe did me entwine' ('Affliction' 1) and God's household, which shows 'curious art in marshalling thy goods' ('Providence'). More often, though, it is the discrete activities which go into creating this comfort which catch Herbert's attention: the making of thread, clothes, fires, beds, food, and gardens. Of God's 'praise, .../ My busie heart shall spin it all my dayes' ('Praise' 3), 'If I have more to spinne,/ The wheel shall go' ('The Glimpse'), and 'reason hath .../ ... of it self, like a good huswife, spunne/ In laws and policie' ('The Pearl'). A 'foolish thought' is dismissed to 'Spin out thy thread, and make thereof a coat' ('Assurance'), and man wears 'stuffe whose thread is coarse and round,/ But trimm'd with curious lace' ('Mans Medley'). Sometimes Herbert, looking 'to clothe the sunne', finds he has accidentally woven himself in, too ('Jordan' 2). Garments are provided ('Who sings thy praise? onely a skarf or glove/ Doth warm our hands, and make them write of love', 'Love' 1) and put off, 'Quitting the furre/ To cold complexions needing it' ('Employment' 2). Other sources of warmth are found, 'as cold hands are angrie with the fire,/ And mend it still' ('Church-lock and key'). Thus, safety protocols are needed: 'I rose, and shook my clothes, as knowing well,/ That from small fires comes oft no small mishap' ('Artillerie'), a scenario which is translated into the context of finding suitable accommodation for God's word, in Herbert's Latin collection 'Lucus' ('Sacred Grove'):

> Could it be that recently as I was sitting by the door
> In the evening I sucked in a falling star;
> And this star, unsuited to lurking concealed
> In a disreputable lodging, is trying to find a way out? ('On Sacred Scripture')[75]

A guest might have expected a warm welcome, given 'that fire which once descended/ On thy Apostles', when God 'didst then/ Keep open house, richly attended', and stars as servants came 'down to know/ If they might mend their

---

[75] 'In S. Scripturas', 'Nunquid pro foribus sedendo nuper/ Stellam vespere suxerim volantem,/ Haec autem hospitio latere turpi/ Prorsùs nescia, cogitat recessum?', in Herbert, Poetry, ed. Drury and Moul, 258–289.

wages, and serve here'. However, now God 'shutt'st the doore, and keep'st within;/ Scarce a good joy creeps through the chink' ('Whitsunday'). A few servants appear disobliging ('I found that some had stuff'd the bed with thoughts,/ I would say *thorns*', 'Love Unknown'), but most are helpful: the bed in 'Miserie' has been made so comfortable that its occupant 'pull'st the rug, and wilt not rise'. Cooking and serving up is done skilfully ('sev'rall baits in either kind/ Furnish thy table to thy minde', 'Affliction' 5), and God has 'prepar'd, and drest' a 'feast' of 'dainties' ('The Invitation'). The sick are physicked: 'I took thy sweetned pill', says a speaker, 'Turning my purge to food' ('Affliction' 1). Out of doors, gardening implements are kept in trim: Time's 'sithe is dull' (more a 'hatchet' than a 'pruning-knife') so needs sharpening ('Time'), and 'watring pots' shed more freely after being pierced with a 'case of knives' ('Affliction' 4).

Above all, it is cleaning in Herbert's poems which absorbs the housekeeper's time. Jeffrey Powers-Beck notes how Herbert uses the same image of sweeping as Perkins does, for working in a vocation:

> Nothing can be so mean,
> Which with his tincture (for thy sake)
>> Will not grow bright and clean.
>
> A servant with this clause
> Makes drudgerie divine:
> Who sweeps a room, as for thy laws,
>> Makes that and th' action fine. ('The Elixer')[76]

F. E. Hutchinson points out that the Country Parson 'holds the Rule, that Nothing is little in Gods service: If it once have the honour of that Name, it grows great instantly'.[77] Nonetheless, Cristina Malcolmson persuasively argues that, in the poem, Herbert defends himself from the degradation he felt in changing from gentleman-scholar to labourer in God's fields.[78] The text was extensively revised by Herbert, and Janis Lull argues that the change from the first version of sweeping 'a chamber, for thy laws' (done as commanded to do) to 'a room, as for thy laws' (done for another reason, but still within the

---

[76] Powers-Beck, *Writing the Flesh*, 73–74. Herbert arrived in Cambridge only seven years after Perkins died there.

[77] Herbert, *Works*, ed. Hutchinson, 248, 541.

[78] C. Malcolmson, *Heart-Work: George Herbert and the Protestant Ethic* (Stanford: Stanford University Press, 1999), 171–173.

law) suggests that 'the revision responds to the Pauline distinction between the letter and the spirit of the law'.[79]

Considering the context of the Country Parson reference underlines Lull's point. While the chapter in which it occurs, 'The Parson in Circuit', focuses mainly on the minutiae of pastoral work, the mention of doing this 'in Gods service' throws Herbert into discussing a limit case: that of entering 'into the poorest Cottage, though ... it smell never so lothsomly' (in Schoenfeldt's splendid pun, 'in the Renaissance one could—in both senses—smell rank'!).[80] Herbert gives three distinct types of reason to impel the minister to do this: the theological (God is present, and so are his flock), the social (the poor especially feel such visits to be 'comfortable'), and as an ascetic nudge to the minister ('in regard of himselfe, it is more humiliation'). In the poem, too, there is a split between extrinsic and intrinsic motivation—cleaning the room and cleaning as prayer—where the former is performed for the sake of the latter.

Wilcox's gloss on 'dust' concentrates on the Bible's sense of it as a basic unit of matter, from which human flesh is formed.[81] It might, however, also be possible to think about the word's dirty connotations in 'The Church-floore', which attempt to threaten the 'sure band' praised there. In return, God mischievously inverts attacks into the helpful completion of chores: Death, 'while he thinks to spoil the room, he sweeps' (like a church warden, sweeping away the dust of slowly decaying monuments and furnishings), and though Sinne stains 'The marbles neat and curious veins', 'all is cleansed when the marble weeps'. These are mundane processes, not mystical or mythical as Strier asserts (corners in old buildings do fill up with dust blown there, and warm air meeting cold stone does precipitate condensation).[82] The fun is in the game of competing intentions being played: God's versus Death and Sinne's. The poem concludes with praise of the 'Architect', which most commentaries focus on—but it might just as well end by praising the Cleaner.[83]

Peering about to spot the dirt is the first step, as Cleaver and Perkins tell their readers. In 'time of service' the attentive congregation will go 'spying' about their hearts, that 'They may weep out the stains by them did rise', and should, since 'Slacknesse breeds worms', 'Shine like the sunne in every corner' ('The Church-porch'). Vermin are spotted: 'hellish moths' 'still gnaw and fret/ ... books' ('Content'), and a sinner foolishly imagines he has 'curtains drawn' (to

---

[79] J. Lull, *The Poem in Time: Reading George Herbert's Revisions of The Church* (Newark: University of Delaware Press, 1990), 97.

[80] Herbert, *Country Parson*, 258; Schoenfeldt, 'Consuming Subjects', 108.

[81] Herbert, *Poems*, ed. Wilcox, xlii, 58–59.

[82] Strier, *Love Known*, 148.

[83] On such architectural readings, see Strier, *Love Known*, 147–150.

60   CLEANING

hide from God's view) which are 'of cloth,/ Where never yet came moth' ('Miserie'). Rubbish is taken out ('How hath man parcel'd out thy glorious name,/ And thrown it on that dust which thou hast made', 'Love 1'). Fortune's 'fine cobwebs' are 'swept ... all away' ('The World'). Laundry is done, as the 'foul' heart is 'dipt and di'd,/ And washt, and wrung' ('Love Unknown'), although close-woven, durable fabrics are recommended for dirty activities: 'Let foolish lovers, if they will love dung,/ With canvas, not with arras clothe their shame' ('The Forerunners'). Herbert's Latin poem on Martha and Mary enumerates all the tasks to be done before Christ enters the house: sweeping, shaking out curtains, lighting the fire, and polishing the furniture.[84] Spills are mopped up: 'Christ left his grave-clothes, that we might, when grief/ Draws tears, or bloud, not want an handkerchief' ('The Dawning'), lines which critics find in bad taste.[85] Their shock value, however, declines if contextualized against other instances of God's pragmatism: dirt is disgusting, so get on and remove it.

Cleaning appears in Herbert as a metaphor for clarification, as an expression of spiritual clarity, and as a physical nudge to focus on God in daily life. When Herbert's catechist uses a household object (such as a hatchet, a bushell, and leaven) to explain his points, for 'things of ordinary use are not only to serve in the way of drudgery, but to be washed, and cleansed, and serve for lights even of Heavenly Truths', the washing done recategorizes the object, from the context of dirty daily life to that of catechetical prompt.[86] So Herbert's reader is repeatedly reminded to segregate, to discriminate, to clean by tidying up: 'Pick out of tales the mirth, but not the sinne./ He pares his apple, that will cleanly feed', 'Pick out of mirth, like stones out of thy ground,/ Profanenesse, filthinesse, abusivenesse' ('The Church-porch'), and 'if there be any ill in [a] custome, that may be severed from the good, [the minister] pares the apple, and gives [his parishioners] the clean to feed on.'[87] The heart should be without a 'noise of thoughts', as these 'defile thy seat:/ For where thou dwellest all is neat' ('The Familie'). Disorder is fought. Herbert asks God to 'give new wheels to our disorder'd clocks' ('Even-song'), perhaps echoing Perkins's image of the mechanism of the clock for those working in their proper vocation. God is implored to mend a disordered prayer life ('Deniall'). In 'Dooms-day', where

---

[84] 'Martha: Maria', in Herbert, Poetry, ed. Drury and Moul, 264–265; Herbert included the poem in the Williams manuscript, see Charles, Life, 92. The Little Academy heard two stories about how the active and contemplative lives were mutually supportive sisters. See Blackstone, ed., Ferrar Papers, 218–221.

[85] H. Vendler, The Poetry of George Herbert (Cambridge: Harvard University Press, 1975), 145–148; C. Bloch, Spelling the Word: George Herbert and the Bible (Berkeley: University of California Press, 1985), 223.

[86] Herbert, Country Parson, 257.

[87] Herbert, Country Parson, 283–284.

'Man is out of order hurl'd', the whirling particles of human dust create a public health hazard:

> Some to windes their bodie lend,
> And in them may drown a friend:
> Some in noisome vapurs grow
> To a plague and publick woe.

Rare exceptions are gratefully noted: the stones enclosing Christ's body are praised for their solemn 'order' ('Sepulchre'), as are Sundays, which bring order and purpose into time ('Sunday'). Robert Higbie and Frank Huntley note how boxes, bags, and cupboards are often used to parcel things up into helpful categories.[88] In 'Man', creation is divided up into different classes to prompt meditation. The earth, for instance, is 'either our cupboard of *food*,/ Or cabinet of *pleasure*'. In 'Mortification', a series of concentric boxes confine the apparently free individual as he grows up and old: swaddling clothes from 'a chest of sweets', his bed, his house, a chair or litter, before a grave. Herbert is confident that he has 'not lost one single tear', since God is careful about storage, allocating each soul 'a bottle' for them, '(As we have boxes for the poore)' ('Praise' 3). Complexities are boxed up: 'The statelier cabinet' of the Trinity and the box of the Incarnation are where God's 'sweets are packt up', separated from 'Sinnes', which 'have their box apart,/ Defrauding thee, who gavest two for one' ('Ungratefulnesse').

As Russell Hillier says, 'trim, clean, and neat' are three of Herbert's favourite adjectives, a trio whose lack of poetic romance has piqued the interest of Herbert scholars.[89] Some focus on the legibility of faith. Gary Kuchar, for instance, argues that Herbert presents poetry as words whose order remedies misreading. 'In Herbert's lexicon, distraction is an antonym of Christ-like neatness', and ministers of the church have a responsibility to explicate the mysteries of faith clearly (albeit in a nuanced way) to its members.[90] Christopher Hodgkins contextualizes Herbert's works in terms of the image in many reformed and conformist texts of cleaning away religious superstition and clarifying

---

[88] For Higbie, this is a protective move; for Huntley, the containers are always threatening to burst open. See R. Higbie, 'Images of Enclosure in George Herbert's *The Temple*', *Texas Studies in Literature and Language*, 15 (1974), 627–398; F. Huntley, 'George Herbert and the Image of Violent Containment', *GHJ*, 8/1 (1984), 17–27.

[89] R. Hillier, '"Th'action fine": The Good of Works in George Herbert's Poetry', *Renascence*, 68/1 (2016), 10.

[90] G. Kuchar, 'Introduction: Distraction and the Ethics of Poetic Form in *The Temple*', *Christianity and Literature*, 66 (2016), 10; G. Kuchar, *George Herbert and the Mystery of the Word: Poetry and Scripture in Seventeenth-century England* (Cham: Palgrave Macmillan, 2017), 5–11, 27–32.

62 CLEANING

worship, to make it comprehensible.[91] Some critics, like Helen Vendler, focus on a soul brought out of anxiety and into divine order.[92] Some focus on doctrine. Herbert's Mary Magdalen knows that 'her sinnes did dash/ Ev'n God himself', but also that her tears will clean him: 'As she had brought wherewith to stain,/ So to bring in wherewith to wash' ('Marie Magdalene'). In an extended reading of the poem, Strier argues that between stanzas two and three Mary moves from weeper (in penitence, looking backwards) to washer (with faith, present-centred). For Strier, the final line, 'And yet in washing one, she washed both', shows Mary has received forgiveness and hence the grace to weep.[93] Coming from a soteriological perspective, Kate Narveson argues that Calvinism's distinction between passive justification and active sanctification appears in Herbert's poems on the cleansing nature of tears and fasting. When Herbert writes about irrepressible 'Tears sullying [God's] transparent rooms' ('Gratefulnesse'), he writes from the point of view of justification, as his body registers the state of his soul which has been washed clean. However, when he writes about fasting he does so from the point of view of sanctification, with its insistence on an ability and duty to fashion the conditions in which godliness flourishes.[94]

Taking Narveson's line, nudges by cleaning would appear to be a form of preparationism. But does Herbert think they work? The early modern period had two uses for the word 'clean': as an emphatic adjective (such as 'clean contrary'), and as a state of purity (generally used in the negative form, 'unclean'). Both express the notion of order created by separating out items.[95] Mary Douglas demonstrates that, in the Old Testament, clean and dirty are categories created for matter in or out of its usual or allotted place. Clean items are those which are proper, suitable, or fitting to their class. The taboo (the potentially untouchable dirty item) arises in situations of doubt, in order to protect a local consensus about how the world is organized. It reduces the intellectual and social dangers of disorder by placing the ambiguous into its own category. Since things, and classes themselves, can be reordered, objects and practices can become successively sacred or taboo, and so evoke responses ranging from humour to horror, Douglas argues.[96] William Miller and William Cohen agree

---

[91] C. Hodgkins, 'The Church Legible: George Herbert and the Externals of Worship', *Journal of Religion*, 71 (1991), 221–223.

[92] Vendler, *Herbert*, 202–230.

[93] R. Strier, 'Herbert and Tears', *English Literary History*, 46 (1979), 239.

[94] K. Narveson, 'Flesh, Excrement, Humors, Nothing: the Body in Early Stuart Devotional Discourse', *Studies in Philology*, 96/3 (1999), 313–333.

[95] L. Mugglestone, '"Next to Godliness?" Exploring Cleanliness in Peace and War', *History of European Ideas*, 45/3 (2019), 323–325.

[96] Douglas, *Purity and Danger*, 48–50.

with her that cultures may use the concept of disgust to police the boundaries of 'us' and 'others', but they focus specifically on the visceral nature of the emotion, which they claim can overcome such boundaries. Cohen unconsciously echoes Della Casa's earlier observation of how dirt can be so psychologically disturbing that it attracts its observer.[97] Miller notes that the vocabulary of disgust tends to be used for hyperbolic moral judgements against day-to-day vices which cannot be clearly separated from accepted practices. Its exaggeration tries to shore up weak walls. The moral quality which particularly evokes an excremental vocabulary is hypocrisy (or, more generally, any form of compromise). Disgust at such half-and-half states, he argues, attempts to cleanse them with fiery indignation, but the observer's attention often ends up clinging stickily to what it is trying to reject.[98]

Herbert can use disgust with dirt to reinforce national and denominational allegiances. 'The Church-porch' advises a reader to

> Leave not thine owne deere-cuntry-cleanlines
> for this ffrench sluttery wch so current goes:
> As if none could bee brave, but who profess
> ffirst to bee Slovens, & forsake their nose. (Deleted lines,
>   Williams manuscript only)[99]

Two of Herbert's poems against Andrew Melville turn the purity of the Puritan against him. 'On Spots and Stains', countering Melville's denunciation of established practices in the church, enquires rhetorically about 'What is the blood of Christ for, if not to wash off the spots/ Which the body's clay spatters too closely upon the soul'. 'On a Certain Puritan' points out the effects of Melville's zeal: 'When you preach in the temples, handkerchiefs are soaked, as are napkins,/ The savage armpit goat, shirts, cloaks, even a woollen overcoat'.[100]

Often, though, while his speakers want to get things clear, they end up being comically exact about how impossible such separation is. Schoenfeldt points out how Herbert uses images of sloshy excrements to talk about the necessity of imposing consistency to get zeal.[101] There are no qualms about mentioning

---

[97] W. A. Cohen, 'Introduction: Locating Filth', in W. A. Cohen and R. Johnson, eds., *Filth: Dirt, Disgust, and Modern Life* (Minneapolis: University of Minnesota Press, 2004), ix–xi.

[98] Miller, *Disgust*, 179–205.

[99] Herbert, *Poems*, ed. Wilcox, 79.

[100] '*De labe maculisíque*', '*Quò sanguis est Christi, nisi vt maculas lauet,/ Quas spargit animae corporis propius lutum*'; '*In Catharum quendam*', '*Cvm templis effare, madent sudaria, mappae,/ Trux caper alarum, suppara, laena, sagum*', in '*Musae responsoriæ*'['The Muses' Reply'], in Herbert, *Poetry*, ed. Drury and Moul, 230–231.

[101] M. C. Schoenfeldt, 'George Herbert's Consuming Subject', *GHJ*, 18/1–2 (1994–1995), 108–110, 112–115, 122–125. See, by contrast, the class distinctions also expressed by charges of filth, M. C.

64   CLEANING

the unmentionable in his quest for cleanliness, poems noting how 'My friend may spit upon my curious floore' ('Unkindnesse'), 'Thy diet, care, and cost/ Do end in bubbles, balls of winde' ('Even-song'), and 'in fulnesse there are sluttish fumes,/ Sowre exhalations, and dishonest rheumes' ('Lent'). In 'The Sinner', the heart is full of 'dregs' mixed with 'spirit and good extract', though the latter 'Comes to about the many hundredth part'. 'The Church-porch' finds that 'The stormie working soul spits lies and froth', and admonishes 'England! full of sinne, but most of sloth' to 'Spit out thy flegme, and fill thy brest with glorie', for 'Who keeps no guard upon himself, is slack/ And rots to nothing at the next great thaw'. *The Temple* ends by asking God to squeeze a sigh out of a gaseous Sin, or make him 'discharge what is behinde' ('L'Envoy'). In 'Miserie', Herbert sarcastically proposes that man 'doth not like this vertue, no;/ Give him his dirt to wallow in all night', preferring to 'wed' 'strange pollutions'. Even when trying to serve God, clarity is a state out of reach of this human 'lump of flesh'. Like Christopher Harvey's speaker, it leaves dirty fingerprints all over clean surfaces:

> As dirtie hands foul all they touch,
> And those things most, which are most pure and fine:
> So our clay hearts, ev'n when we crouch
> To sing thy praises, make them lesse divine.

As the poem repeats, seven times ('foolishnesse', 'foolish man', 'a foolish thing, a foolish thing' 'Folly', 'fool'd', 'follies'), such dirt is the result not of out-and-out vice, but of a lack of clarity and focus. Disorder is a sort of bad faith: 'No man shall beat into his head' a plain fact, for he acts 'as though he knew it not,/ His knowledge winks'.

Schoenfeldt shows how *The Country Parson* details situations in which dirt lies side by side with divinity. For instance, the bread used for holy communion is sacred, but is nevertheless checked for mould: the minister 'takes order with the Church-Wardens, that the elements be of the best, not cheape, or course, much lesse ill-tasted, or unwholsome'.[102] The soul is made of 'wretched earth', yet

> Where once I scorn'd to stand,
> That earth is fitted by the fire and trade

Schoenfeldt, 'The Art of Disgust: Civility and the Social Body in *Hesperides*', *GHJ*, 14/1–2 (1990–1991), 127–154; S. Greenblatt, 'Filthy Rites', *Daedalus*, 111/3 (1982), 1–16.
[102] Herbert, *Country Parson*, 258; Schoenfeldt, 'Consuming Subjects', 108.

> Of skilfull artists, for the boards of those
> Who make the bravest shows ('The Priesthood').

Herbert's heart is an untidy place 'where in/ One box doth lie both ink and sinne', both the fault and the means to overwrite it ('Good Friday'). On his deathbed, Herbert dismissed his church renovation as only being 'a good work, if it be sprinkled with the bloud of Christ'.[103] Nothing he had done could finally be declared as clean or dirty.

Sometimes Herbert tries a good rummage to get clarity: 'Dare to look in thy chest; for 'tis thine own:/ And tumble up and down what thou find'st there' ('Church-porch'). Careless prayer and refusing to listen to an inward prompt are revealed as the sins at issue by a little methodical tidying: 'Go search this thing,/ Tumble thy breast, and turn thy book./ If thou hadst lost a glove or ring,/ Wouldst thou not look?' ('The Method'). And yet, despite all this effort, disorder seeps back: 'Where are my lines then? my approaches? views?', the speaker of 'Dulnese' grumbles about misplaced objects (concluding that 'Sure thou didst put a minde there, if I could/ Finde where it lies'), leaving God to 'cleare' things up.

The final fate of an individual's soul may be a known unknown, and unchangeable—at least from a human point of view—but Herbert's poems find his behaviour less clearly clean or dirty. Those who have been cleansed can enter 'The Church', but, as is sometimes forgotten by commentators, so too can those who are not, but passionately desire to become so:

> Thou, whom the former precepts have
> Sprinkled and taught ...
>   ... come not here:
> Nothing but holy, pure, and cleare,
> Or that which groneth to be so,
> May at his perill further go. ('Superliminare')

If the volume of energetic cleaning which goes on in Herbert's poems is recognized, it suggests that he feels a lot of ambiguity about the current state of his soul. And, as Della Casa, Douglas, Miller, and Cohen point out, this creates both fascination and humour. Hopes and fears about getting clear of sin are repeatedly aroused, allayed, and aroused again, putting the soul in one category then another, and back again.

---

[103] Herbert, *Poems*, ed. Wilcox, 43.

66   CLEANING

Theodore D. Bozeman finds a 'precisionist strain' among zealous Protestants, who were committed to working at the limits of human capacity and endurance in being heroically exact in doctrine and morals. More of such piety might be expected to lead to less doubt in one's faith. However, Bozeman points out, in practice the opposite was the case. The more intense and refined the analysis of one's conscience, the less assurance one felt.[104] Herbert's poems show the unremitting nature of heart housework. His desire to keep himself orderly is rarely brought to a satisfying end. Doubt about whether he has, in fact, been reclassified from damned to saved provokes his most energetic nudges to get things clear and clean—no magical weightlessness here, just the trudge of eliminating smudge through nudge.

[104] T. D. Bozeman, *The Precisianist Strain: Disciplinary Religion and Antinomian Backlash in Puritanism to 1638* (Chapel Hill: University of North Carolina Press, 2004), 3–6, 145–155.

3

Building

1 Ideal Spaces for Worship

The Reformation did not necessarily limit the variety of sacred spaces in which one might worship, though such locations as convents, priories, shrines, crosses, hermitages, and pilgrimage routes vanished. Instead, the sense that daily life itself could be led as a form of prayer increased the possibilities for recognizing new holy spaces.[1] Moreover, since the polemical and aesthetic aims of Laudianism were based on a vision of the divine presence in the world, an appropriate ritual response to that presence was indicated. Seeing the physical 'church as the house of God had certain very practical consequences', says Peter Lake, both in making it as fitting a space as was possible for human skill to accomplish and in using it to amplify the response of those who experienced that space. There should be a sensitive use of God's 'creatures', such as stone, wood, paint, and fabric, to further these two aims.[2]

Thus, Giles Fleming (rector of Waddingworth, Lincolnshire) argues that 'the comelinesse, and beauty of the house of prayer, erecteth and lifteth up the minde into a more solid and due consideration of those holy exercises which we goe about; solemnely, even in all things, mightily working (though insensibly) upon the minds of men'.[3] John Browning (at the time rector of Little Easton, Essex) asks

doth not the reverent entrance of one that entereth, as he should, stir up the fainting devotion of them that pray? Doth not the devout kneeling of those that are about us, put us also in mind of the duty, and earnestnesse of our prayers. And so, whereas the Priest preacheth to the eare only, every one in

---

[1] W. Coster and A. Spicer, 'Introduction: The Dimensions of Sacred Space in Reformation Europe', in W. Coster and A. Spicer, ed., *Sacred Space in Early Modern Europe* (Cambridge: Cambridge University Press, 2005), 4–10.

[2] P. Lake, 'The Laudian Style: Order, Uniformity, and the Pursuit of the Beauty of Holiness in the 1630s', in K. Fincham, ed., *The Early Stuart Church, 1603–1642* (Stanford: Stanford University Press, 1993), 164–168. On priming decisions through affecting the senses, see Thaler and Sunstein, *Nudge*, 110.

[3] G. Fleming, *Magnificence Exemplified: And, the Repaire of Saint Pauls Exhorted Unto* (1634), 42.

George Herbert and the Business of Practical Piety. Ceri Sullivan, Oxford University Press.
© Ceri Sullivan (2024). DOI: 10.1093/9780198906841.003.0003

68 BUILDING

this his devotion, and by his example (which is most forcible) preacheth to each other others eye.

Againe, this bodily reverence, as it addeth heat of devotion to others; so it is truly an incentive of devotion to our selves: for the body, as it receiveth life and motion from the soule, so it returneth also a further life by motion to it againe: as strings touched in the same instrument, move one another; or as the bodies warmth warms the cloathes, which reciprocally preserve, and returne the bodies warmth againe.[4]

Robert Skinner (royal chaplain-in-ordinary, and rector of Launton, Oxfordshire) appeals

> to common experience, for do we not find ourselves otherwise affected, when we come into a naked deformed, ruinous Temple, adorned with nothing but dust and cobwebs, and when we come into a goodly reverent beautifull Church, wherein we may behold on every side remarkeable testimonies of devout Magnificence? Doth not the very Fabricke and fashion, and solemn accommodation beget in our hearts a religious regard and venerable thoughts?[5]

One R. T. assumes that the 'humane soule ... is ... so weake of understanding that without the helpe of our senses we understand nothing'. He talks of how, in a cruciform or rectangular church, 'the man who enters the West doore from farre beholding the Altar ... shall find his devout soule, more wrapped with divine awe and reverence, more inflamed with pure and holy zeale, in the delay and later approach unto it, than if at first he had entered upon it all'. Windows placed high 'differ more from profane buildings, [and] keep our thoughts from wandring abroad, whilst our eyes have nothing but Heaven, and heavenly objects to behold, and besides cast an excellent light for the paintings on the wals'. Stained glass windows, in particular,

> adorn the Church with a glorious light, and moderate that bright light, which is a hinderance to devotion ... For devotion requires collected spirits which light diffuses ... And we find it by experience that in our light Churches, did not wee close our eyes, wee could hardly keepe our thoughts from distractions till the end of a short collect.

---

[4] J. Browning, *Concerning Publicke-Prayer ... Six Sermons* (1636), 25.
[5] R. Skinner, *A Sermon Preached Before the King at White-Hall* (1634), 29.

The chancel should have a higher roof and be more adorned than the nave, 'that when we shall enter into this place more holy & divine thoughts may possesse our minds, occasioned by the differing structure, and more glorious ornaments', and so on.[6]

In such celebrations of sacred space, the architecture and furnishings help create a cognitive niche which transports the worshipper into the realm of the numinous. This chapter argues that Herbert's churches likewise help him worship God—but the register and the timeframe which he uses are very different. For most of his adult life Herbert needed to know concrete details about contemporary construction techniques, expertise acquired over the course of his lengthy and expensive church and rectory repairs at St Mary the Virgin in Leighton Bromswold, Huntingdonshire, and the Wiltshire properties of St Peter's at Fugglestone, its attached chapel of St Andrew's at Bemerton, and Bemerton Rectory. Other (luckier) authors can relish the feelings produced by entering finely modelled and sensitively lit churches; Herbert has to think about paving, glass, pulleys, and cement. They can allow themselves to be lost to the world; he has to be present to the construction work around him. To the existing roles Herbert is credited with—of devout minister, lyrical musician, and witty courtier—might be added the more banal one of property manager.

The Temple registers Herbert's attempts to turn physical architecture into a form of godly choice architecture. This chapter first points out the volume of references to building work in Herbert's poems, then outlines his experience in construction and maintenance. It concludes by examining how two groups of poems (on monuments and windows) reflect on how these features of a church fail or succeed in nudging their speakers in the right direction.

2 The Reality

Some recent Herbert commentary has inspected some of the concrete things and places in the poems. Paul Dyck points out how things are labelled with scriptural tags, and shows how 'The Church' starts and ends with a communion table, a physical spot where God re-enters his creation.[7] Anne Myers thinks that the aphoristic and didactic style of 'The Church-porch' expresses the common uses for this room, where contracts were made, catechizing and

---

[6] R. T., *De templis: A Treatise of Temples* (1638), 122–123, 190, 196–197, 199.
[7] P. Dyck, 'Locating the Word: The Textual Church and George Herbert's *Temple*', in D. W. Doerksen and C. Hodgkins, eds., *Centered on the Word: Literature, Scripture, and the Tudor-Stuart Middle Way* (Newark: University of Delaware Press, 2004), 224–244; P. Dyck, 'Approaching the Table: Invitation and the Structure of Herbert's "The Church"', *GHJ*, 35/1–2 (2011–2012), 45–54.

70 BUILDING

other teaching took place, alms were distributed, and so on.[8] Drawing on contemporary engineering texts, Roberta Albrecht shows the virtues hoisting a soul to heaven in 'The Pulley' to be rundles (rollers or pivots), with a gearing ratio of 1:6.[9] Kathleen Swaim argues that the 'season'd timber' of 'Vertue' burns down to 'coal' (charcoal), cleansed of the impurities that create cinders when wood is fired.[10] Such lively readings display Herbert's sense of fun, where he relies on God to 'reinvent weakness as a mechanical advantage', in Albrecht's phrase.[11]

However, no one has yet brought together a fuller list of *The Temple*'s references to construction materials and techniques. The quantity of these is striking. Cement is integral to 'The Altar' and 'The Church-floore'. 'The Glimpse' mentions how lime is slaked to start a hot chemical reaction, before sand and clay are added to produce cement. There is a 'plummet' for measuring distance and for ensuring a true line in erecting walls (in 'Prayer' 1), and 'quarries' of stone to make them with (in 'The Sinner').[12] In 'The Pulley' the soul, potentially weighted down on earth by many gifts from God, will be tossed up to heaven by the counterweight of restlessness (no slow and deliberate haul here). In 'Justice' 2 the scales of justice change into 'buckets, which attend/ And interchangeably descend,/ Lifting to heaven from this well of tears'. Water flows from the 'pipe' of 'The Water-course'. In 'The World' the 'inward walls and Sommers' (that is, horizontal load-bearing beams, such as those which support rafters) are being undermined by the invasive 'Sycomore' (not necessarily the biblical tree; it could also be the common sycamore, *acer pseudoplatanus*, a pioneer species often found around recently ruined buildings). Moreover, the addition of 'Balcones' (such as that hung onto the west wall of the Little Gidding chapel to hold an organ) and 'Terraces' has 'weakened all by alteration'. Perhaps bits could be held up by a 'Holdfast', a scaffold clamp? Broken paving stones were often a problem in church buildings (for instance, in 1607 and 1634 the paving inside Salisbury Cathedral was reported as defective). The neatly laid and firm paving of 'The Church-floore' is a credit to the 'Architect'.[13] Tiling is praised in 'The Priesthood', where 'earth and clay'

---

[8] A. Myers, 'Restoring "The Church-porch": George Herbert's Architectural Style', *English Literary Renaissance*, 40/3 (2010), 427–457.

[9] R. Albrecht, '"The Pulley": Rundles, Ropes, and Ladders in John Wilkins, Ramon Lull, and George Herbert', *GHJ*, 30/1–2 (2006–2007), 1–18.

[10] K. Swaim, 'The "Season'd Timber" of Herbert's "Vertue"', *GHJ*, 6/1 (1982), 21–25.

[11] Albrecht, 'Rundles', 8.

[12] M. F. Moloney, 'A Note on Herbert's "Season'd Timber"', *Notes and Queries*, 202 (Oct. 1957), 434–435.

[13] T. Cocke and P. Kidson, *Salisbury Cathedral: Perspectives on the Architectural History*, Royal Commission on the Historical Monuments of England (London: H. M. S. O., 1993), 17–18; 'Salisbury 1634',

is translated by the 'fire and trade/ Of skilfull artists'. A 'winding stair' (a spiral staircase hung onto the walls of a tower) comes to mind when Herbert is reaching for an analogy for fiction in 'Jordan' 1. The 'pillars' 'On which heav'ns palace arched lies' ('Sunday') are usually explained as arched trellising around a garden (thus picking up the poem's following reference to the 'fruitfull beds', separated by bare paths). But the phrase 'heav'ns palace' comes into focus more if the lines are read as a reference to the 'pillars' of a church aisle, on which the rafters rest. 'The Church-porch' tells its reader to 'crumble not away thy soul's fair heap' and to be steady, for lasting 'Houses are built by rule'. The bankrupt's 'crackt name ... in the church-glasse', by contrast, will be all that is left to memorialize him. 'The Thanksgiving' lists public building works which the speaker intends to complete: a hospital, a chapel, and mended roads. 'The H. Communion' refers to the early modern architectural innovation of a series of private rooms, which lead further and further away from the building's public space. There is some complicated carpentry in 'Confession', where the poet, 'master' in his 'trade', makes tills in boxes, boxes in chests, and chests in closets, to hide his heart away from affliction. This is in vain, though: a 'scrue' and awl of grief can 'winde' into any 'piece of timber', and 'no smith can make such locks, but they have keyes'. In 'Ungratefulnesse', unlike the heart's locked 'box', 'two rare cabinets' of grace are 'unlockt', as they are again in 'Praise' 3, where 'boxes for the poore' and 'chests' are opened for topping up with Christ's tears. Those streaming tears remind the poet of 'streamers neare the top/ Of some fair church to show the sore/ And bloudie battel' (pennons hung outside a church tower).[14]

The sayings about building work which Herbert collected in *Outlandish Proverbs* (published in 1640) are stolid about expecting that costs will burgeon, but even then not bodging a job: 'The house shewes the owner', 'Building and marrying of Children are great wasters', 'A good bargaine is a pick-purse', 'Ill ware is never cheape', 'Never had ill workeman good tooles' (turned on its head in 'Church-porch' as 'The cunning workman never doth refuse/ The meanest tool'), 'Good cheape is deare', 'It costs more to doe ill than to doe well', 'Hee that repaires not a part, builds all', 'An old friend, a new house', 'Building is a sweet impoverishing', 'Things well fitted abide', 'A little lett lets an ill workeman', and 'Good workemen are seldom rich'.[15] One poem, 'Man', opens conversationally

---

Fourth Report of the Royal Commission on Historical Manuscripts, 1 (London: H. M. S. O., 1874), 129.

[14] Herbert, *Works*, ed. Hutchinson, 532.

[15] G. Herbert, *Outlandish Proverbs, Selected by Mr. G. H.* (1640), in Herbert, *Works*, ed. Hutchinson, 321, 323, 329, 333, 334, 337, 346.

72 BUILDING

with this sort of proverb about building works: 'My God, I heard this day,/ That none doth build a stately habitation,/ But he that means to dwell therein'.

Of course, none of these references are conclusive evidence of personal experience. After all, Herbert can mention Mount Etna ('Sinnes Round') without anyone assuming he had toured Sicily. Scriptural images of the temple or a house of prayer, such as those expounded in *The House of God, the Sure Foundation, the Stones, the Workmen and Order of the Building* by Matthew Brookes (minister at Great Yarmouth), might have provided Herbert with architectural analogies (including God's instructions about Noah's ark, the tabernacle built by Moses, or the parable of houses built on rock or sand).[16] Thus 'Sion', for instance, starts with a description of Solomon's temple as an illustration of the inner temple: 'now thy Architecture meets with sinne;/ For all thy frame and fabrick is within'. As Stanley Fish demonstrates, godly writers often turned to the metaphor of building work when talking about constructing a reformed self through catechizing and other pious means.[17] It was common to describe the gathered godly as God's true temple.[18] *Bethel: or, A Forme for Families in Which all Sorts ... are so Squared, and Framed by the Word of God ... for Usefull Pieces in God's Building* by Matthew Griffith (rector of St Mary Magdalen, Old Fish Street, London) starts off with a 'Plat-forme of the Whole Building', developing the image of how 'Gods building' is 'A well-order'd familie'.[19] *The Spirituall Architecture. Or, the Balance of Gods Sanctuary* by Robert Barrell (curate at Maidstone, Kent) teaches its reader 'how to build up thy selfe to be an house or temple for the Lord'.[20] Robert Bagnall, rector of Hutton in Somerset, describes ministers as humble labourers erecting the temple of the spirit in their hearers.[21] William Perkins argues that one of the principal duties of the general calling of a Christian is to 'further the good estate of the true Church of God' by prayer and by 'the worke of edification', as enjoined by 1 Thess. 5.21 and Jude 5.20. 'The Church of God is a temple made without hands, the foundation is Christ, and every member of Christ with all that pertain to Gods election are living stones'. Builders such as pastors and teachers cut and lay the

---

[16] S. Hanley, 'Temples in *The Temple*: George Herbert's Study of the Church', *SEL 1500–1900*, 8/1 (1968), 121–135; J. D. Walker, 'The Architectonics of George Herbert's *The Temple*', *ELH*, 29/3 (1962), 289–305. Classical temples have also been considered, see M. E. Rickey, *Utmost Art: Complexity in the Verse of George Herbert* (Lexington: University of Kentucky Press, 1966), 5–15.

[17] S. E. Fish, *The Living Temple: George Herbert and Catechizing* (Berkeley: University of California Press, 1978), 54–77.

[18] A. Spicer, 'Holiness and *The Temple*: Thomas Adams and the Definition of Sacred Space in Jacobean England', *The Seventeenth Century*, 27/1 (2012), 4–7; Coster and Spicer, 'Sacred Space', 7–8.

[19] M. Griffith, *Bethel: or, a Forme for Families* (1633), a1r.

[20] R. Barrell, *The Spirituall Architecture. Or, the Balance of Gods Sanctuary* (1624), A4r.

[21] R. Bagnall, *The Stewards Last Account* (1622), A2r–v.

2 THE REALITY 73

stones, and those who cannot do this 'further the buildings either by carrying of burdens or by making of morter'. This, Perkins explains, is done by drawing people we know personally to the love of the true religion by 'admonitions, exhortations, consolations', and the like.[22]

However, it is the unusually technical and contemporary idiom which Herbert uses, from how to make cement to what summers do, which sets his work aside from these contemporary commentators. Most householders at some time have to grapple with understanding something about building techniques, units of measurement, costs, and quality criteria for a range of construction materials, and about wage rates for skilled and unskilled labour. *Vade mecums* were published for the seventeenth-century novice builder, covering the qualities of mortar and lime, timber and stone, brick and glass, and the basic structures of a building, from collars to rafters, and bearing-loads to balconies, such as *The City and Country Purchaser and Builder, A Platform for Purchasers, Guide for Builders, Mate for Measurers*, and *The Art of Fair Building* (Figure 3.1).[23] Herbert's poems use their register.

There are a number of reasons why this might be so. First, Herbert worked within a precise regulatory framework for the maintenance of church property, one which focused more on repairs than on reforms. As Nigel Yates has shown, the Reformation tended to provoke a change of use for church space, rather than a change in structure.[24] The two main 'rooms' of the church, the chancel and the nave, became distinguished by function rather than by personnel (for instance, both clergy and laity now took communion in the chancel), so buildings rarely needed remodelling. Instead, church regulations focused on good repair. Numbers 80 to 88 of the 1604 Canons dealt with 'Things appertaining to Churches', two of which were concerned with their fabric. Number 85 required it to be 'kept in sufficient Reparations', with (in the following order) windows 'well glazed', floors 'paved, plain, and even', and the churchyard fenced. These are recognized weak spots in large and ancient

---

[22] Perkins, *Vocations*, 15–18.

[23] The Great Fire of London prompted the production of many advice books on the costings and quality assessment of building materials and construction, such as W. Leybourn, *A Platform for Purchasers, Guide for Builders, Mate for Measurers* (1668) on mortar, 106–107; paving, 107–110, 116–117; timber, 110–112; locks, 113; glass, 113–115; and summers, 132; S. P., *The City and Country Purchaser and Builder* (1667) on tiles and bricks, 51, 56–59; lime, 51, 55; timber, 52; summers, 52, 59–60; winding stairs, 66; paving, 68; iron balconies (note the weight of these, and the care needed to calculate if a wall would bear them), 69; P. Le Muet, *The Art of Fair Building* (1623), trans. R. Pricke (1670), illustrates summers, cross braces, great and window posts, collars (horizontal beams connecting a pair of rafters, to stop them from sagging), compass rafters, and stays [H8r].

[24] N. Yates, *Buildings, Faith, and Worship: The Liturgical Arrangement of Anglian Churches, 1600–1900* (1991; Oxford: Clarendon Press, 2000), 30–36.

74 BUILDING

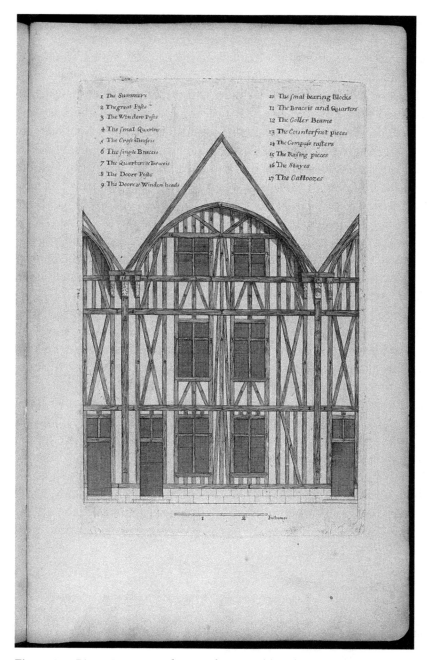

Figure 3.1 Pierre Le Muet, *The Art of Fair Building* (1623), trans. R. Pricke (1670), Bodleian Library, University of Oxford, Vet. A3 b.35, H8r.

public buildings (even today, parish officials acquire expertise in the funding streams, regulations, and practical aspects of maintaining them). Canon 86 required personal episcopal inspections every three years, and compelled churchwardens to levy the parish to cover the costs of any necessary repairs unearthed.[25] Visitation questions inquire of the churchwardens and minister about whether the church and minister's house are 'in good reparations ... decently and comly kept'.[26] There is also a section on security, checking with the churchwardens and minister about whether the parish chest of alms for the poor had three separate locks and keys.[27] As Hutchinson points out, *The Country Parson* covers the same agenda as these visitation articles by putting first things first when a minister is appointed to serve a church.[28] 'First he takes order, that all things be in good repair; as walls plaistered, windows glazed, floore paved, seats whole, firm, and uniform, especially that the Pulpit, and Desk, and Communion Table, and Font, be as they ought, for those great duties that are performed in them'. Commentators on this passage tend to focus on the concluding statement about the church furnishings, since it enriches discussions of doctrinal and devotional attitudes to God's word, but the preceding insistence on structural maintenance should also be noted.

Second, when visiting his family in London, Herbert would have become aware of a multitude of costly church repair works there, both in hand and foreseen. The planned 1608 restoration of St Paul's was budgeted at over £22,500. There were a series of royal initiatives to campaign for funds to repair the building; the king himself led a procession to Paul's Cross to inaugurate the campaign of 1620.[29] New glazing was installed in the cathedral in the following decade. A major restoration of 1633–1642 was initiated by an enormous gift of £10,000 by the former Levant Company magnate Sir Paul Pindar.[30] Nor was the cathedral the only beneficiary of 'reparations'. J. F. Merritt shows how, contrary to the image promulgated by Laudian polemic, there was an increase in church repair and rebuilding over James I's reign. During this period, for instance, sixty-three of the London parishes paid significant amounts (up to ten times the usual annual parish expenditure) on enlarging naves, moving

---

[25] Bullard, ed., *Canons*, 88–90.

[26] Fincham, ed., *Visitation Articles*, 1.159–60.

[27] Articles for Salisbury (1628, 1635), Norwich (1619), and Lincoln (1607, 1618, 1622), in Fincham, ed., *Visitation Articles*, 1.160, 173–176.

[28] Herbert, *Country Parson*, 246, 559.

[29] J. Doelman, *King James I and the Religious Culture of England* (Woodbridge: D. S. Brewer, 2000), 78–79.

[30] N. Llewellyn with J. Schofield, 'Post-Medieval, 1530–1666', in J. Schofield, *St. Paul's Cathedral Before Wren* (Swindon: English Heritage, 2011), 193–195.

76 BUILDING

walls, rebuilding chancels, adding galleries, repairing steeples, and reglazing windows.[31]

The extent of such building work prompted official guidance on funding it, if the parish was unable to do so itself. 'A Proclamation for preventing the decayes of Churches and Chappels for the time to come' (11 October 1629) alleges that there is a general decay of chapels and churches in many parts of the realm, and is suspicious that parishioners deliberately overlook dilapidations until they become serious, 'out of hope to obtaine some generall Collection, whereby to spare themselves, and to get the worke, which they are bound to doe [out of parish rates] by law, to bee done by the common purse of others'. The proclamation emphasizes that no more such collections under letters patent will be authorized, except in the case of acts of God, such as fire or tempest. It ends by requiring surveyors not to rely on documents presented by churchwardens (who might be trying to spare themselves and their neighbours the cost of repair), but to inspect the buildings in person.[32]

The third reason for Herbert's familiarity with the register of building may have been his own renovations. On 5 July 1625 he was installed as non-residentiary canon of Lincoln Cathedral and prebendary of Leighton Ecclesia, Huntingtonshire. There was some churn in occupancy before and after his period of tenure, which might have affected funding and the overseeing of any necessary major repairs of the parish church of St Mary's. Herbert's predecessor, Christopher Pasley, was only in place for four months. The prebend was vacant on 8 August 1634, and the next recorded incumbent was Herbert Thorndike (who had deputized for Herbert as university orator), installed on 12 April 1636.[33] The prebend's responsibilities were to preach or cause to be preached an annual sermon at Whitsun at Lincoln Cathedral, recite Psalms 31 and 32 privately every day for the good of the parish, and pay a seventh of his income for the post over to the residentiary.[34] However, he was not bound to take charge of parochial duties, nor to keep the church in repair. At some point Herbert tried to get Nicholas Ferrar to take the position (Amy Charles suggests this was as late as 1630), but the Ferrars suggested instead a partnership in which Herbert as prebendary raised funds for rebuilding and the Ferrar brothers oversaw the works.[35] Herbert's initial demurral suggests he was aware

---

[31] Merritt, 'Church-Building', 940–942.
[32] J. F. Larkin, ed. *Stuart Royal Proclamations*, 2 vols. (Oxford: Clarendon Press, 1983), 2.248–50.
[33] 'Prebendaries: Leighton Ecclesia', *Fasti Ecclesiae Anglicanae 1541–1857. Volume 9: Lincoln Diocese* (1999), 85–87 (http://www.british-history.ac.uk/report.aspx?compid=35195).
[34] Charles, *Life*, 121–122.
[35] Charles, *Life*, 150–152; Blackstone, ed., *Ferrar Papers*, 58–59.

of the magnitude of that task, which he took on at last as an act of piety, not as a duty of the prebendary, binding himself to act with a solemn vow.[36]

For nearly two decades no services had been said at St Mary's, according to Ferrar's preface to *The Temple*.[37] The south aisle of the church had been demolished in 1606, and the roof of the nave had fallen in. Izaak Walton noted that the sort of public collection regulated in 1629 had been tried for St Mary's, but unsuccessfully.[38] So the restoration group tried their personal connections, turning first to patrons of the parish, acquaintances, and family members. Herbert's letter to his brother Henry, of autumn 1630, says that he has already spent £200 on (unidentified) building works, even though he has not yet received a sum of money due to him (Hutchinson presumes this refers to the Bemerton tithes). On 23 March 1632, Herbert wrote to Henry, pleased with the latter's success in enlisting aid for the building fund from Katherine Clifton, Duchess of Lennox (Baroness Clifton of Leighton Bromswold), and taking up Henry's offer to approach the Earls of Manchester and Bolingbroke.[39] Herbert himself was apparently adept at cajoling money out of connections: Walton says he doubled to £100 a contribution from the Earl of Pembroke by a 'witty and persuasive' letter.[40] Herbert remained involved with the project all his life, bequeathing £15 to the building fund at his death on 3 March 1633.[41]

As Nicholas Ferrar had planned, the renovation of St Mary's was supervised by his brother John, drawing on his experience of the restoration work at Little Gidding, and perhaps using the same group of workmen.[42] Woodnoth acted as treasurer, personally paying the workmen. He already had financial expertise as a freeman of the Goldsmith's Company, running a concern large enough to employ two or three apprentices at a time, and perhaps had useful contacts to tap for donations. Herbert clearly valued his financial nous, for he appointed Woodnoth executor of his own will.[43] However, the money was so slow to come in that much of the actual work was not done until long after Herbert had moved to Bemerton, in April 1630. Charles reads 'The Crosse' as referring to the decision to rebuild St Mary's (the only cruciform church of the three),

---

[36] I. Walton, 'The Life of Mr. George Herbert', in A. W. Pollard, ed., *The Complete Angler and The Lives of ... Herbert* (London: Macmillan, 1901), 386–388.

[37] Herbert, *Works*, ed. Hutchinson, 4.

[38] Walton, 'Life', 386–388.

[39] Herbert, *Works*, ed. Hutchinson, 375–379, 582. Since the Lennox household was interrupted every week, as all services for the whole parish had to be held in their hall because of the state of the church (Blackstone, ed., *Ferrar Papers*, 58), the donation may not have been entirely disinterested.

[40] Walton, 'Life', 387.

[41] Herbert, *Works*, ed. Hutchinson, 382.

[42] A. L. Maycock, *Nicholas Ferrar of Little Gidding* (1938; Grand Rapids: W. B. Eerdmans, 1980), 129–132.

[43] Walton, 'Life', 388; Charles, *Life*, 168–169.

78 BUILDING

citing 'not onely I,/ But all my wealth, and familie might combine/ To set thy honour up, as our designe'.[44] She takes the lines following these ('much delay,/ Much wrastling, many a combate') as a note about Herbert's weak health. But they could also be an allusion to the financing problem, perhaps also reflected in the defensive tone about procrastination in 'The Answer' to 'all,/ Who think me eager, hot, and undertaking,/ But in my prosecutions slack and small'.

Even before he took on St Mary's, Herbert would already have heard much about the trials of renovations. In 1624 Mary Ferrar had bought the manor of Little Gidding from Esmé, Lord Aubigny, afterwards Baron Stuart of Leighton Bromswold, then the third Duke of Lennox. On arriving at the manor, Mrs Ferrar went straight to the church to pray, but could barely get through the door as the church was being used as a barn. The woodwork was decayed, and the glass gone from the windows. The manor house was in a similar state. It took years for both buildings to be refloored, reglazed, repanelled, and to hang a balcony at the west end of the church for the organ.[45]

Given this volume of building work, it is understandable that the Little Academy regularly turns to construction metaphors when thinking about how to create a godly life. The Moderator says that everyone should express their 'Agreements in the Foundation, before wee go foreward with the Building' of such a significant project. As in renovating the Little Gidding chapel, when everyone laid a brick, 'and they, that through Age or Absence could not doe it themselves had a Brick laid by some other hands', so too should happen in 'building up our selves a Spiritual house & Temple'. The Cheerful urges discretion: 'a just weight layd upon the summers within poyseth the Building & makes it stronger; but that, which is overheavy, makes it fall & ruin'. When the Academy loses some of its main actors, they lament that this gives 'no lesse a shake to the business, then the taking away of Groundsels & the beating down of the maine walls doth to the frame of a building'. However, the members resolve to begin meeting again, 'squaring out & rearing the Frame according to the condition & Quantity of the stable & durable materials' (that is, household members who are usually present).[46]

The Ferrars and Woodnoth threw workmen at the St Mary's site in the summer of 1632: eighteen masons and labourers and ten carpenters were on the

---

[44] Charles, *Life*, 128–129.

[45] Blackstone, ed., *Ferrar Papers*, 24–25, 27–29; T. Cooper, '"Wise as serpents": The Form and Setting of Public Worship at Little Gidding in the 1630s', in N. Mears and A. Ryrie, eds., *Worship and the Parish Church in Early Modern Britain* (Farnham: Ashgate, 2013), 203–210.

[46] Williams, ed., *Conversations at Little Gidding*, 177, 179, 181; Blackstone, ed., *Ferrar Papers*, 106, 109.

job by the end of July, John Ferrar reported.[47] John notes two letters from Herbert to Nicholas about the process: Herbert 'goes on in the discourse of the building the Church, in such & such a forme as N. F. advised … and letting N. F. know, all he had, & would doe, to gett moneys to proceed in it', and 'so he goes on in his advice, for the ordering of things, to that business'.[48] John does not give details, but some evidence of the renovation work can be gathered from the existing fabric of the church and rectory buildings. The north aisle was demolished, and new north and south walls built to extend the line of the chancel. This reduced the space available for the seated congregation but had the advantage of giving the church a pronounced cruciform shape. The north and south doorways to the old aisles were retained to become the doorways for new north and south porches, with new side walls (in coursed Welden rubble) built back from the doorways to the new nave wall (thus making the porches the width of the old aisles). The church was reroofed, necessitating new tie beams and braces, as well as coverings (a rain-water head on the south side is dated 1632, and one on the north, 1634).[49] The red and yellow glazed tiles still on the floor of the north transept date from the 1630s. Finally, a pulpit, reading desk, dwarf screen, and seating were installed.[50]

Herbert was more closely involved with the renovations of the Fugglestone and Bemerton properties, which were nearly concurrent with that at St Mary's. St Peter's has no remaining sign of seventeenth-century work (bar some box pews which may be of that period), but St Andrew's and the Rectory have.[51] Walton says that Herbert had to repair the chancel of the chapel of St Andrew's, and to rebuild three parts of the Rectory when he took office.[52] Charles, however, doubts that the Rectory needed much doing to it, other than to repair the minor damage consequent on leaving a building empty for ten years.[53] Yet given that two thirds of its surviving walls (of knapped flint and rubble, with ashlar dressings) date from the earlier seventeenth century, Walton's account may have substance. St Andrew's shows little sign of

---

[47] John Ferrar to Nicholas Ferrar, 30 July 1632, Blackstone, ed., *Ferrar Papers*, 276.
[48] Blackstone, ed., *Ferrar Papers*, 77–78, 79.
[49] Royal Commission on Historical Documents, *An Inventory of the Historical Monuments in Huntingdonshire* (London: H. M. S. O., 1926), 177–180, plate 99; N. Pevsner, *Bedfordshire and the County of Huntingdon and Peterborough* (Harmondsworth: Penguin, 1968), 282–284.
[50] The current tower, financed by the fourth Duke of Lennox, probably dates to 1640 (four of its bells are dated 1641), A. Taylor, 'The Seventeenth-century Church Towers of … Leighton Bromswold (?c.1640)', *Architectural History*, 27 (1984), 289–290.
[51] Royal Commission on Historical Monuments (England), *Ancient and Historical Monuments in the City of Salisbury: Vol. 1* (London: H. M. S. O., 1980), 163, 42–43; Institute of Historical Research, *Wiltshire*, 6.48–49.
[52] Walton, 'Life', 397, 399.
[53] Charles, *Life*, 153–154.

80 BUILDING

seventeenth-century stonework (just the south doorway and a small opening in the south of the chancel), but this evidence points neither way since there was a wholesale restoration of the church in 1860. Some of the structural wood-work, however, dates from about 1630: five pairs of trussed roof rafters, and some oak panelling (now incorporated into a modern chest), which suggests major repairs were made.

It seems probable from the physical evidence, then, that from the summer of 1630 until the autumn of 1632 Herbert had in hand or in prospect three or even four restoration projects on large public buildings, the most complex of which was planned at a distance, completed by proxy, and took a large amount of cash, emotional energy, and time. That Herbert himself thought he had done a proper job is suggested by the verse he left on the mantel of his hall chimney, which asks his successor to spend on the poor what will be saved by living in such a solid 'new House'.[54] Church reconstruction, not poetry, was what Woodnoth called a work of merit, the 'good work' referred to by Herbert on his deathbed and in Ferrar's preface to *The Temple*.[55] It would be unsurprising if such work did not influence the register of the poems. A brief instance of this might be 'Prayer' 1's reference to the sound of 'church-bels beyond the starres heard'. When Herbert arrived at St Peter's he found two new bells, cast in 1628 by John Danton, which were called 'Love God' and 'Praise God'.[56]

A more extended example might be the vocabulary of purchase and sale, often discussed by commentators on 'Redemption' and 'Obedience', whose readings either reflect on St Paul's declaration of how Christ's atonement paid the debt due from humanity for sin (Coloss. 2.14) or look at the register of contemporary general business contracts.[57] Less noted, however, is that Herbert is using the specific register of manorial land valuation, and that there were estate surveys of both Bemerton and Little Gidding in 1632. This was an extensive process, which in the case of Bemerton (one of the Pembroke manors) had not been undertaken since 1567. In spring, the two surveyors, Robert Drewe and William Kent, checked the estate's documents (especially the previous surveys, the court book, and lease book) against those of the ten-ant (namely, the indentures of leases of enfeoffment, or copies of the court

---

[54] Walton's report, in C. A. Patrides, ed., *George Herbert: the Critical Heritage* (London: Routledge and Kegan Paul, 1983), 113.

[55] Herbert, *Works*, ed. Hutchinson, 4.

[56] The bells of St. Mary the Virgin post-date Herbert's restorations there (though perhaps not his plans, given that the fourth Duke of Lennox financed the bell tower, and his mother had seen a 'book' about the renovations), Institute of Historical Research, *The Victoria History of the County of Wiltshire*, 18 vols. (London, 1953–2011), 6.48.

[57] B. Knieger, 'The Purchase-Sale: Patterns of Business Imagery in the Poetry of George Herbert', *Studies in English Literature, 1500–1900*, 6.1 (1966), 111–124.

roll). In particular, the surveyors looked at the details of the terms on which the tenancies were held, the payment made when a tenancy changed hands, and the annual rent. This was a legal rather than a field survey. However, Drewe and Kent (consulting with the estate steward about the physical state of the property and cross-referring to the book of rates held by the parish clerk or local overseer of the poor) also calculated the value of the tenancy, for use in drawing up the entry fines to be charged to any future new tenants. The Fugglestone survey was taken on 14 February 1632, examining two tenancies by indenture and twenty-four by copy, and the Wilton survey three weeks later on 5 March, covering sixteen tenancies by indenture. One of the tenants, William Abyn, is registered as holding for four lives a garden plot abutting St Andrew's land.[58]

In autumn 1632, too, the holdings of the manor of Little Gidding were renegotiated. The Ferrars, as new owners of the manor, had found out that glebe land had been sequestered from the diocese in the original enclosure a century earlier. In September 1632, by a decree in chancery, Mary Ferrar returned to the diocese land worth £10 a year. A private paper by her about this prays 'Bee graciously pleased, Lord, now to accept from thy handmayd the restitution [of land] ... as an earnst & pledge of the total resignation of her self & hers to thy service vouchsafe to receive ... this small portion of that large Estate, which thou hast bestowed upon her'. She asks God to 'redeeme' his 'right' in his 'possessions' of 'Earth' and of her heart, so she may become his 'Inheritance'.[59]

The allegory of 'Redemption' is one in which the 'tenant' of the 'rich Lord' of a 'manour' asks for the lease to be varied according to the worth of the land, but has first to find his landlord, who is taking 'possession' of another piece of 'land' bought earlier (that is, he is completing the purchase by physically standing on it). The governing metaphor of 'Obedience' uses the same words as Mary Ferrar: the poet desires to 'Convey a Lordship' (that is, of a manor), passing by 'speciall deed' all the land and what it bears, without 'reservation', in an 'action' that is registered in a 'court of rolls'. Moreover, he hopes, the purchase will be doubled by a reader willing to 'passe his land' over, also. The idiom reappears in 'Love Unknown', where the tenant of 'A Lord' has a 'lease' on 'grounds which may improve'. He holds it only for two lives, and admits he often defaults on its terms.

---

[58] E. Kerridge, ed., *Surveys of the Manors of Philip, First Earl of Pembroke and Montgomery, 1631–32*, *Wiltshire Archaeological and Natural History Society: Records Branch*, 9 (1953), x–xii, 49–55, 82–85.
[59] Blackstone, ed., *Ferrar Papers*, 69.

82 BUILDING

Contemporary knowledge about Herbert's work as a renovator may have influenced the way his early editors ordered and titled his poems. His building work is mentioned by all his early biographers: Nicholas Ferrar, Barnabus Oley, Thomas Fuller, John Aubrey, and Izaak Walton.[60] The Williams manuscript does not include 'The Church-floore' or 'The Windows'. In this manuscript, too, 'Church-lock and key' is entitled 'Prayer', the poem's first line speaks of 'stops' not 'locks', and the poem is placed well before 'Church-monuments'. In the Bodleian manuscript, however, a building sequence begins to appear, comprising of 'Church-monuments' (then 'Church-musick' and 'Anagram'), then 'The Church-floore', then 'The Windows'. In the 1633 first edition, 'Anagram' is moved elsewhere, thus firming up the building sequence.[61]

His contemporaries' responsiveness to building work in *The Temple* might also have been heightened by the fact that the collection was often bound with Christopher Harvey's *Synagogue* (usually, from the first edition of 1640 to that of 1650, and always so for the next 200 years). Paul Dyck argues that binding Harvey and Herbert's poems together meant that *The Temple* was partly interpreted through Harvey's determination to support a high church approach to sacred space (in the later edition, Harvey uses the slightly aggressive phrase 'why not' repeatedly, as in 'The Font ... I say, why not', 'Pray'r by th'Book ... Why not'). The same line of argument might also be used about the concrete buildings, since about a quarter of the poems in the 1640 *Synagogue* show Harvey's robust enthusiasm for images of a kickable object ('A Stepping-Stone to the Threshold of Mr. Herberts Church-porch', 'The Church-yard', 'The Church-stile', 'The Church-gate', 'The Church-wall', 'The Church', and 'The Church-porch'). The 1679 edition extended this feature to the furnishings ('The Font', 'The Pulpit', 'The Bible', 'The Reading Pue', 'Church-utensils', 'Communion Plate', and 'The Communion Table').

Harvey's response to Herbert is notable for the way he points to a piece of church property, then states exactly how to use it to think about a feature of godly life:

> Seest thou that stile? observe then how it rises
> Step after step, and equally descends:
> Such is the way to winne celestial prizes;
> Humility the course begins and ends.[62]

---

[60] Patrides, ed., *Critical Heritage*, 60, 78, 88, 89, 103–104, 112–113.
[61] Herbert, *Works*, ed. Hutchinson, li, lvi–v, 66 fn.
[62] C. Harvey, *The Synagogue, or the Shadow of The Temple* (1640), 3; C. Harvey, *The Synagogue, or the Shadow of The Temple* (1679), 11, 14; Dyck, 'Approaching the Table', 48–49.

There is little description of any quality other than that needed to establish a parallel with a spiritual quality. Harvey is imperious about the manner in which the reader is to engage with these objects. She is instructed to look, view, turn towards, walk round, and even sit on them. This is not a church which inspires 'more holy and divine thoughts', in R. T.'s words, 'mightily working (though insensibly) upon the minds of men', in those of Fleming. Nothing sacramental is called to mind, nothing transcendent: all is conscious, conscientious concept-building, using the physical materials to hand.

Might the way that Harvey builds an extended mind—however flat-footedly—suggest that Herbert's repeated references to construction could be read as more than a result of his own hard-won experience in church repairs? The next two sections look at his poems on monuments and glass as instances of failed and successful nudges respectively, to consider this possibility.

3 Obdurate Monuments

While Herbert seems to have had a relatively free hand in his work on the walls, roofs, windows, floors, and doors of the churches, he had to be cautious about touching the monuments. There are few now at the three churches, either from the 1630s or before. St Peter's has a Purbeck marble chest tomb of a lady with her hands on her breast, but no inscription. At St Mary's there are three monuments in the north transept: a fragment of a large stone crest (possibly part of a seventeenth-century monument), and two family tombs in alabaster. One is an altar tomb with the recumbent effigies of Sir Robert Tyrwhit (d. 1572), wearing plate armour with his head on a mantled helm and a lion at his feet (both arms and legs are lost), and his second wife, Elizabeth (d. 1578), wearing a French cap and long cloak.[63] The central bay of the south side of the chest bears the arms of the Tyrwhits. In bays on either side are a child and two swaddled infants; the coat of arms is repeated on the west end of the chest. The effigy of the Tyrwhits' daughter, Katherine (d. 1567), is nearby on a second altar tomb.

The Tyrwhit family would have loomed large in Herbert's plans for renovations. Leighton Bromswold manor was held by the church until 1548 then sold to Sir Robert Tyrwhit, who settled it on Katherine, at her marriage to Sir Henry D'Arcy. In 1591 the manor was settled on their daughter, Katherine, at her marriage to Sir Gervase Clifton. In 1613 it was settled on their daughter, Katherine, at her marriage to Esmé, Lord Aubigny; this Katherine died in 1637,

---

[63] Royal Commission on Historical Documents, *Huntingdonshire*, 179.

84   BUILDING

after Herbert's renovations were complete. The monuments in St Mary's are important records of the Tyrwhit tradition of passing the manor down from mother to daughter, on the latter's marriage.[64]

Moreover, the monuments are tangentially associated with two more famous monuments to Protestantism. Elizabeth Tyrwhit was, from 1537, a gentlewoman of the privy chamber, attending the strongly Protestant Katherine Parr on her deathbed, and later appointed as governess to a resentful Princess Elizabeth. John Foxe's *Actes and Monuments* relates how, in 1546, opponents of the reform agenda attacked Parr's three closest associates. Two of these were Lady Anne Herbert (afterwards Countess of Pembroke) and Tyrwhit, whom the queen held, 'for her virtuous disposition, in very great favour and credite'.[65] By archiepiscopal instruction a copy of *Actes and Monuments* was chained in the parish church, so anyone might read about the parish's most famous Protestant woman.[66] Tyrwhit was also a noted Protestant scholar and one of the first women to publish an English private prayer book, *Morning and Evening Praiers, with Divers Psalmes Himnes and Meditations* (1574). This was used by Thomas Bentley for the second section of his *Monument of Matrones* (1582), with a dedicatory epistle to Queen Elizabeth which dwells on the structural image he shares with Foxe: 'out of the admirable monuments of your owne Honourable works ... one entire and goodlie monument of praier, precepts, and examples meet for meditation, instruction, and imitation'. The epistle to the reader explains these 'rare and excellent monuments, of good record, as perfect presidents of true pietie and godlinesse in woman kind to all posteritie ... in this Monument'.[67]

Before starting work on St Mary's, Herbert would have scanned the area for potential patrons or people who might object to the work, and would naturally be circumspect in plans for related physical monuments. It is highly likely that he would have learnt about the Tyrwhit family history, especially since Foxe mentions the Herbert and Tyrwhit families together. A fifty-year-old copy of Bentley's *Monument of Matrones* would not normally have come

---

[64] Institute of Historical Research, *The Victoria History of the County of Huntingdon*, 3 vols. (London, 1926–1938), 3.88.

[65] 'Tyrwhit [née Oxenbridge], Elizabeth', *Oxford Dictionary of National Biography* (http://www.oxforddnb.com/view/article/46929); H. and R. Tyrwhitt, *Notices and Remains of the Family of Tyrwhitt ... 1067 to 1872* (1858; 1872), 22–26; J. Foxe, *Acts and Monuments Online* (1583), book 8, 1267–1268 (http://www.johnfoxe.org/index.php?realm=text&gototype=modern&edition=1583&pageid=1267).

[66] J. Roberts and E. Evenden, 'Bibliographical Aspects of the *Acts and Monuments*', *Acts and Monuments Online*, fn. 19 (http://www.johnfoxe.org/index.php?realm=more&gototype=modern&type=essay&book=essay2); Herbert, *Country Parson*, 246.

[67] T. Bentley, *The Monument of Matrones* (1582), 'To Queene Elizabeth', B1r, B1v, 103–138; see also the poem by 'L. S.', '*Hic aeterna pij cernis monumenta laboris*', B7r.

Herbert's way, but the Tyrwhit family might have had a copy to show their new minister, along with Katherine Tyrwhit's prayerbook.

Visitation questions covered the state of repair of monuments in a church.[68] Nigel Llewellyn notes their vulnerability, due more to general wear and tear than to iconoclasm. Inscriptions could not be completely sealed onto the stone and so tended to peel off; monuments might be moved so as to better organize the available space or because the person commemorated was now remembered differently; valuable materials of tombs were wanted for other uses (plasterers coveted alabaster's gypsum, for instance); extruding elements (like praying hands) were often carved separately and fixed on with wooden dowels which rapidly perished, and so on. Occasionally the commissioner of a monument might leave money for its maintenance, or a guild or fraternity to which the dead person had belonged might fund this. Mostly, though, it was down to the parish minister and clerk to tidy up what had been chipped, rotted, or rubbed off.[69] Herbert, like any parish official, had to inspect for decay on a regular basis.

In 1631 the antiquary John Weever surveyed the poor state of many of the tombs of England. He quotes Horace and his admirers (specifying Edmund Spenser among them) on the well-worn topos of how texts live longer than monuments. Weever argues that tombs could be useful teachers, if kept in repair:

> the frequent visiting, and advised reviewing of the Tombes and monuments of the dead ... with the often reading, serious perusall, and diligent meditation of wise and religious Epitaphs or inscriptions, found upon the tombes or monuments, of persons of approved vertue, merit, and honour, is a great motive to bring us to repentance ... They are externall helpes to excite, and stirre up our inward thoughts.[70]

The 'vertue, merit, and honour' which Weever talks about have as much to do with rank as morality. The place where a monument was sited, the materials it was made of, and the artistry involved in fashioning it were as eloquent as any inscribed genealogy in demonstrating the power of both the dead person and

---

[68] Fincham, ed., *Visitation Articles*, 1.161.

[69] N. Llewellyn, *Funeral Monuments in Post-Reformation England* (Cambridge: Cambridge University Press, 2000), 161–163, 263, 268–269.

[70] J. Weever, *Ancient Funerall Monuments within the United Monarchie of Great Britaine, Ireland, and the Islands Adjacent* (1631), 1–5, 9, citing Horace, *Odes*, 3.30.1–5.

86 BUILDING

the commissioner.[71] Weever imagines a sliding scale of site and style according to rank: from being buried outside the church (with no monument), to inside the church (with a flat ledger stone), to near or inside the chancel (perhaps with an effigy).[72] There could be, in Llewelyn's phrase, some 'spatial bullying' involved in decisions about this. In St Paul's Cathedral the tombs of two of Herbert's kinsmen, William Herbert, first Earl of Pembroke, and Sir Philip Sidney, were both cast into the shade by the scale and magnificence of that erected for Sir Christopher Hatton in 1591. The latter got a lot of adverse comment, such as a pasquil pinned near it on how 'Philip [Sidney] and Francis [Walsingham] have no tomb/ For great Christopher takes all the room'.[73] At a more domestic level, the Little Gidding community also showed itself attuned to the significance of where tombs were placed: Nicholas asked to be buried a coffin's length from the door of the chapel, so that John, as older brother, could be buried in front of him when the time came.

The Tyrwhit tombs at St Mary's do not celebrate the virtues of mother, husband, or daughter; they celebrate the family coat of arms, in costly alabaster. Moreover, the size and site of the Tyrwhit tombs effectively turns the north transept into a private chapel. Large tombs take up valuable floor space (at a premium because a Protestant congregation appreciated sitting rather than standing to listen to lengthy sermons), and space was already tight in St Mary's, as a result of Herbert's alterations. The Tyrwhit monuments are in the north transept, where substantial demolition work was going on. It would have required repeated discussion between overseers, workmen, and funders about whether to re-site them, or about how to protect them if left in place.

Another amateur builder arrived at Bemerton in 1630, one who had already got a reputation as a patron of fine funerary monuments. The family seat of the earls of Pembroke, Wilton House, lay just to the north of St Peter's. Lady Anne Clifford, Countess of Dorset and Montgomery, married Philip Herbert, the fourth Earl of Pembroke, in June 1630. For the following five years she spent her summers at Wilton.[74] Clifford and George Herbert were on good terms: he visited her for an hour in October 1631, and he sent her a friendly note that December.[75] The Appleby triptych of her portrait, which she commissioned in 1646, includes an image of Herbert's published works. Clifford was

---

[71] Llewellyn, *Monuments*, Ch. 3. On the uproar caused by a violation of rank in tomb placement, see 'State Trials in the Reign of Cha[r]les the First, A.D. 1627–1640', *Cobbett's Complete Collection of State Trials*, 33 vols. (1809–1812), 3.column 552.

[72] Weever, *Monuments*, 10–12.

[73] Llewelyn with Schofield, 'Post-Medieval, 1530–1666', 187–189.

[74] Herbert, *Works*, ed. Hutchinson, 583.

[75] Blackstone, ed., *Ferrar Papers*, 267; Herbert, *Works*, ed. Hutchinson, 376–377.

a noted restorer and erector of monuments, and open-minded about experimenting with different styles as they became fashionable.[76] By the time she was living at Wilton her commissions included a Tuscan-pillared table tomb in jet and white marble (1612, to her cousin, Frances Bourchier), an alabaster ledger tomb with effigy (1617, to her mother, in the same style as that to Elizabeth I in Westminster Abbey and probably by the same sculptor, Maximilian Colt), and a monument to Spenser (erected in 1620, also in the Abbey). For the last, Clifford replaced a wall tablet, whose Latin inscription linked Spenser with Chaucer, with a standing monument declaring Spenser to have had 'a divine spirrit [which] needs noe othir witnesse then the works which he left behinde him'.[77] The tomb she later commissioned for herself, in St Lawrence, Appleby-in-Westmorland, dwells triumphantly on her lineage (the reason she retained her disputed inheritance).

Any discussion between Clifford and Herbert about church monuments would not have been one-sided. Herbert's mother put up, in St Nicholas's, Montgomery, a massive and sophisticated canopied transi-tomb to herself and her first husband, Richard, four years after his death in 1596. The tomb, possibly designed by Walter Hancock, has the husband and wife lying on the top slab; below lies a shrouded figure of Richard; their eight children are depicted praying for them. Above, Vanity and Time are surmounted by an achievement of the Herbert arms (shield, helm, crest, and mantling). The Latin inscription focuses on recommending that the reader observe what virtue, piety, and the love of good can do, but about six sevenths of the English inscription commemorates the rank and lineage of Magdalen and her own mother.[78] Yet despite these extensive preparations for a lasting memorial, Magdalen was not buried there when she died in 1627. Herbert was only seven when the first family tomb went up in 1600, too young to be consulted about its style or inscription. In 1627, however, her second husband, Sir John Danvers, and her sons, including George, presumably would have considered the possibility of using the existing monument. Nevertheless, they decided to bury her where she had lived with Danvers, in the parish of All Saint's, Chelsea.[79] Her

---

[76] Later, in 1654, she erected a monument to her former tutor, the poet Samuel Daniel. R. Spence, *Lady Anne Clifford: Countess of Pembroke, Dorset, and Montgomery (1590–1676)* (Stroud: Sutton, 1997), 38–39, 66–68, 151–155, 191, 200–203.

[77] W. Camden, *Reges... et alii in ecclesia collegiate B. Petri Westmonasterii sepulti* (1600; 1606), 70–71; https://www.westminster-abbey.org/abbey-commemorations/commemorations/edmund-spenser).

[78] Montgomeryshire Genealogical Society, *Montgomeryshire Records. Parish of Montgomery: St. Nicholas and Non-Conformist Churches. Memorial Inscriptions* (1996), 14–15. Powers-Beck describes the tomb in detail, see *Writing the Flesh*, 8–23.

[79] W. H. Stewart, *Chelsea Old Church*, rev. K. A. Esdaile and R. Blunt (London: Oxford University Press, 1932), 52.

88 BUILDING

monument there was probably modest, for there are no traces of it either in situ or in accounts of the church.

To summarize Herbert's experiences with tombs: in summer 1632 the work at St Mary's was going strong, including dealing with the owners of the Tyrwhit tombs, which had to be protected if the funding stream was to last. Herbert was in regular contact with a notable commissioner of monuments, Clifford. He had recently reviewed his own family tomb, a bulky block of family history, rich in inscription and heraldic images. The Herbert tomb cites the first standard topos, celebrated by Weever, that it records the 'virtue' (both in rank and merit) of the deceased; the Clifford Spenser tomb cites the second standard topos, lamented by Weever, that words are more lasting memorials than stones.

In 'Church-monuments', the body is set down by the speaker to learn to

> finde his birth
> Written in dustie heraldrie and lines;
> Which dissolution sure doth best discern,
> Comparing dust with dust, and earth with earth.
> These laugh at Ieat, and Marble put for signes,
>
> To sever the good fellowship of dust,
> And spoil the meeting. What shall point out them,
> When they shall bow, and kneel, and fall down flat
> To kisse those heaps, which now they have in trust?

A loving (and perhaps slightly patronising) soul treats its body as Wallington treats his figurine of Death-in-a-coffin. Twice it anticipates going off to do some more elevated work ('While that my soul repairs to her devotion' and 'Deare flesh, while I do pray'). In the meantime, it proposes to create a cognitive niche—quite literally—by sitting the body down next to the monument, as though part of the latter's sculpture, to 'intombe' it. The body is arranged into a decent posture (what, in a congregation, Wolberg calls a 'teachable attitude').[80] The 'heap of dust' to which the body is introduced is not only another's dead body, but also the monument itself, to which death 'Drives all at last'. Such tombs had been handled by Herbert in his church renovations, tombs detailing the virtues of rank, but liable to decay themselves. Having settled the body in place, the soul points out what it should learn in this 'school'. First, the rank

---

[80] Wolberg, 'Posture and Spiritual Formation', 60. See also J. Craig, 'Bodies at Prayer in Early Modern England', in Mears and Ryrie, eds., *Worship and the Parish Church in Early Modern Britain*, 173–196.

inscribed on the stones will lose meaning, then the 'Ieat, and Marble' displaying this 'dustie heraldrie' will 'bow, and kneel, and fall down flat'. Just so will flesh, contained in the hourglass of the human figure, turn to dust and trickle down, before time crumbles. First the meaning (the virtue of rank) will go, then the signs (the words) communicating that meaning, then the physical material which forms those signs.

Critical attention has perhaps been a bit too quick to follow the direction pointed out by the soul. Joseph Summers traces how sentences, stanzas, and their topics dissolve across the poem.[81] Stanley Fish thinks the poem undoes the claim of any 'creature' (persons, spaces, objects, and even time and actions) to a separate existence from God, losing any meaningful distinctions between them in an 'exercise in tautology' by 'comparing dust with dust, and earth with earth'.[82] Barbara Harman sees mounds of dust burying themselves in themselves, in a circular process of origin to end to origin.[83] For Richard Strier and Christopher Hodgkins, Herbert's poems on the physical church tend to make the items themselves 'vanish', an 'internalising tendency' making them metaphorical from the start, and 'seldom literally present to the poem's speaker', in the words of Hodgkins.[84]

Such comments register the enormous imaginative effort which the soul makes to create a vivid image of grinding everything it can think of down to the smallest fragments possible: on one side, people of rank, the signs of that rank, and the material of those signs, and on the other, the reader of those signs, the flesh of that reader, and the time the reader is given to read. The claim made by Weever and on the Spenser tomb about the lasting qualities of words beyond memorials is not quite correct: some 'thing' must be kept in trim, to contain or bear those words. The monuments' dissolution is spoken of as being for the future (something which Herbert critics do not dwell on). At present, though—thanks, in part, to the sort of renovation work Herbert was doing around the Tyrwhit tombs—the poem's monuments are still in good shape, the dust is still 'in trust', and social distinctions are still maintained.

---

[81] J. Summers, *George Herbert* (London: Chatto and Windus, 1954), 134–135.

[82] S. E. Fish, *Self-Consuming Artifacts: The Experience of Seventeenth-Century Literature* (1972; Berkeley: University of California Press, 1974), 164–170, 207–215.

[83] B. Harman, *Costly Monuments: Representations of the Self in George Herbert's Poetry* (Cambridge, MA: Harvard University Press, 1982), 112–120.

[84] R. Strier, *Love Known: Theology and Experience in George Herbert's Poetry* (Chicago: University of Chicago Press, 1983), 146–151; Hodgkins, 'Church Legible', 217–241; C. Hodgkins, *Authority, Church, and Society in George Herbert. Return to the Middle Way* (Columbia: University of Missouri Press, 1993), 165. Even the titles of the poems do so, over the church architecture sequence, Anne Ferry argues. See 'Titles in George Herbert's "little Book"', *English Literary Renaissance*, 23/2 (1993), 314–344.

90   BUILDING

Moreover, these monuments do not offer the elevating lessons which Weever praises, Bentley uses as a guiding metaphor, and which dominate the Latin inscription on Richard Herbert's tomb. Instead, their inscriptions are focused on the secular aspect of lineage, which the Clifford and Tyrwhit monuments, and the English portion of Richard Herbert's tomb, celebrate. Moreover, they are at the top end of Weever's scale according to expense and rank: vertical (since they can 'fall down'), either free-standing or wall-mounted, and with extensive ornamentation and inscription. So the soul cannot rely on them to point out to the body any edifying descriptions and representations of the lasting value of a virtuous life. Thus, it has to create the opposite image, that of dissolution. The question of 'What shall point out them,/ When they shall bow, and kneel, and fall down flat?' is spelled out by the soul as a nudge: an easily accessible picture, put strongly so as to come easily to mind to restrain the body, when the latter 'shalt grow fat,/ And wanton in ... cravings'.

Yet though the soul's visionary effort deserves a response, it does not get one. Even in terms of genre, an address to the body would usually initiate a dialogue between it and the soul, the two agreeing with each other or arguing fiercely, as in Andrew Marvell's 'Dialogue between the Soul and the Body' and Henry Vaughan's 'The Evening-Watch: A Dialogue', 'Resurrection and Immortality', and 'Death. A Dialogue'.[85] Here, however, after the body has been nudged into a teachable posture it remains silent and immobile. When the soul returns from its prayers, the body will be just as it was and where it was before, a lump next to other lumps. Hence, the soul is nervously and increasingly strident about the intended edification: six times it emphasizes that the body must 'take acquaintance' in this 'school', 'may learn/ To spell', 'learn here', 'mayst know', 'Mark here', and 'mayst fit'. Hence, the table of topics in the 1656 edition of *The Temple* reads the poem as a *memento mori*: 'Monuments, mortal, as well as men' and 'Tombs, what use is to be made of them'.[86] Herbert himself had recently occasion to recollect how the figures of he and his siblings had been placed on a tomb to observe, for as long as the monument lasted, the contrast between the living and dead flesh of his father.

However, for all the response the body gives, the conclusion of the poem might as well be read as a rousing *carpe diem* rather than a *memento mori*. While the intombing and trusting are in the present, the edification is for the future and still only a possibility. Indeed, far from obediently noticing how the 'tame ... ashes' in front of it are free from 'lust', the body might well be

---

[85] R. Osmond, 'Body and Soul Dialogues in the Seventeenth-Century', *English Literary Renaissance*, 4/3 (1974), 399–400.
[86] G. Herbert, *The Temple* (1656), I11v, K4v.

tempted to draw the opposite lesson, since it is invited to 'take acquaintance' of its future bedfellows as though this will be a temptingly sociable event. The moment when monuments 'shall bow, and kneel, and fall down flat/ To kisse those heaps, which now they have in trust' is read by Wilcox as 'a process of increasing reverence, reminding us of the acts of prayer and devotion which are proper to being in church'.[87] But it could also be the moment when respect and trust are thrown away and the party starts to swing. The 'blast of deaths incessant motion' creates a 'good fellowship of dust', with particles giddily enjoying the 'meeting', where they 'laugh' and will 'fall down flat', shattering each 'glasse'.

Given the body does not budge, then, this is not likely to be a successful nudge. But perhaps instead the poem might be read as a warning to those of us who hope to use the world around us as part of our extended mind, without too much input from ourselves (the fantasy that the contents of a book can be absorbed by putting it under one's pillow before falling asleep, for instance)? While things can be used to think with, they cannot be left as though they can think alone, while the so-called superior part goes off to do some blue skies research.

4 Playing with Glass

Playing about with glass makes for a much more illuminating nudge. Church regulations and episcopal visitations want the windows to give good light indoors, and check on this with the parish's churchwardens, minister, and schoolmaster.[88] Herbert's poems about windows, however, ignore function and focus on how to look at their shapes, material, and colour, as ways to create a devotional state of mind.

The only evidence about the glass in Herbert's churches comes from John Aubrey's description of Bemerton (likely to be reliable because Aubrey was a kinsman of Herbert and a regular visitor to Wilton). Referring to Herbert's 'Coloss. 3.3', Aubrey notes that 'in the Chancell are many apt sentences of the Scripture. At his Wive's Seate, *My life is hid with Christ in God* (he hath verses on this Text in his Poems). Above, in a little window-blinded, with a Veile (ill painted) *Thou art my hideing place*. Psalm 32.7'.[89] Aubrey's editor suggests the

---

[87] Herbert, *Poems*, ed. Wilcox, 237.

[88] Fincham, ed., *Visitation Articles*, 1.160; 'Salisbury 1634', *Fourth Report of the Royal Commission on Historical Manuscripts* 1 (1874), appendix, 127–129.

[89] J. Aubrey, *Brief Lives*, ed. K. Bennett, 2 vols. (Oxford: Oxford University Press, 2015), 1.694, 2.1659–1660.

92 BUILDING

latter feature was a blind, varnished to make it transparent, with the biblical tag painted on it. Critics have pointed out the first text at Jane Herbert's seat as being of incidental interest, but do not notice what was painted above it.[90] Read together, however, the two inscriptions can be seen to form a call and response which makes the location of the hidden soul clear: first a teasing 'where is it hid?', and then a happy 'here!'

This dialogue between the seat text and the window text mirrors the diagonal acrostic of 'Coloss. 3.3', which forces the reader to use a gaze which is both 'straight' and 'doth obliquely bend'. There is much debate among Herbert scholars about whether to read the poem down or across first. In fact, empirical experiments in eye movements show that skilled readers tend to do both at once when looking to understand a text rapidly. They scan a text for headings, paragraph structure, font changes, or key words to locate potentially relevant information, then read more carefully when such regions are found. Visual acuity decreases as a function of distance from a location which is fixated on by the eye. The visual field consists of the fovea at the centre (covering an area roughly equal to the width of a thumb held at arm's length from the eye), the parafovea (information from which will be relayed to the brain as fuzzy), and the periphery (barely registered by the brain). Saccades (quick, ballistic eye movements) allow readers to move the fovea to the word they wish to process with the highest efficiency, and decisions about when and where to do so are to a large extent under the control of cognitive processes. In skilled readers, around ten per cent of the time saccades are regressions, back to a previous word fixed on in order to repair a fault in comprehension (to be distinguished from line sweeps, moving back to the right, one line down).[91] In the case of the poem 'Coloss. 3.3', a skilled reader will fixate first on the biblical citation, then drop down to the centre of the subtitle ('is hid with'), and then to the italicized centre of the block of text ('Is Hid, In Him'), particularly when reading the first edition, where the first two words also benefit from wider blank spaces before them, which draws the eye. Each of these groups of words is about a thumbnail size, when held at arm's length. The parafovea will deal more fuzzily with the words radiating out from this central riddle about hiding. Meanwhile, there is a tension between regressions and line sweeps in the vertical and diagonal readings, which would cause frequent saccades, thus also pulling against a steady comprehension of the meaning.

---

[90] For instance, Herbert, *Poems*, ed. Wilcox, 303.

[91] K. Rayner, E. R. Schotter, and R. Treiman, 'So Much to Read', So Little Time': How Do We Read, and Can Speed Reading Help?', *Psychological Science in the Public Interest*, 17/1 (2016), 7, 9, 25.

Moreover, the minor changes of pronouns in the Pauline text, which will appear in the parafovea, are registered by the eye and transmitted to the brain as fuzzy information, which might add to the initial mystery of what is hidden where. There are four versions of the verse: the biblical original of Coloss. 3.1–3, which might be remembered by a scripturally literate reader ('seek those things which are above … your life is hid with Christ in God'), the poem's subtitle ('Our life is hid with Christ in God'), the poem's italicized text ('My Life Is Hid, In Him That Is My Treasure'), and the version at Mrs Herbert's seat ('My life is hid with Christ in God'). There is, however, only one answer, which—as the original biblical text, Coloss. 3.1, urges—must be sought 'above' the seat, in the window: 'Thou art my hideing place'. A game of hide-and-seek (where I, you, and we go searching around for what 'is hid', using 'one eye' to 'aim and shoot at that which Is on high') is ended when God is found and directly addressed, triumphantly. To realize this, one would have to be reading both the texts at once, from a distance (not sitting in the seat itself). Thus Mrs Herbert herself was being put forwards as an example—and delicately complimented— every time someone in the church read her husband's two labels about her! If Aubrey's example is typical of the use made of other 'apt sentences' at Bemerton, then Herbert's church would have been a place of playfulness as well as edification.

Aubrey only notes texts, but story windows did not disappear with the Reformation. In the 1607 visitation to Salisbury Cathedral, Bishop Cotton was told that its glass and lead demanded continuous repair, but its authorities still invested in three new windows in 1620, which showed scenes in the life of St Paul.[92] Edmund Howes (continuing John Stow's annals of London's history) felt that coloured glass in churches was worth recording, such as the 1613 windows of St Stephen Walbrook, 'pleasantly repaired with new coullored Glasse made only for that purpose'.[93] However, some narratives in glass could cause offence. Some commentators on Herbert's 'The Windows' briefly refer to Henry Sherfield, the Recorder of Salisbury, who 'reformed' the windows of St Edmund's there.[94] For decades a pre-Reformation window at St Edmund's had irritated the vestry: it showed God the Father as a little old man in a blue and red coat, it mixed up the order of the works done during the week of Creation, and its God was using a pair of compasses to create a properly circular sun and moon (as if he needed to rely on geometrical instruments). The Bishop of Salisbury, John Davenant, had forbidden the vestry to replace the

---

[92] Cocke and Kidson, *Salisbury Cathedral*, 17.
[93] Merritt, 'Church-Building', 955.
[94] C. Davidson, 'George Herbert and Stained Glass Windows', *GHJ*, 12/1 (1988), 33–44.

94 BUILDING

window with white (clear) glass, so in October 1630 Sherfield locked himself
into the church, took a pike, climbed precariously onto the edge of a bench,
and picked out small and discrete sections of the offending glass (he then fell
off his perch, and had to spend a month in bed). Clearly, he was not aiming to
smash the whole window, otherwise he would not have been secretively bal-
ancing up in the air wielding a heavy pole; he could just have lobbed a large
stone from outside.

The incident was taken as an affront to church discipline and doctrine.
Depositions of witnesses were taken in January 1631, and by 6 February 1632
the case had been kicked upstairs to the Star Chamber. Making specific reference to the 1604 Canons, the Attorney General pointed out that the vestry's
main function was to keep the church in good repair, and that there was 'a great
deal of difference between repairing and reforming'.[95] The prosecution carica-
tured Sherfield as a wild-eyed, strong-armed iconoclast. The defence argued
that Sherfield's care in picking out a few quarries of glass suggested he was sane,
and believed he was carrying out God's will in erasing inaccurate or impossible representations. Shifting ground, it also noted that the material damage was
slight: the whole window had only cost about 40s, and the dislodged quarries
were worth no more than 18d. After a brief trial, Sherfield was found guilty,
fined £500, and instructed to make submission to the bishop; the king himself
commanded that this apology be as full as possible. The bishop, cautiously,
asked for the form of submission to be drafted by the Privy Council. This was
provided by the Attorney General on 8 April, and Sherfield recited it a week
later. All the clergy located near Salisbury, which presumably included Herbert, were summoned to hear him do so. Herbert had two other connections
to the case. He probably knew Sherfield personally, since St Edmund's and St
Andrew's are only two miles apart, and both men were on committees in the
1624 parliament.[96] Moreover, Sherfield's counsel for defence had been Edward
Herbert, George's uncle.

Sherfield's submission presumably incited Salisbury parishioners to troop
to St Edmund's to see the notorious window, before going back to their own
parish church to do some beady-eyed checking up. 'Love-joy' features two
such theological aesthetes, gazing at a painted window showing 'a vine drop

---

[95] *Calendar of State Papers Domestic (1629–31)*, 495; *Calendar of State Papers Domestic (1631–33)*,
267, 530, 536, 538–539, 571–572; *Calendar of State Papers Domestic (1633–34)*, 19, 21; 'State Trials',
3.columns 519–562; P. Slack, 'Religious Protest and Urban Authority: the Case of Henry Sherfield,
Iconoclast, 1633', *Studies in Church History*, 9 (1972), 295–302.

[96] C. R. Kyle, 'It will be a Scandal to show what we have done with such a number': House of Commons Committee Attendance Lists, 1606–1628', in C. R. Kyle, ed., *Parliament, Politics, and Elections
1604–1648*, Camden Fifth Series 17 (2001), 205, 220.

grapes with *J* and *C*/ Anneal'd on every bunch'. The two observers play the duck/rabbit game by showing themselves entirely uninterested in whatever story is painted on the glass (say, Noah's vineyard in Gen. 9.20, or the fruitful wife of Psalm 128.3, or Christ's image of himself as a vine in John 15.5, or a eucharistic symbol). Nor do they look through the glass. Instead, they put words to the letter-shapes made by the glass (the word 'Anneal'd' makes it clear that it is these, not the curved leading around the quarries, which form the letters). Setting aside the unlikely notion that each bunch comes with a grape that has a descriptive label (as in today's supermarket), either these letter shapes appear in the bunch's tendrils (Hutchinson's suggestion) or in the curving profile of one grape against another.[97] Neither viewer is 'loth/ To spend [his] iudgement' on creating a reading from the aspect of the window which they have agreed to focus on. The poem stresses the individuality of the readings: 'I cast', 'I saw', 'I ... said', 'It seem'd to me'. Many of Herbert's poems show a superior correcting another's understanding of a text or situation (as do the friends in 'Love Unknown' and 'The Holdfast', for instance).[98] Here, however, both speakers' points of view are approved ('Sir, you have not miss'd'): a few quarries of glass have not become a Star Chamber matter. Since the grapes do not bear labels (either of words or initial letters), the viewers can select whatever facet—here, shape—which will reveal the best of what they want to find in looking at the window. This facet allows them both to accept that the substance of Jesus Christ and his grace of joy and charity are both present at the same time, making the poem an instance of what Whalen calls 'the potentially sacramental dimension of ordinary reality', where 'a thing can be another thing while not ceasing to be itself'.[99]

Little Gidding suffered from some less charitable shape-spotting over its windows. Church wardens might prudently imagine that clear glass was the safe choice when reglazing, but this was not necessarily so. Iconoclasts and iconophiles alike could scout out crosses everywhere (as Donne does, seeing them in the shapes of seagulls and breast-stroke swimmers).[100] Herbert may have heard about Nicholas Ferrar's prudent response to someone who asked whether the family was going to reglaze the Little Gidding chancel window (of clear glass) with glass painted with a crucifix. Had such a window been

---

[97] Herbert, *Works*, ed. Hutchinson, 518.

[98] On a mid-century sub-genre of window poems, which attacks those who do not distinguish between sign and signified, see A. Smyth, '"Art Reflexive": The Poetry, Sermons, and Drama of William Strode (1601?–1645)', *Studies in Philology*, 103 (2006), 444–451.

[99] Whalen, *Immanence*, 124.

[100] J. Donne, 'Of the Cross': *The Poems of John Donne*, ed. R. Robbins, 2 vols. (Harlow: Pearson Longman, 2008), 2.7–14.

96 BUILDING

there when the family arrived they would have left it, said Ferrar, austerely; not being so, they would not add it without due authority. Even so, his visitors were undeterred, and enthusiastically continued to spot more potential crucifixes (including those made by the leading around the rectangular panes of glass).[101]

Sometimes Herbert concentrates on the material of the windows. Early modern painted glass has a very different look to that of the deeply coloured and thick pot-glass of medieval windows. In the latter, small individual pieces in one colour are set in leaded patterns that follow the main features of a subject, mosaic-style. By contrast, coloured glass from the mid-sixteenth century onwards tends to be made of large hand-blown panes which have been painted with a complete scene. To do this, compounds of ground powdered glass, mixed with a fusable medium, are painted onto clear glass, and then fired. The process allows more realistic, pictorial, and complex treatments of characters and landscapes, but the larger, thinner glass also has weaker tints, so the glass tends to lack fire.[102]

Two poems are interested in what the colour of the physical glass does to the view and hence the interpretation of an object. Recent studies of colour psychology show it to be a very effective (albeit context-specific) nudge, partly for evolutionary advantages, to signal mood, intent, or engagement. Colour both carries meaning and can have an important influence on affect, cognition, and behaviour; the 'red effect' is particularly strong.[103] 'Justice' 2 plays with coloured panes, looking at God's hand through 'sinne and errour', which 'through their glasse discolour' it. The hand seen through this pane 'did burn and glow' red, and the 'dishes' of the 'ballance' it holds are distorted into 'two great pits', full of hell fire, no longer weighing and judging the souls in them, but pre-emptively punishing them. Herbert then gazes at the hand through 'Christs pure vail' of 'white' (clear) glass, an imputed grace which turns the hand white too, and allows an alternative shape to the dishes to come into view, as alternately rising and falling buckets of penitential 'tears'. Here, the colour

---

[101] The gossip is undated. See Blackstone, ed., *Ferrar Papers*, 72–74.

[102] P. Cowen, *A Guide to Stained Glass in Britain* (London: Michael Joseph, 1985), 15–18, 50–55, 202–203; C. Winston, *Memoirs Illustrative of the Art of Glass-Painting* (London: John Murray, 1865), 108, 124–125. On the visual qualities of the glass from the two processes, see R. O. C. Spring, *The Stained Glass of Salisbury Cathedral* (Salisbury: Friends of Salisbury Cathedral, 1979), 15–18, figs. 1–11.

[103] A. J. Elliot and M. A. Maier, 'Color Psychology: Effects of Perceiving Color on Psychological Functioning in Humans', *Annual Review of Psychology*, 65/1 (2014), 95–120; A. J. Elliot and M. A. Maier, 'Color-in-Context Theory', *Advances in Experimental Social Psychology*, 45 (2012), 61–126; R. Mehta and R. J. Zhu, 'Blue or Red? Exploring the Effect of Color on Cognitive Task Performance', *Science*, 323 (2009), 1226–1239.

change nudges the speaker into a new perspective, as justified confidence can replace his 'fears'—though it still permits the latter to be glimpsed through the first pane, if the viewer chooses to move his eyes.

The same refocusing appears in 'The Elixer', only one stanza of which remained unchanged through the poem's two major revisions:

> A man that looks on glasse,
> On it may stay his eye;
> Or if he pleaseth, through it passe,
> And then the heav'n espie.

Wilcox, arguing that this stanza contains the poem's 'unchanging central idea', cites 1 Cor. 13.12, 'for now we see through a glass darkly; but then face to face'. However, given the poem elevates the status of cleaning, the film on the window which makes it into an object of attention itself might well be dirt (or at least the irregularities in hand-made glass). The first line of the poem asks God to help to 'In all things thee to see', including in—not just through—the impurities. Although the stanza encourages a saccade between the earthly 'drudgerie' of grubby glass needing to be made 'bright and clean' and the 'divine' meaning of doing so, focusing on a near object (the glass) still allows the parafovea to register something of the far, and vice versa. Which to fixate on is a decision free for man to make 'if he pleaseth', but (as in 'Justice' 2) God can be seen in both fixations, more or less clearly, not just in the view through the window of the heavens.

In 'Justice' 2 Herbert moves his head to see a static object through different quarries. In 'The Elixer' and 'Coloss. 3.3' his head stays still, but he varies the focal point of his eyes. In 'Love-joy' the eye and the viewer stay still but the interpretation varies. Initiating all these changes is left to the viewer, 'if he pleaseth'. Glass is a useful piece of choice architecture because the material encourages the reader to fixate on the most profitable aspect, but still gives her freedom to choose other perspectives, which are in view albeit not in focus.

However, the viewer's choice is given up to God in 'The Windows', which takes a view of church light which appears to reflect what R. T. says about how stained-glass windows 'adorn the Church with a glorious light, and moderate that bright light, which is a hinderance to devotion ... For devotion requires collected spirits which light diffuses'. Both poem and R. T. are interested in the effects of light on the non-image forming faculties of the eye: how brightness or dimness increases conscious alertness to the exterior circumstances or meditative interiority. Understandably, then, interpretations of this poem

98 BUILDING

often start with St Paul's statement that 'we all, with open face beholding as in a glass the glory of the Lord, are changed into the same image from glory to glory' (2 Cor. 3.18) to move into considering the Laudian debate about the beauty of holiness.[104] Such discussions then focus on the relationship between the devout image and the thing it refers to, rather than on the medium on which that image rests, and ask about the effects of the minister living out the lessons of his sermons, himself an image in God's story.[105]

However, the poem does not necessarily encourage viewers to look through the glass to the minister's life. The 'life' to be observed in 'Doctrine and life' may be read, as Herbert tells God earlier, as 'thy life', God's life. Herbert's attention is on the material of the glass. Although natural man is merely 'brittle crazie glasse', God can allot him the 'glorious and transcendent place' of expounding the 'eternall word'. The viewer can still look through the glass to the object outside, though her view of this will be distorted by the crackling inherent to poor glass, so the film between eye and object is apparent, and the latter therefore 'shows watrish, bleak, & thin'. Herbert has his own period's glass in mind, since the figure of the preacher still shows up, however watery when there is no light behind the window (medieval glass, by contrast, shows up as dark and opaque, not watery, when there is no light).

Neither 'colours and light' are at the command of the preacher: the poem stresses that these are God's qualities, bestowed at will ('dost him afford'). It is God's choice whether or not to 'anneal in glasse' his 'storie', so that 'the light and glorie/ More rev'rend grows, & more doth win'. The moving qualities of 'colours and light' result in 'strong regard', an absorbed and sustained gazing at the effect of light on the glass. This develops in the viewer a sense of 'aw' at the presence of God, where his sunlight glows and disappears, at his divine will. By contrast, the occasion for sitting in the church, the sermon, is casually dismissed at the end of the poem as an ephemeral distraction: 'speech alone/ Doth vanish like a flaring thing,/ And in the eare, not conscience ring'. Throughout, the viewer has the choice of what to focus on (the story on the glass, the glass itself, objects seen through the glass, or the light illuminating the glass)—all are present, simultaneously—but would be wise to fixate on the aspect which will give the most grace-filled experience.

---

[104] For instance, R. G. Shafer, 'Herbert's Poetic Adaptation of St. Paul's Image of the Glass', *Seventeenth-century News*, 35 (1977), 10–11; J. Kronenfeld, 'Probing the Relation Between Poetry and Ideology', *John Donne Journal*, 2/1 (1983), 55–80.

[105] Vendler, *Herbert*, 80.

To conclude: in his building poems, Herbert exemplifies how to make choices about which view will prove most productive, not limiting the reader to just one focal point. In doing so, he turns *The Temple* into a work in progress, where the reader is encouraged to decide how to make a devotional cognitive niche for herself, using the physical materials to hand.

4

Conversing

1 Conversational Prowess at Little Gidding and Bemerton

The primary problem for Protestants when conversing with God is that all their talk ends in asking for his favour even to ask for his favour to talk to him (or, less happily, in admitting that this grace appears not to have been received). Under the *sola fide* paradigm, what may set out to be praise, or thanks, or discussion shrivels into petitions, granted or denied. Making requests of another is embarrassing, Penelope Brown and Stephen Levinson point out, because both speaker and addressee can lose face if no agreement is reached.[1] This chapter points out the comedy of manners produced when Herbert's exquisite conversational tact in nudging God for a response meets God's blunt rebuttal. Herbert speaks in the sociable way recommended by the period's courtesy manuals; God speaks in the rebarbative way modelled by godly dialogues of the period. The former approach (though not the rules of polite speech) has been noted by Herbert scholars, particularly in relation to 'Love' 3; the latter, however, has not—and it provides much of the comedy of the poems. This chapter draws on the detailed linguistic strategies revealed by the manuals and the dialogues, to show how Herbert's God puts Herbert's speaker into place, not vice versa.

Sociologists and anthropologists are interested in the characteristically indirect nature of approaches and responses made in a hierarchical relationship. Brown and Levinson formulate a ladder of modes of petition: at the bottom end is a decision not to ask at all, at the top is a bald demand without any amelioration of the embarrassment of a possible refusal. In between are three sorts of tactics to minimize the threat to face: by asking privately or evasively (so the existence of the approach can be denied by both parties), by negative politeness (which details restraints on the appeal, minimizing the proposed imposition), and by positive politeness (which suggests the benefits to both sides if it were to be granted). In the first group (off-record requests) come

---

[1] P. Brown and S. Levinson, *Politeness: Some Universals in Language Usage* (Cambridge: Cambridge University Press, 1987), 102, 131, 214.

George Herbert and the Business of Practical Piety. Ceri Sullivan, Oxford University Press.
© Ceri Sullivan (2024). DOI: 10.1093/9780198906841.003.0004

hints, clues, presuppositions, under- or over-statements, tautologies, ironies, metaphors, rhetorical questions, ambiguities, generalizations, and ellipses. All these techniques sidle around the actual petition, using a degree of calculated vagueness to allow either side to pretend that the asker is not needy or that the hearer may not be in a giving mood. In the second group of tactics (minimizing the proposed imposition) come hedging, expressing pessimism about agreement, showing deference about the addressee's power to act on the request, apologizing for impinging on the hearer's time or generosity, stating one's reluctance to ask, describing the overwhelming need that prompts the request, and attempting to impersonalize the situation by using the passive voice and indefinite or plural pronouns. In the third group of tactics (claiming cooperation) come attention to the addressee's interests, in-group identity markers, agreement on as much as possible before the request is made (dwelling on safe topics), skirting round disagreement, making jokes, expressing optimism that the request will be granted, and asserting possible reciprocity. All these mildly manipulative nudges express a social anxiety that may or may not be sincere but which it is profitable to pretend to feel, in a situation where a subordinate approaches a superior.

The opposite situation, where inferiors are given instructions which they do not want to comply with but have no right to refuse, provokes similarly indirect discursive manoeuvres.[2] Fantasies of vengeful open speaking of command or denial are elaborated in private, but face on both sides is maintained in public. This avoids precipitating outright rebellion, which on one hand would suggest the superior's weakness, and on the other, elicit punishment of the inferior for non-compliance. James C. Scott argues that there are common modes of indirect verbal resistance to maintain face in this situation: dissimulation, feigned ignorance, slander, false compliance, gossip, implied complaints, euphemisms, rumours, and unwelcome silences. These methods sustain long-running and grinding low-level conflicts over small details, without ever bringing dissent into the open. Grumbling, for instance, cannot be deemed insubordinate (its words cannot quite be heard, or are not explicit about the real problem), yet it forces the superior to spend time and effort in clarifying commands and in ensuring they are carried out. Through these nudges, both ranks maintain their public image as super- or sub-ordinate, but test the limits and stability of this hierarchy.

---

[2] J. C. Scott, *Weapons of the Weak: Everyday Forms of Peasant Resistance* (New Haven: Yale University Press, 1985), xvi–ii, 241–303; J. C. Scott, *Domination and the Arts of Resistance: Hidden Transcripts* (New Haven: Yale University Press, 1990), 3–15, 136–182.

102   CONVERSING

It is these sidling modes of management, upwards and downwards, which Herbert's speakers try out when dealing with God. This chapter first discusses the importance that well-structured conversation was given at Little Gidding and Bemerton. It then contrasts secular and godly advice on dialogue, especially when speakers come from different ranks. The final section looks at how the urbane speaker of many of the poems, attempting to fudge over the fact he is trying to nudge God into bestowing grace, is sharply put into his place by God's home truths, in a comedy of embarrassment.

As a student at Cambridge, Nicholas Ferrar's tutors and friends noted his ability to call on a store of relevant examples and stories to persuade his hearers to act properly. One of them later said that, in discussion, he and others were like 'good Taylors, we can take measure of a Man, if he come to us, & bring us Cloath, & shall fitt him well, & cutt it out for him. But N. F. I may compare to one of those Burchin-Lane Taylors', who stock such a number of ready-made garments that they can suit any customer at once. During Ferrar's continental tour in 1613, his skill at conversation was praised. Expatriate Englishmen at Hamburg thought 'he understood the art of dialogue well, and without the pedantry of assuming and imposing upon the company he would lead the discourse to some useful consideration of virtue or vice'. At Leipzig, Ferrar learned shorthand, then spent successive fortnights at the workshops of different trades (including those of painters, weavers, dyers, and smiths), noting down their talk. One result was that he increased his conversational flexibility, based on a sort of equality with those he spoke with; he was said to 'treat with artisans in their proper terms: he could maintain a dialogue with an architect in his own phrases; he could talk with mariners in their sea terms.'[3] Once Ferrar was established at Little Gidding and receiving guests, this skill came into its own. One visitor, the Bishop of Lincoln, admired the way Ferrar could introduce useful stories during conversations to settle disputes or make a telling point while maintaining amity.

Herbert too was noted for his conversational prowess, particularly in challenging interlocutors without alienating them. Patrick Collinson has argued that the incidental services of a minister, both professional (such as visiting the sick, the needy, and wrong-doers) and administrative (such as charitable works), tend to be underplayed by today's scholars in favour of preaching and clerical formation, even though the occasional offices were probably more

---

[3] Blackstone, ed., *Ferrar Papers*, 14–15 fn. 2, 53, 80–82; Muir and White, eds., *Ferrar*, 99–102. Ferrar's tour is described in more detail in Ransome, *Web of Friendship*, 33–35.

1 CONVERSATIONAL PROWESS AT LITTLE GIDDING AND BEMERTON   103

valued by parishioners.[4] Herbert's incidental advice and exhortation were what his biographers focused on. Barnabus Oley's 1652 biography, prefacing Herbert's collected works, admired his skill in the 'the Fraternall duty of reproof', one of 'most difficult offices of Christian Prudence'. 'This Authour had not only got the courage to do this, but the Art of doing this aright'. In Oley's view, Herbert's ministry and his poems habitually used the same pastoral technique: discussing some neutral situation, then transferring what his interlocutors said about this 'in a Figure' to a godly interpretation of that before him.[5]

But indirect rebuke was not the only discursive talent for which Herbert was praised. Isaac Walton's life of Herbert, published in 1670 and revised in 1675, described the family as conversable. Herbert's mother, Magdalen, had 'great and harmless wit', 'cheerful gravity', and 'obliging behaviour', and Herbert had a 'civil and sharp wit, and ... a natural elegance' in speech. His habitual 'aspect was chearful' (even if he were unwell, when he would prescribe himself 'cheerful conversation'), and he would relieve the poor 'chearfully'.[6] Walton relates four incidents in which Herbert used such amiable pragmatism in his pastoral work. He was visited by a poor and elderly woman, who, 'after she had spoke some few words to him ... was surpriz'd with a fear, and that begot a shortness of breath'. Herbert repeatedly reassured her that he would hear her 'with patience' as well as help her financially, 'and this I will do willingly, and therefore, Mother, be not afraid to acquaint me with what you desire'. He sat her down with him, and took her hand while listening to her. Walton comments, in parenthesis, that 'it is some relief for a poor body to be but hear'd with patience', and Herbert's tact sent the woman home with a 'chearful heart'. On his regular walk to Salisbury, Herbert overtook a gentleman and 'took fair occasion to talk with him, and humbly begg'd to be excused, if he ask'd him some account of his faith'. Herbert gave two grounds for this: 'though you are not of my Parish, yet I receive Tythe from you by the hand of your Tenant', and 'I am the bolder to do it because I know there be some Sermon-hearers, that be like those Fishes, that always live in salt water, and yet are always fresh'. After catechizing the gentleman, Herbert suggested some rules for pious living, in such 'a loving and meek manner' that the gentleman often tried to walk with him again. Meeting a fellow minister on a journey, and falling into 'some

---

[4] P. Collinson, 'Shepherds, Sheepdogs, and Hirelings: The Pastoral Ministry in Post-Reformation England', in W. J. Sheils and D. Wood, eds., *The Ministry: Clerical and Lay* (Oxford: Basil Blackwell, 1989), 189–191.

[5] G. Herbert, *Herbert's Remains*, ed. B. Oley (1652), B9r–v.

[6] Patrides, ed., *Critical Heritage*, 94, 98, 107, 122.

104   CONVERSING

friendly Discourse' on professional topics, Herbert 'took occasion to say' that 'the decay of Piety' of which the minister complained was a fault that 'must lye at our doors', as brother ministers. Walton's fourth story is of how, on the way to Salisbury, Herbert took off his coat to help a poor man with a foundered horse. The man blessed Herbert and Herbert blessed him back, then gave him money and told him 'That if he lov'd himself, he should be merciful to his Beast'. When Herbert arrived at his friends' house, they reproached him for demeaning himself. He answered that 'the thought of what he had done, would prove Musick to him at Midnight ... and I praise God for this occasion: And now let's tune our Instruments'.[7] Walton gives a great deal of space to such seemingly insignificant details because he wants to show Herbert's conversational tact, of the sort highlighted by Brown and Levinson: putting himself on the same level as the poor people he helps (sitting down, holding hands, working alongside them, and blessing them), or, with those of the same rank as himself, excusing what could be seen as an impertinence (making a jokey analogy to fish in the sea, claiming he was merely paying back an obligation incurred, appealing to a professional *esprit de corps*, and turning the company's attention onto a practical communal task to avert potential argument).

The importance of calibrating the appropriate approach to a conversation is registered in *The Country Parson* and 'The Church-porch'.[8] Being ordained should change the quality of a minister's talk: 'before [chaplains] are in Orders, they may be received for Companions, or discoursers; but after a man is once Minister' he is raised in rank, and must be bold enough to reprove even the master of the house—but discreetly. Such expediency is the keynote of the rest of the manual's advice on speech. The minister is to keep his word strictly, not just because it is right, but because country people know that honesty 'is the Life of buying, and selling', and if the minister does not recognize this, 'he wil quickly be discovered, and disregarded: neither will they beleeve him in the pulpit, whom they cannot trust in his Conversation'. The parson must seek to know a little of everything, even 'tillage, and pastorage', 'because people by what they understand, are best led to what they understand not', and so he listens to learn about things, for 'to put men to discourse of that wherein they are most eminent is the most gainful way of conversation'. Herbert held the post of orator of the University of Cambridge from 1620 to 1628, but he goes out of his way, in his pastoral work, to avoid taking the directorial, monologic approach of the set speech.

---

[7] Patrides, ed., *Critical Heritage*, 112, 120–121.
[8] Herbert, *Country Parson*, 226, 228.

1 CONVERSATIONAL PROWESS AT LITTLE GIDDING AND BEMERTON 105

During divine service his minister uses a conversational intonation, volume, and pace, not a ritualized one, speaking in a way which is 'treatable, and slow; yet not so slow neither, as to let the fervency of the supplicant hang and dy between speaking, but with a grave livelinesse, between fear and zeal, praying yet pressing'. On their side, members of the congregation are expected to answer as though they are really listening, 'not in a hudling, or slubbering fashion, gaping, or scratching the head, or spitting even in the midst of their answer, but gently and pausably, thinking what they say'. The sermon uses the same mutual performance of attending to the other person's interest in what is being said: the preacher keeps 'a diligent, and busy cast of his eye on his auditors', to ensure that he speaks in an interesting way, but also to show the congregation that he is aware of who amongst them is attending to him.[9]

Herbert's ministry of conversation was not confined to parochial occasions. As Malcolmson says, in no 'social activity does he participate as an individual divorced from his clerical responsibilities'.[10] Nor does his household. His wife 'among her neighbours is the beginner of good discourses, his children among children, his servants among other servants; so that ... all are preachers'.[11] However, Herbert is amusingly frank about how wearing such an instrumental approach may be for his interlocutors. Thus, the parson 'mingles other discourses for conversations sake, and to make his higher purposes slip [in] more easily'. On a journey, 'those he meets on the way he blesseth audibly, and with those he overtakes, or that overtake him, hee begins good discourses, such as may edify, interposing sometimes some short, and honest refreshments, which may make his other discourses more welcome, and lesse tedious'. In general conversation, though always on the watch to reprove foolish or evil statements, he uses 'suppling' words to point them out, such as 'This was not so well said, as it might have been forborn; We cannot allow this: or else if the thing will admit interpretation; Your meaning is not thus, but thus; or, So farr indeed what you say is true, and well said; but this will not hold'. If the minister sees a conversation going awry in charity or purity, then 'he either prevents it judiciously, or breaks it off seasonably by some diversion. Wherein a pleasantness of disposition is of great use, men being willing to sell the interest, and ingagement of their discourses for no price sooner, then that of mirth'. As Herbert pragmatically concludes, showing some 'mirth' is necessary, as 'all men shun the company of perpetuall severity'.

---

[9] Herbert, *Country Parson*, 231, 232–233.
[10] Malcolmson, *Heart-work*, 38–39.
[11] Herbert, *Country Parson*, 240, 251, 252, 268.

106 CONVERSING

'The Church-porch' has conventional ethical injunctions against boasting about drunkenness or lechery, swearing, and repeating stories which contain 'Profanenesse, filthinesse, abusivenesse', but the greater part of the poem's advice on conversation is about social subtleties. A speaker is advised to have solid matter to discuss and to not be over-sensitive. He should refrain from laughing often, which looks foolish (and especially 'Lesse at thine own things laugh; lest in the jest/ Thy person share', for 'Many affecting wit beyond their power,/ Have got to be a deare fool for an houre'). Vary the content to suit the hearer: bring into 'thy discourse, if thou desire to please:/ All such is courteous, usefull, new, or wittie'. Again and again, Herbert insists that conversation involves mutual attention. Listening to another on his area of expertise 'dost thy self and him a pleasure', so ask questions to enhance the relationship (the quality of the responses is not relevant): 'steal from his treasure/ What to ask further. Doubts well rais'd do lock/ The speaker to thee'.[12] Turn-taking in speech is key, for 'A civil guest/ Will no more talk all, then eat all the feast'. Listen even to the angry: 'he that lets/ Another chafe, may .../ Mark all his wandrings' and 'Mark what another sayes: for many are/ Full of themselves, and answer their own notion'. Likewise, the thirty or so proverbs about conversation collected by Herbert urge concision or silence: 'Gossips are frogs, they drinke and talke', 'Talking payes no toll', 'Give loosers leave to talke', 'Speak fitly, or be silent wisely', 'More have repented speech then silence', and so on.[13]

Fish discusses the way Herbert's poems and *The Country Parson* are conversational in their approach to catechism, bringing the ignorant to realize a truth by their own reason, not by hearing it stated.[14] As Fish admits, though, even the most Socratic of catechisms is not at heart a conversation, since the minister aims to draw out specific points. There is only a surface equality in the discussion. Looking at the poems from the point of view of secular advice on the art of conversation may show why, for all the worry about worldly aims, there is still an appreciation of the pleasure and skill in dissolving hierarchies to allow 'the quick returns of courtesie and wit' ('The Pearl') and the 'trade in courtesies and wit' ('Employment' 2).

---

[12] Herbert offered similar advice to his younger brother Henry, in a letter of 1618. See *Works*, ed. Hutchinson, 366.

[13] Herbert, *Outlandish Proverbs*, numbers 275, 485, 602, 625, 682; see also 53, 104, 151, 246, 265, 278, 435, 526, 554, 645, 649, 672, 674, 694, 709, 727, 761, 767, 799, 838, 856, 926, 998.

[14] Fish, *Living Temple*, 24–44.

2 Advice on Amiable Conversation

Oliver Morgan has recently used the methodology of inter-actional linguistics to analyse the ways in which dialogue in drama is organized: how speakers know when to speak and when to fall silent (a sequencing problem, whose basic rule he summarizes as 'speak when spoken to'), how asides alter dialogue, and what governs the relative length of speeches within a conversation. He does not find such methods discussed in the language theory of the early modern period (interested in the rhetoric of the single speaker, not in the to and fro of conversation), and thinks them barely mentioned in civility theory.[15] However, this section argues that such matters as signalling when and who should speak (by the posture, gaze, expression, and gesture of the body, and the pitch, pace, intonation, stress, and volume of the voice) were discussed in the period as part of a training in civil manners, particularly when dealing with cross-rank interactions.

The period's courtesy theory, as Peter Burke, Anna Bryson, and Jennifer Richards among others have shown, is intensely interested in the social advantages of displaying skill in civil conversation.[16] Advice literature is preoccupied with how verbal tact should be used for both cooperative and competitive means, following Cicero's discussion of conversation in *On Duties* (a staple school text). Cicero argues that while conversation draws on some of rhetoric's techniques, it does not have oratory's over-riding purpose of dominating the listeners present to make them feel, judge, or act in a particular way: good talk, he says, is not a private monopoly. Concerned to put the agreeable in the service of the good, Cicero thinks that all those involved in a discussion have the responsibility to keep it going by such amiable and egalitarian means as speaking undogmatically, taking turns, not being malicious or slanderous, never boasting or focusing on their own concerns, keeping to a subject as long as (and only as long as) it continues to interest most of the company present, and showing neither over-mastering passion nor indifference to others' points or to the subject being pursued.[17]

---

[15] O. Morgan, *Turn-Taking in Shakespeare* (Oxford: Oxford University Press, 2019), 24–42.

[16] P. Burke, *The Art of Conversation* (Cambridge: Polity Press, 1993), 90–108; A. Bryson, *From Courtesy to Civility: Changing Codes of Conduct in Early Modern England* (Oxford: Clarendon Press, 1998), 152–168; J. Richards, *Rhetoric and Courtliness in Early Modern Literature* (Cambridge: Cambridge University Press, 2003), 1–42.

[17] M. T. Cicero, *On Duties (De officiis)*, trans. W. Miller (Cambridge, MA: Harvard University Press, 1913), 1.37–38.

108 CONVERSING

As Richards shows, early modern advice follows suit, urging behaviour which admitted rivalry but managed it for productive and sociable ends.[18] A best-selling treatise by Desiderius Erasmus, taught to the youngest boys at school and often translated, reminds them to be unobtrusively helpful in keeping a conversation going: speaking merrily and lightly at table, allowing others to speak freely without the fear of being reported elsewhere (the ravings of Herbert's 'The Collar', with its speaker pounding 'the board', sound like the sort of loose talk over dinner which Erasmus wants guests to forget the next day), smiling and listening to interlocutors, responding in kind, allowing speakers to finish what they are saying, looking at the person one addresses, and using their correct names and titles, only gainsaying another's points if absolutely necessary (and then, very gently), speaking in words rather than just gesturing, and withdrawing if other guests want to talk privately.[19] Francis Bacon admires this sort of well-conducted conversation. While 'The Honourablest Part of Talke, is to give the Occasion; And againe to moderate and passe to somewhat else; For then a Man leads the Daunce', one should also ask questions, giving 'other Men their Turnes to speak', or even, exceptionally, redirecting the conversation when it is being hogged by one person, 'As Musicians use to doe, with those, that dance too long Galliards'.[20] The tutor James Cleland advises his young readers not to be 'captive' to their own mood, but to fit that of others present. All interlocutors are to be welcomed by countenance, word, and gesture, and all present must make an effort to speak engagingly ('when you have saluted your friend, I meane not that yee shoulde stand still dombe, admiring his or your own brave cloathes ... or to beate your bootes with a rod, [or] bite your nailes' in silence, and so on).[21] Some 'General maximes of conversation' by the French courtier Nicolas Faret urge participants to be 'supple' and open to the positions taken by their company:

one of the most infallible marks of a minde well bred, is to be thus universall, and susceptible of many formes, so as it bee with reason, and not through

[18] Richards, *Rhetoric and Courtliness*, 28–29.
[19] D. Erasmus, *The Civilite of Childehode*, trans. T. Paynell (1560), C3r–C4r. *De civilitate morum puer* was read in the third and fourth forms of the grammar schools at Bury St Edmund's, Bangor, and Winchester during Elizabeth's reign, and recommended for petty school use by the educational theorist Charles Hoole. See T. W. Baldwin, *William Shakspere's Small Latine & Lesse Greeke*, 2 vols. (Urbana: University of Illinois Press, 1944), 1.298, 305, 330; C. Hoole, *The Petty Schoole, Shewing a Way to Teach Little Children to Read English* (1659), 33.
[20] F. Bacon, 'Of Discourse', in M. Kiernan, ed., *The Essayes or Counsels, Civill and Morall* (Oxford: Clarendon Press, 1985), 103–105.
[21] F. Cleland, *Hero-paideia, or the Institution of a Young Noble Man* (1607), 168, 189.

2 ADVICE ON AMIABLE CONVERSATION 109

lightnesse or weaknesse. There is a rusticity and stupidity [for someone] to be so tied to his owne complexions, as hee can never yeild in any point.[22]

This stretches to the sort of topics to be dealt with, which should be such as all present can join in. William Cornwallis's essay 'Of Discourse' criticizes those who cannot follow others' leads in the conversation; 'for Mercenary and Mechanicke, it skilles not, it becomes them well to discounter themselves by theyr speech, but a Gentleman should talk like a Gentleman, which is, like a wise man: his knowledge should be generall.'[23] Della Casa's *Galateo* likewise urges speakers to remember the pleasure of their listeners, and not to fall into anger, melancholy, obscurity, or self-concern (topics guaranteed to bore any listener are the speaker's own family, dreams, and successes!).

Della Casa is particularly concerned with how interlocutors should be mutually concerned to save face. They should maintain a demeanour of pleased engagement, whether listening or responding. Looking inattentive is ill-bred. Offering 'advyce unrequested' is an insult ('what is it els but to vaunt youre selfe wiser then he is, whom you do counsell: nay rather, it is a playne checke to him, for his Ignorance and Folly'). Rebuking others for faults, he thinks, turns one into an unpleasant combination of physician, confessor, judge, censor, schoolmaster, and father. Open contradiction has a 'bitter taste'; better to 'say, I cannot tell how to say it: Then say: you ar deceived: Or, it is not true: Or, you know it not'. Interrupting another's speech is an irritating habit (like pullets pecking corn from other birds' beaks), as is tempting the company to ignore the current speaker, or only half listening, or staying coldly silent during the discussion.[24] The same concern for preserving the credit of interlocuters appears in the translation of an anonymous French conduct book, *Youths Behaviour, or Decency in Conversation Among Men*:

when another speaketh, take heed that through thee hee bee not neglected by his auditors; and be attentive, turning not thine eyes here and there, nor busie thy selfe in ought else. If any drawl forth his words, help him not therein, nor prompt him, bee it not that hee intreat thee so to doe, or that it were in private, or that thou hadst great familiaritie with him. Likewise interrupt him

---

[22] N. Faret, *The Honest Man: or the Art to Please in Court*, trans. E. Grimeston (1632), 259.

[23] W. Cornwallis, *Essayes* (1600), G3v–G4r.

[24] Della Casa, *Galateo*, 16–17, 60, 62, 81, 84. Herbert's use of another prominent courtesy text, Stefano Guazzo's *The Civile Conversation* (1574), trans. G. Pettie (1581), has been examined, but Guazzo focuses on 'conversation' in terms of company, not discussion. See K. Wolberg, 'George Herbert's *The Country Parson* and Stefano Guazzo's *The Civile Conversation*', *GHJ*, 27/1–2 (2003–2004), 105–118; John Lievsay, *Stefano Guazzo and the English Renaissance, 1575–1675* (Chapel Hill: University of North Carolina Press, 1961), 141–144.

110   CONVERSING

not, nor answer him, untill hee have brought his speech to a period. Being in the midst of a discourse, aske not of what one treateth, since that it is a draught of authoritie; but thou mayst well intreat gently, that hee proced, if thou perceivest that for thee hee hold his peace ... If any one had begun to rehearse a History; say not, I know it well: and if he relate it not a-right, and fully; shake not thy head, twinkle not thine eyes, and snigger not thereat; much lesse maist thou say, It is not so, you deceive your selfe.[25]

Face-saving is important because it is 'a greater signe of contempt and disdaine, to scorne a man, then to do him an open wrong', since it makes him of no account, says Della Casa.[26] De Sales also thinks that to scoff at another is 'one of the greatest offences that a man can committ against his neighbour' by words, since it is done without an eye to gain, and out of 'meere despight and contempt'.[27]

Complex social manoeuvres result from grossly mismatching interlocuters. S. R.'s *Courte of Civil Courtesie* recommends that a superior yields precedence to a lower-ranked person who is eminent for knowledge, skill, or virtue, but does so with 'a modest audacity ... neither too lowde nor whisperyng, [so] as the rest of the company may well perceive: it is the vertues, and not the man that is preferred', and the courtesy is offered as a self-respecting mark of respect for the other's abilities, not out of 'sheepishe simplicitie'. S. R. suggests graceful phrases which will make this condescension clear to everyone present, such as 'Not I by your leave' or 'On, on I pray you, you bee next the door'. In an inferior's house, S. R. explains, if expected to converse with a yet more socially inferior person (however rich), then one should move seats, 'wherby the [host] shalbee (in sylence) taught to consyder better an other time'. If the host looks abashed then the guest should cover over the *faux pas* gracefully; if, however, the host does not notice the snub then the guest should 'gird him' firmly. In deciding whom to speak with when in company, the guest should wait for the higher-ranking people (or at least equals) to approach him first. If none offer to do so, then it is better he sits alone, 'with a steddy and assured countenaunce, as though ... studying some matter of waight, or harkening to others talke if it bee not secret: then to accompany him selfe with sutch as bee unworthy of his company'. Rather than fidgeting, he should sit silently but alertly, ready to take part in a conversation if a 'word or looke bee addressed' to him by a superior. The latter will allocate the turns in discussion, so he should be watched to see if

---

[25] *Youths Behaviour, or Decency in Conversation Amongst Men*, trans. F. Hawkins (1646), 33, 39.
[26] Della Casa, *Galateo*, 62.
[27] De Sales, *Devoute Life*, 400, 420.

he also is making conversation out of politeness or from a real wish to talk, 'and when [the inferior] seeth his better pawse, so that hee turne not awaywarde (as though hee would begon from him) to invent some matter of himself, to lengthen talke'.[28]

Yet considerations of rank may make it impertinent to use such conversational tact. Della Casa thinks

> they bee ... very tedious to men, and their conversation & maners are very troublesome: who shewe too base and abject a minde in their doings. And where the chiefest and highest place is apparantly due unto them: they will ever creepe downe to the lowest. And it is a spiteful buisynes to thrust them up: For they will straight jogge backe againe, like a resty jade ... When wee meete at a doore ... they will not (for all that you can doe) in any case enter before you, but so traverse the ground, go backe, and so fray and defend with their arms and their handes: that at every thirde steppe, a man must be ready to wage battell with them.[29]

A contemporary guide on how to 'converse with persons of ... quality' imagines this sort of inverse (and tedious) competition, as when making 'Complements at sitting downe to the Table':

ALEXANDER Come my Masters, please it you that wee wash our hands?
THE INVITED After you Sir, if it please you.
ALEXANDER Leave Ceremonies, for I cannot abide them. Let us wash, if it please you.
THE INVITED Sir, they are not Ceremonies when a civill and due respect commands them. You shall be first if it please you.
ALEXANDER Well, well, seeing you will not be ruled, let us wash together.
THE INVITED Sir, it should not be so, but your desire has all authoritie upon us.
ALEXANDER And what, my masters, will you not please to sit?
THE INVITED It shall be after you, Sir, if it please you [and so on, while the dinner gets cold].[30]

Indeed, Della Casa argues that gestures of courtesy are only open to those of a certain rank:

[28] S. R., *The Courte of Civill Courtesie* (1577), 1, 2, 3, 7, 8, 9.
[29] Della Casa, *Galateo*, 40.
[30] *The Mirrour of Complements ... to Converse with Persons of Worth and Quality* (1635), 48–49.

112   CONVERSING

neither must handy crafts men, nor men of base condition, buisie them selves
to much, in over solemne Ceremonies to greate men and Lordes... It is not
lookt for in such ... It seemes that in such, they seeke & looke rather for
obedience and duetie, then honour ... He thinks the servant doth make a
doubt whether he is a master or no, as if it were not in him to imploy him, &
command him.[31]

Strier castigates the stanzas on conversation in 'The Church-porch' for promoting self-interest as a guiding principle. They are 'purely strategic': their
'ideal of social behaviour is to get maximal returns from minimal outlays'
of engagement. Strier is particularly critical of Herbert's rhetorical question
about responding angrily in a discussion ('Why should I feel another mans
mistakes/ More, then his sicknesses or povertie?'), thinking it suggests that
Herbert discourages empathy.[32] However, if the courtesy handbook's approach
to egalitarian principles in conversation is considered, these stanzas read less
like self-preservation and more like advice not to make points in anger, which
is a 'discourtesie' showing neither 'wisdome' nor 'love'. Strier argues elsewhere that admonitions about civility in 'The Church-porch' are influenced by
early seventeenth-century devout humanism, which tried to reconcile social
concerns and gospel teaching, and was summed up in Francis de Sales's *Introduction to a Devoute Life*.[33] De Sales argues against the Pauline position that
most pleasant conversation is a vice (Ephesians 5.4); instead, he thinks, good
conversation is an expression of neighbourly charity. Strier concludes that
while Herbert does not want to follow de Sales in turning sociability into a
virtue, he is willing to offer an overtly Christian courtesy handbook.

Looking at Protestant texts of practical divinity may, however, make Herbert
seem closer to de Sales than this suggests, since they are not far behind secular manuals in urging urbanity in discussion. *The True Watch, or a Direction
for the Examination of our Spirituall Estate*, a popular work by the schoolmaster and devotional writer John Brinsley, asks its readers to reflect on sins of the
tongue. It moves between blunt moral injunctions against evil talk (lying, blas-
pheming, flattering, and so on), to warnings about sophisticated mishandling
of words (such as 'reporting mens bare wordes or actions without their intent
and meaning, wresting or any way perverting them'), to positive approval of

---

[31] Della Casa, *Galateo*, 51. Erasmus offers similar advice against being 'opiniative' through such
courtesy competitions. See *Civilitie*, C4r.
[32] Strier, 'George Herbert and the World', 227–232.
[33] R. Strier, *Resistant Structures: Particularity, Radicalism, and Renaissance Texts* (Berkeley: University of California Press, 1995), 84–110; de Sales, *Devoute Life*, 384–427.

2 ADVICE ON AMIABLE CONVERSATION   113

making sensible and amiable conversation ('using but few, and wise speeches for in many wordes are much vanitie ... Striving to cheerefulnesse and affability in all our speeches, as our Saviour' did).[34] Abraham Jackson counsels the godly apprentice to show 'reverence' for his master by 'giving him such titles, and using such formes as are fit: as Sir, and forsooth, &c., and 'not presuming sawcily to contradict his sayings, or ... interpose' an unasked-for opinion. If the apprentice is commanded to do something immoral he must refuse; but

> in refusing to obey, you must take heed of sturdy and insolent behaviour; you must beware of provoking words; you must expresse your unwillingnesse in milde speeches, and intreat him not to urge you to that which goes against your conscience to doe: as being expressely forbidden by Gods Word.[35]

Christians, like courtiers, should speak in a way which promotes amiability, as a way to keep in cheerful charity with their neighbours. Richard Greenham (a famed adviser in practical divinity, until 1591 rector of Dry Drayton, Cambridgeshire, then lecturer at Church Church, Greyfriars, London) calls it an 'unchristian courtesy' to leave one speaker to bear all the responsibility for discussion at dinner, so suggests a series of tactics to rustle up matter for table talk: ask questions of the others present, or (if this fails) talk about the communion of the saints, or (if this fails) complain of one's own stupidity, and 'even of ... dulnes and deadness ... raise quicknes and life of speech again.'[36] For Perkins, one of God's graces of the tongue is urbanity, 'a grace of speech whereby men in seemely manner use pleasantnesse in talke for recreation, or for such delight as is joyned with profit to them selves and others'. There are times when it is right to laugh and relax in speech (with the usual caveats).[37]

Of course, where possible, talk should be morally profitable. De Sales recommends one discern, from the outset, the tendency of any discussion. Setting aside evil conversation (to correct which, one must 'use mildnes, warines, and dexteritie'), there are three sorts:

> there be some kind of conversations, profitable for nothing, but for meere recreation, which are made by a simple turning or abstracting of our mindes from serious affaires: for such, though a man must not be totallie addicted

[34] J. Brinsley, *The True Watch, or a Direction for the Examination of our Spirituall Estate* (1606), 71, 74.

[35] Jackson, *Pious Prentice*, 59, 111–112.

[36] R. Greenham, 'Practical Divinity': *The Works and Life of Revd Richard Greenham*, eds. K. L. Parker and E. J. Carlson (Aldershot: Ashgate, 1998), 144.

[37] W. Perkins, *A Direction for the Government of the Tongue* (1593), 44–47.

114   CONVERSING

unto them, yet we may lend them so much leasure, as is convenient for recreation.

There are also those which are civil in intent, aimed at keeping amity among neighbours. Both of these types of talk can be undertaken in moderation, but they should always give way to the third type, 'profitable recreations'; 'with devout, and virtuous persons ... a soule that happeneth to be in virtuous companie, cannot choose but be partaker of their good qualities.'[38] Richard Rogers remembers as the highlight of February 1587 a 'most sweet journey' of two days made with a fellow minister, with 'much time bestowed in the way about our christian estat'. Conversely, six months later when he rode to London with his wife, because they did not set themselves from the start 'to passe the time profitably, ... we wandringe by litle and litle in needlesse speach', his 'zeal' of grace was 'abated', even though 'no great default [was] committed.'[39]

3 Dialogues of Reproof and Refutation

Even when it comes to admonitions about an interlocutor's opinions or actions, practical divinity is, at first, as irenic as the secular texts. Perkins urges 'meekenesse in reproofes' from speakers, who are to act like 'Chirurgeons ... who being to set the arme or legge that is forth of joynt, handle it so tenderly, that the patient shall scant feele when the bone falles in againe'. He suggests four methods to do this: telling a story that includes the error in disguise, calling attention to the opposite virtue (with, perhaps, an oblique reference to the sin), reproving oneself for the same fault, and finally (should it be necessary to reprove the failing directly) using 'prefaces, that wee doe it of love, that wee wish well to the partie, that wee speake as considering our selves, that wee also are in daunger of the same fault: and partly by framing the reproofe out of the worde of God, that the partie may see him selfe, rather to be reprooved by God, then by us' (as Jackson also suggests).[40] Such methods of rebuke save face by indirection (hinting at the fault and suggesting that someone else has pointed it out) and by positive politeness (making common cause with the sinner).

Edward Reyner, rector of St Peter at Arches, Lincoln, repeats and develops the advice by Perkins, noting that 'there is great skill in shaping reproofs'. The speaker should remember that 'Reproof is a bitter pill, which should be

---

[38] De Sales, *Devoute Life*, 385, 386, 426.
[39] Knappen, ed., *Puritan Diaries*, 53, 58.
[40] Perkins, *Government of the Tongue*, 37–39.

rolled in the Sugar, or lapt up in the pap of love', and done 'not from an arrogant humour of censuring, nor from an ambitious desire of credit', nor 'in an imperious, domineering, provoking, exasperating manner, but in a mild, winning way, as it were, subjecting our selves' to those chidden. For Reyner, the style of reproof depends on the parties' relative rank, age, temper, and degree of acquaintanceship, demanding one calibrate exactly when to speak mildly and privately, and when to do the opposite.[41] Advice on maintaining good relationships in a godly household, by Robert Cleaver (rector of Drayton, Oxfordshire), likewise suggests varying the rebuke according to the severity of fault committed and the attitude of the transgressor. Faults committed out of ignorance, accident, oversight, and a mistaken desire to please may deserve only mild admonition. More serious actions (such as unjustly acquiring others' goods or being 'negligent in increasing' one's own) may be rebuked by using the words of God. These will provoke salutary shame and fear, if uttered in 'zeale of Gods glorie' and 'love' for the person endangering his soul by his error.[42]

On the whole, though, admonishing others in public was, Greenham thought, best done by neutral indirection, for instance, by saying to the company generally 'my bretheren such a syn hath passed from this place, the giltles need not to bee offended [by hearing about it,] the person gilty is to repent of it'. When considering whether to rebuke anyone, Greenham offers a preliminary checklist designed to reduce the impertinence: is there ground in the Bible for the rebuke, does it stand with your calling to reprehend the other person, might someone else be better placed to do so, who else may hear the rebuke (damaging the sinner's credit), and, finally, can you 'put on the person of the offendor, that as you spare not his sin because of zeale of gods glory, so you pres it not too far beecaus of compassion of a brother'?[43] If the answer to any of these is no, stay silent.

Some Protestant dialogues illustrate cooperative correction. For instance, *The Preachers Plea, or, a Treatise in Forme of a Plain Dialogue, Making Known the Worth and Necessary Use of Preaching* by Samuel Hieron, vicar of Modbury, Devon, has participants who courteously accept emendation and even direct rebuke and admonition from each other: 'I am not a little glad to heare this from you', 'Blessed be God, you have well satisfied me in this', 'You cannot content me better, then if you shall undertake to discourse therof', 'You have

---

[41] E. Reyner, *Rules for the Government of the Tongue* (1656), 174, 175, 181.
[42] Cleaver, *Householde Government*, 49–56.
[43] Greenham, *Works*, 153, 154.

116 CONVERSING

said the very truth', 'Truly sir, it is even so', 'Yes verily', 'I conceive you well', and 'I am (I thanke you) well satisfied for this'.[44]

The best-sellers in this genre, however, are not so uniformly amiable. There is no point in correcting the trivial-minded, the foolish, the mad, the scornful, and the obdurate, say Perkins and Reyner; 'enemies of religion', 'fooles and pratlers' are just not worth speaking to.[45] However, the hardened or open sinner may be trumpeted at: 'such a one is a knotty piece, there is need to take the hard mallet and wedges of reproof to rive him', according to Reyner.[46] George Webbe, vicar of Steeple Aston, Wiltshire, and a distinguished preacher, notes that 'it is the Apostles rule, that we should have no fellowship with the unfruit-full works of darkenesse, but rather reprove them: As our Saviour sharply reproved Peter', and I. B's *A Dialogue Betweene a Vertuous Gentleman and a Popish Priest* has as its epigraph the biblical text that 'Thou shalt not hate thy brother in thy heart, but thou shalt playnely rebuke thy neighbour, and suffer him not to sinne' (Leviticus 19.17).[47] In *The Country Parson*, Herbert largely varies his style of rebuke according to the sensitivities (based on rank) of the people involved.

> Those that the Parson findes idle, or ill imployed, he chides not at first, for that were neither civill, nor profitable; but always in the close, before he departs from them: yet in this he distinguisheth; for if he be a plaine countryman, he reproves him plainly; for they are not sensible of finenesse: if they be of higher quality, they commonly are quick, and sensible, and very tender of reproof: and therefore he lays his discourse so, that he comes to the point very leasurely, and oftentimes, as Nathan did, in the person of another, making them to reprove themselves.

There is an exception, though: 'when the offence is publicke, and against God, I am then to follow the Apostles rule, 1 Timothy 5.20. and to rebuke openly that which is done openly'.[48] Such plainness could be dangerous, and not just to either side's reputation. Rogers prayed for 'wisdome and grace' when about to deal with a 'company of bad felowes', and 'by means of that did, in reasoning with one young man who is become a veary Atheist, receive a sensible blessing

---

[44] S. Hieron, *The Preachers Plea, or, a Treatise in Forme of a Plain Dialogue, Making Known the Worth and Necessary Use of Preaching* (1604), 4, 8, 9, 12, 14, 16, 20.
[45] Perkins, *Tongue*, 64–65.
[46] Reyner, *Tongue*, 172–174.
[47] G. Webbe, *The Araignement of an Unruly Tongue* (1619), 166.
[48] Herbert, *Country Parson*, 248.

3 DIALOGUES OF REPROOF AND REFUTATION   117

of my prayer that I was not thrust through by him for being earnest against his atheisme.[49]

Such extreme situations often invigorate the Protestant printed dialogue, a subgenre popularized in a denunciation of luke-warm Christianity by George Gifford, curate of All Saints-with-St Peter, Maldon, Essex. In *A Briefe Discourse of Certaine Points of the Religion, which is Among the Common Sort of Christians, which May Bee Termed the Countrie Divinitie*, Zelotes catches up with Atheos on a twenty-mile journey, and within two pages is quizzing Atheos about the quality of his minister (briskly concluding he is 'more meete for too keepe swine, then too bee a Sheaphearde over the flocke of Christ'), and then about the state of Atheos's own faith. It never occurs to the interlocutors to break off the conversation with polite vagueness. Atheos has two characteristic responses. The first is to complain about the way Zelotes twists his words: 'you take all thinges wrong, yee doe not heare [me] say so', 'you put in a greate deale more then I sayde, and take mee still at the woorst', and 'I trust I knowe, and I meane well, God knoweth my meaning howsoever you take me'. The second is to tell Zelotes to mind his own business: 'let me alone: I beleeve as well as you, take care for your selfe; you shall not answere for me', and 'it were good that you Puritanes shoulde consider your selves'.[50]

Gifford's approach was followed in the best-selling dialogue by Arthur Dent (rector of South Shoebury, Essex), *The Plaine Mans Path-way to Heaven. Where Every Man Shall Cleerly See, Whether He Shall Be Saved or Damned*. Its four participants (a godly minister, a zealous and a lax layman, and one who scorns religion) attack each other without mercy: 'You shew your selfe to be a notable Infidell' and one of the 'rankest Atheists that ever I talked withall' (Theologus to Antilegon), 'you are all of the spirit: you are so full of it, that it runneth out at your nostrils' (Antilegon to Theologus), 'all holy exercises of religion are … as vineger to your teeth and smoke to your eies' (Theologus to Asunetus), 'one of these folke of God which know their seats in heaven' (Antilegon to Philagathus), 'I had not thought any man had beene so ignorant, as I now perceive this man is' (Philagathus to Asunetus). Even Asunetus, Dent's lax Christian, is pricked into protesting against such sharp rebuttals: 'I have heard all your speech hitherto, and like reasonably well of it, but now I can forbeare no longer, my conscience urgeth me to speake … you goe too far'.[51] No quarter

---

[49] Knappen, ed., *Puritan Diaries*, 54. Rogers lists ways to speak winningly, to bring people back to grace. See *Seven Treatises*, 371–372.

[50] G. Gifford, *A Briefe Discourse of Certaine Points of the Religion, which is Among the Common Sort of Christians, which May Bee Termed the Countrie Divinitie* (1581; 1582), 2v, 14r–v, 20v–21r, 79v, 83r.

[51] A. Dent, *The Plaine Mans Path-way to Heaven. Where Every Man Shall Cleerly See, Whether He Shall Be Saved or Damned* (1601; 1607), 18, 135, 266, 267, 273, 324. On Dent's debt to Gifford, and

118   CONVERSING

is given in a similar dialogue by I. B., where the zealous layman is so unyield-
ingly direct about the consequences of the errors of a minister whom he meets
that the latter falls sick:

[GENTLEMAN .]How doe you (M.Par) me thinks your collour doth begin to
    change.
[PARSON .]Oh, oh, oh.
GEN. What are you not wel, that you looke so ill?
PAR. Oh, sicke, sicke.

Though the Gentleman offers first aid (ginger, aqua vitae, and a visit to the
physician), the Parson gasps that it is his 'sinnes' which trouble him, and
gallops off to reform his life.[52]

Virginia Cox argues that elite humanist dialogues represent the act of debate
to reflect on the matter discussed, how this could be transmitted, and how it
might be responded to. There may be a degree of counterpointing between
these aims, as an invitation to the reader to pursue independently the positions
presented. Such playful, sceptical, and witty dialogue is held in private places
between well-educated and leisured friends.[53] By contrast, Roger Deakins and
Antoinina Bevan Zlatar point out, the Protestant dialogue is highly opposi-
tional and instrumental. The conversations occur in public places (on the
road, for instance, or at an inn), not in a secluded space. Characters are relative strangers to each other rather than part of an in-group. They are treated
according to their teachability and not their rank, so the obdurate are fair targets for 'deliberate rudeness': they are openly rebuked or ridiculed by their
interlocutors with a 'host of rhetorical figures of disparagement, ranging from
scoffs and negative similes to irony', followed by marvel 'at the adversary's fool-
ishness or iniquity', says Zlatar. Such disputes are public, blunt, and egalitarian,
with no certain outcome in terms of their conversion plot, though the reader
is left in no doubt about which is the right side.[54]

Contradiction was a learned and enjoyable skill. Grammar school boys
practised adversarial disputations, at first copying models and then inventing

---

imitators of Dent, see C. Haigh, *The Plain Man's Pathways to Heaven: Kinds of Christianity in Post-
Reformation England, 1570–1640* (Oxford: Oxford University Press, 2007), 2–3.

[52] I. B., *Vertuous Gentleman and a Popish Priest*, J8v.

[53] V. Cox, *The Renaissance Dialogue: Literary Dialogue in its Social and Political Contexts, Castiglione
to Galileo* (Cambridge: Cambridge University Press, 1992), 5–6.

[54] R. Deakins, 'The Tudor Prose Dialogue: Genre and Anti-Genre', *Studies in English Literature,
1500–1900*, 20/1 (1980), 5–23; A. Bevan Zlatar, *Reformation Fictions: Polemical Protestant Dialogues
in Elizabethan England* (Oxford: Oxford University Press, 2011), 1–29, 203 ff; I. Green, *Print and
Protestantism in Early Modern England* (Oxford: Oxford University Press, 2000), 372–378.

3 DIALOGUES OF REPROOF AND REFUTATION 119

their own.[55] School exercises included writing as another (a woman, a carter, a city, a beast, a tree, the stars) to gain experience in taking up binary positions in a debate, not to imagine and hence empathize with opponents' positions.[56] Pedagogues such as John Brinsley call on Quintilian's image of how orators, like wrestlers, learn various moves, 'so that they have a stock of "numbers" from which they can apply one or two, as occasion offers'.[57] Michel de Montaigne dwells on how, in debate, 'occasion, company, yea the change in my voice, draws more from my minde than I can finde therin, when by my selfe I ... endevor to employ the same'. Indeed,

> if I conferre with a stubborne wit, and encounter a sturdy wrestler, he toucheth me to the quicke, hits me on the flanks, and pricks me both on the left and right side: his imaginations vanquish and confound mine. Jelousie, glory and contention, drive, cast and raise me above my selfe. And an unison or consent, is a qualitie altogether tedious and wearisome in conference.[58]

At university, public disputations were conducted with zeal as 'a form of academic blood sport'. A 'natural academic predisposition to argumentativeness' tended to favour public refutation, where 'quite evident personal dislike combined with detestation of opposing viewpoints and encouraged academics with the upper hand to seek the public humiliation of their opponents'.[59] A visitor to Cambridge in 1600 noted how the respondent in a masters' disputation mounted such a 'violent attack', in which the proposer's position was 'belittled' and 'undermined ... with so much animus, that the other man went quite red with mortification'.[60] Moreover, disputation was a spectator sport; the Cambridge authorities that year had to issue orders to listening students against 'standinge upon stalles, knockinge, hissinge and other immoderate behaviour', as they responded to weak or telling points.[61]

---

[55] Baldwin, *Shakspere's Small Latine*, 2.366–72.

[56] J. Deitch, '"Dialogue-wise": Discovering Alterity in Elizabethan Dialogues', in H. Ostovich, M. V. Silcox, and G. Roebuck, eds., *Other Voices, Other Views: Expanding the Canon in English Renaissance Studies* (Newark: University of Delaware Press, 1999), 46–73.

[57] J. Brinsley, *Ludus literarius: or, the Grammar Schoole* (1612), 205–206, 281; M. F. Quintilian, *The Education of the Orator* (*Institutio oratoria*), trans. D. A. Russell, 5 vols. (Cambridge: Harvard University Press, 2001), 12.2.12–13.

[58] M. de Montaigne, *The Essayes*, trans. J. Florio (1603; 1613), 51, 519.

[59] V. Morgan with C. Brooke, *A History of the University of Cambridge. Vol. 2: 1546–1750* (Cambridge: Cambridge University Press, 2004), 128–131. See also P. Mack, 'The Dialogue in English Education of the Sixteenth Century', in M. T. Jones-Davies, ed., *Le Dialogue au Temps de la Renaissance* (Paris: Jean Touzot, 1984), 189–212.

[60] Z. Waldstein, *The Diary of Baron Waldstein: A Traveller in Elizabethan England*, trans. and ed. G.W. Groos (London: Thames and Hudson, 1981), 99.

[61] Morgan, *Cambridge*, 130.

120 CONVERSING

Comparing written Protestant dialogues with the sorts of inter-personal exchanges between the godly and ungodly recorded in court and visitation books, Christopher Haigh argues that the acrimonious tone of dialogues such as Dent's accounts is precisely why the genre was popular: contempt for worldly values could spill over into contempt for the persons who held these values.[62] Joseph Puterbaugh shows how the heroes of John Foxe's *Actes and Monuments* dramatize dissent as the word of God moving in the martyrs, which models how to separate truth from falsehood. Foxe includes many debates, in university, prison, and tavern, in which the faithless maintain the courtesies and conventions of formal dispute but the godly blank their interrogators' lines of argument. Frank speaking is cherished for developing a Protestant spiritual identity and propelling church reforms.[63]

At Little Gidding, the Academy's meetings tended to start with a story on a set theme, followed by a semi-formal exposition by the teller, and then a vigorous open debate. Ferrar registers interlocutors' sensitivity to non-verbal signals which cue delivery and response, noting when speakers and listeners look up or down, sigh, blush, pause, turn away, gesture, interrupt, are silenced or urged to speak. The Academy's discussion about how the Spanish king Charles V had retired from worldly affairs is an example of how free the speakers feel to rebut each other's positions and even to argue *ad hominem*. At one point, the discussion turns to how the young Submisse is hoping to enter the service of a great lady. The Guardian initially supports her, but then her mother, the Moderator, distinguishes between going into service in order to be useful (a godly labour) or for the social advantages given and gained (unlawful, as taking honour from God). The Guardian thanks the Moderator for this: to have 'rectified both mine owne & your understanding is, I assure you, of so much comfort, as I feele not at all the Batterie of that shame, whereunto this sudden retraction justly seemes to have exposed mee in the necessarie inferences of rashnes, ignorance, or unconstancy'. However, the Resolved then launches an ambush on the Moderator, opening with back-handed praise of the Guardian about how

the cheerfull redeeming of a mans Errors by ingenuous Confession being the best proofe, that can be given both of a good heart & of a sound head. He must needs love truth well, thats ready to buy it as the price of his best Credit; &

---

[62] Haigh, *Plain Man's Pathways*, 4–6, 12–13, 122–139.

[63] J. Puterbaugh, '"Truth hath the victory": Dialogue and Disputation in John Foxe's *Actes and Monuments*', in D. Heitsch and J-F. Vallée, eds., *Printed Voices: The Renaissance Culture of Dialogue* (Toronto: University of Toronto Press, 2004), 137–156.

4 CONVERSATION IN *THE TEMPLE* 121

needs feare no shame for his weaknes, thats supported by the worth of such a disposition. The imitation whereof wee shall aequally applaude, as wee doe expect from our judicious Moderator.

From me say SHEE halfe starting.

However strong you make it, I am sure (sayd the Resolved) your own Judgement testifieth it will bee necessarie to call back those Passionate disgraces, wherewith ... you have contemptuously affronted the whole order of free & Gentlemen Attendants.

[But] you take the errour & purpose the amends (sayd the Resolved) in a quite contrarie way, then I had hoped ...

The contradiction of your discourses ... intangle my thoughts, as in a Laberinth.

Other brisk attacks surround this passage of arms: the Patient tries to break into the discussion, but 'your turn comes shortly (said the Moderator)'; the Moderator's contemptuous response to the Resolved's conclusions is that 'The Mountaine hath at last brough forth a Mouse'; the Affectionate determines on 'the administring of this Physikec [bitter advice] to the Submisse, whereunto her owne indisposition of Minde, & many opportunities so well served at this present, as I doubt wee shall afterwards repent, If we do not at this time make use of them'; the Moderator denies the Submisse any chance to save face, literally: 'I read in her countenance the Challenge both of unkindenes & revenge for so publique an imputation in a matter wherein she thinketh herselfe perhaps most free'.[64] The godly conversation of the Little Academy is designed to reveal the truth, not please the participants.

4 Conversation in *The Temple*

Herbert shows himself getting the tone wrong when talking to God, again and again, as he tactfully nudges God to respond. However, he also shows God ruthlessly reframing the situation, moving away from any hint that Herbert and he could form a sort of egalitarian and sociable in-group, and favouring the sort of rudeness which the Protestant dialogues reserve for the unregenerate: either aggressive rebuke of the hardened sinner or—even worse—dismissive silence towards the enemy of religion or the fool.

---

[64] Williams, ed., *Conversations at Little Gidding*, 136, 139–141, 144, 155.

122   CONVERSING

In *The Temple*, conversation is generally stated—not implied, as happens in most lyric verse—to be in progress, with Herbert using speech tags such as 'said'. Such verbs are often arranged in adjacency pairs, sorted according to function, which makes it clear when and in what mode replies will be: 'questioning'/'answer'd' ('Love' 3), 'demand'/'began' and 'ask'd/answer' ('Peace'), 'calling'/'reply'd' ('The Collar'), 'threatned'/'told' ('The Holdfast'). Herbert also distinguishes the volume and tone of speech: characters whisper ('Jordan' 2), rave ('A Parodie'), cry out ('Ephes. 4.30'), mutter ('A true Hymne'), speak pulingly and shrilly ('The Familie') or in a 'simpring' way ('Affliction' 1), and prattle ('Conscience'). They gesticulate for emphasis. At a cheerful 'Dooms-day', for instance, one 'member jogs the other,/ Each one whispering, Live you brother?', and the speaker of 'The Collar' pounds the table as he 'rav'd and grew more fierce and wilde'. Sometimes an overheard or prospective conversation gives an opening for comment, as in 'My God, I heard this day,/ That none doth ... ' ('Man'), 'So that we need not say, Where's this command?' ('Vanitie' 1), Fortune 'spinning phansies ... was heard to say' ('The World'), and when God's 'words were then, *Let me alone*' ('Decay'). Some speakers use pointedly colloquial phrasing. In 'Good Friday', 'sinne may say,/ *No room for me*, and flie away'. In 'Miserie', the drunkard declares that '*Man is but grasse,/ He knows it, fill the glasse*', refusing restraint with 'Not he: he knows, where he can better be,/ As he will swear'. The quality of reception may also be noted: Time at first listens 'patiently', but after some while starts 'chafing' ('Time'), and the speaker of 'The Holdfast' is struck silent and 'amaz'd' by what is said, being 'Much troubled'.

Moreover, the physical presentation of these poems in the early versions suggests their compositors and scribes wanted to point out these moments as conversational. In the first edition of *The Temple*, direct speech is usually indicated by italics, as in 'Redemption' ('Who straight, *Your suit is granted*, said'), 'Jordan' 1 ('Who plainly say, *My God, My King*'), 'Even-song' ('Saying to man, *It doth suffice*'), 'Church-musick' ('Yet say sometimes, *God help poore Kings*'), and 'Affliction' 3 ('there came forth, *O God*').[65] In the Bodleian manuscript, four of the five poems distinguish these phrases by letter size (the exception is 'Even-song').[66] In the Williams manuscript (which antedates the Bodleian

---

[65] G. Herbert, *The Temple* (1633), 32, 48 56, 57, 64.
[66] G. Herbert, *The Temple: A Diplomatic Edition of the Bodleian Manuscript (Tanner 307)*, ed. M. di Cesare (Binghamton: Medieval and Renaissance Texts and Studies, 1995), 57, 83, 96, 108.

manuscript by some years), the same happens in 'Jordan' 1 and 'Redemption' (entitled 'The Passion').[67]

Speech in the poems has been examined for its dramatic and courtly qualities.[68] For instance, Simon Jackson thinks *The Temple's* desire for visual and musical harmony echoes the aim of court dramatic performances.[69] Herbert's courtly register, Michael Schoenfeldt argues, shows the strain of separating secular from godly discourse when both modes share a similar aim, of praise for those above in a hierarchy, expressed in a nearly identical vocabulary of submission.[70] But remembering the period's advice on when to use tact and when not widens these studies by admitting the disobliging aspect to conversation in *The Temple*.

Often, conversation in the collection is an amiable and cooperative process. God may be willing to utter some kindly (albeit brief) words to act as conversation-stoppers on anxious internal dialogue. At death, God will say '*It doth suffice:/ Henceforth repose; your work is done*' ('Even-song'), and an anxious tenant is briefly reassured ('*Your suit is granted*') in 'Redemption'. Even where there is some necessity to command, God saves face all round. 'Love' 3 stages the sort of circular, self-deprecatory courtesy contest at table which Erasmus and Della Casa found so tedious. The guest is welcomed in, but draws back; the guest is asked what he needs, but answers that he needs someone better than himself to enter; the guest is told he is worthy, but replies that he cannot even look at his host; the guest is told the host enables this, but answers that he has disabled his sight; the guest is told it has been reenabled, but answers that he will, in that case, serve the host. The period's conversation theory would label the inferior in this exchange as rude: claiming independence by what Strier calls 'manipulative courtliness'.[71] Even then, though, as Fish and

---

[67] G. Herbert, *The Williams Manuscript of George Herbert's Poems. A Facsimile Reproduction*, intro. A. Charles (Delmar: Scholars' Facsimiles and Reprints, 1977), 25r, 53r. This manuscript does not include 'Even-song' or 'Affliction' 3, and font size is not varied in 'Church-Musick'.

[68] The family was closely involved with the drama of the period. The third and fourth earls of Pembroke acted in Jacobean court masques, and, as successive Lord Chamberlains, oversaw the office of Master of the Revels. George Herbert's younger brother, Henry, held the latter office from 1623. Henry and Edward (George's eldest brother) each wrote a play. From mid-1626, Herbert spent about a year with Henry at Woodford, Essex, during which time Henry licensed Philip Massinger's *The Roman Actor* and *The Judge*, James Shirley's *The Brothers*, William Davenant's *The Cruel Brother*, and the unattributed *The Great Duke of Florence*. See N. W. Bawcutt, ed., *The Control and Censorship of Caroline Drama. The Records of Sir Henry Herbert, Master of the Revels, 1623–73* (Oxford: Clarendon Press, 1996), 6–7, 164–166.

[69] S. Jackson, 'The Visual Music of the Masque and George Herbert's *Temple*', *English Literary Renaissance*, 45 (2015), 377–399.

[70] M. Schoenfeldt, *Prayer and Power: George Herbert and Renaissance Courtship* (Chicago: University of Chicago Press, 1991), 22.

[71] Strier, *Resistant Structures*, 112.

124 CONVERSING

Schoenfeldt point out, when Love stops answering doubts and invites the guest to 'sit down ... and taste my meat', he maintains a polite fiction to cover a naked command, a request which 'constrains in proportion to the politeness through which it is expressed'.[72]

Although neighbours and parishioners rarely appear in the poems, friends frequently do, as Constance Furey shows, and relations with them are worked at with accommodating courtesy.[73] In 'Love-joy', for instance, 'One standing by' politely asks for the speaker's opinion about a window. This opening remark turns into a face-savingly indirect test of whether the speaker understands his faith by discussing an impersonal object in this light (as Oley says Herbert did in his ministry). The speaker (enjoying the invitation to 'spend [his] judgement', as courtesy manuals predicted he would) gives a right but incomplete account (the grapes stand for '*Joy* and *Charitie*'). This is corrected by agreement (another courteously indirect nudge): 'Sir, you have not miss'd,/ ... It figures JESUS CHRIST'. In 'To all Angels and Saints', parenthetical apologies appear (as in 'Artillerie'), as Herbert excuses himself from appealing for help to these 'glorious spirits'. He would if he could, 'But now (alas!), I dare not', so he finds common ground with them in God's 'injunction', '('Tis your own case)', so 'we dare not' flout it. Herbert further saves face all round by claiming that he would certainly be willing to 'disburse' praise of them too, if only he could find written authority from God to do so.

That is not true, however, of all conversations in *The Temple*: participants can abuse, contradict, and ignore each other, in the register of the Protestant dialogues. This might be expected, say, between opposing personifications such as appear in 'A Dialogue-Antheme', where Christian and Death taunt each other ('where is thy glorie?', '*Go spell and reade*', '*Let losers talk*', and 'Spare not, do thy worse'). Perhaps, too, it is not surprising when it comes from Herbert. John Olson suggests that antagonistic biblical dialogues lie behind moments in Herbert's poems in which figures rail at God, and can only hear his voice when they fall silent.[74] Sometimes Herbert, as master of his thoughts, tries to silence rebellious mutterers. In 'Assurance', for instance, he addresses his sudden suspicion that he is not saved by repeating back the speech by a Thought: 'Thou said'st but even now'. Herbert relates the subsections of the Thought's argument, then answers each, robustly: 'And what to this?', 'What is thy aim?', 'I see, I know,/ I writ thy purpose long ago'. He not only threatens to report

---

[72] Fish, *Living Temple*, 134; Schoenfeldt, *Prayer and Power*, 205, 213, 217.
[73] C. Furey, *Poetic Relations: Intimacy and Faith in the English Reformation* (Chicago: Chicago University Press, 2017), 61–71, 86–87.
[74] J. Olson, 'Biblical Narratives and Herbert's Dialogue Poems', *GHJ*, 12/1 (1988), 17–28.

4 CONVERSATION IN *THE TEMPLE*   125

the Thought's speech to God, he acts on that threat, immediately: 'I will to my Father,/ Who heard thee say it. O most gracious Lord,/ If ... '. Then he turns back to dismiss the Thought ('go on'). In 'Ephes. 4.30', Herbert's heart is instructed to 'Cry out, Get hence' to 'sawcie mirth'. 'The Familie' includes a 'noise of thoughts', voicing 'loud complaints and pulling fears', 'wranglers' of 'distemper'd fears'. These notions are rebuked again in 'Content' ('Peace mutt'ring thoughts', 'cease discoursing soul', and 'Do not thy self or friends importune') and in 'Conscience' ('Peace pratler', 'chatting fears', 'pratlers' who 'persistest and 'carp', where Christ's passion is the only act that can leave these talkative thoughts 'not a word'). Such 'corrective self-address', argues Cooley, means 'the speaker takes upon himself elements of the disciplinary function, relieving God of the necessity to exercise violent correction'.[75]

However, the rebarbative tone which turns an interlocutor's would-be nudges to sludge sounds very strange when coming from God, though this is rarely commented on. In 'Dialogue', Herbert starts with the face-saving gesture of running down his own little efforts in offering his life to God ('if' my soul was worth it, of course 'should I then' offer it, 'but ...'). The credit being saved here is God's, since Herbert is minimizing the obligation he is implying that God would be under, in accepting a richer contribution. The usual and courteous counter-move to this would be for God to praise the offered gift, perhaps hyperbolically (as in, 'you're too good'). Instead, God responds to the underlying condescension, unwilling to take such face-saving at face value. He starts by flatly contradicting the implication that Herbert has anything to give (briefly pausing midway to add a scornful epithet): '*What (childe) is the ballance thine?*' Then he rudely asserts his superior knowledge of the potential '*gains*' (which '*onely he,/ ... can see*') in owning Herbert's soul.

Herbert hastily repairs God's breach of the social surface by making another face-saving gesture, that of vagueness (he 'can see no merit', it is 'beyond my savour', 'the reason then is thine' not 'mine', the only way forwards is to 'disclaim the whole designe', and 'resigne'), a passive form of contradiction much recommended by the courtesy manuals. This turns God sarcastic: he has, after all, already very clearly laid out, four times, who owns the soul in question. By pretending not to understand, Herbert is using a tactic by which inferiors refuse their superior's claims, in a way that avoids being disciplined for non-cooperation. Scornful replies, as the manuals say, are much more hurtful than rebuke since they assume the interlocutor is not worth contradiction. So

---

[75] R. W. Cooley, *'Full of all knowledg': George Herbert's Country Parson and Early Modern Social Discourse* (Toronto: University of Toronto Press, 2003), 167.

God, here, first sardonically agrees with Herbert that, if the latter were to be willing to leave it all to God, then that would indeed be 'all'—and then flatly denies that he is getting even that modicum, given Herbert's *'repining'*. Midway through God's follow-up to this (a needling reminder of all he has done for Herbert), the latter's inappropriate courtesy is abandoned, as Herbert indecorously breaks across God's words to, even more indecorously, tell him to be quiet: *'left all joyes to feel all smart*—/ Ah! No more: thou break'st my heart'. Such rudeness is the honest expression which God has been bludgeoning him for.

The same dynamic between the two ideals of good conversation structures 'Artillerie'. Herbert, a self-approvingly prudent housekeeper, shakes his clothes free from a shooting star, 'as knowing well,/ That from small fires comes oft no small mishap'. God surprises him by a sudden rebuke for not understanding that the star was his (adding a gratuitous insult on how this sort of ungracious behaviour is thoroughly typical of Herbert): *'do as thou usest, disobey/ Expell good motions from thy breast'*. This irritable response is listened to tactfully, Herbert consciously exercising his patience and courtesy with the same sort of mild protest that the lax Christians put up in Protestant dialogues, about having their words and intentions twisted by the godly into appearing sinful. Internally protesting against the unreason of God not telling him that the star was a messenger, he hastens to repair the conversation by an 'If' and some deference ('Dread Lord'), as courtesy manuals advise. If it is true that Herbert goes wrong so often, he will certainly change his ways from now on, 'For I will do, or suffer what I ought'. Then (with an air of owing something to himself) he hints that God himself can be even more inattentive in dialogue ('My tears and prayers night and day do wooe,/ ... yet thou dost refuse'). 'Submission' shows the same indirect move, calling attention to the fact that he is not rebuking God, though he could do so:

> But that thou art my wisdome, Lord,
> And both mine eyes are thine,
> My minde would be extremely stirr'd
> For missing my designe.

In 'Artillerie', Herbert parenthetically and apologetically retreats after this indirect rebuke, trying to save God's face by denying any right to make such a parallel between their speeches: 'Not, but I am (I must say still)/ Much more oblig'd to do thy will,/ Then thou to grant mine'. He then attempts to minimize his imposition on God, by voicing a request for the favour of being listened to ('Thy promise [to hear] now hath ev'n set thee thy laws'). The final stanza makes a weak claim for cooperation between him and God, since both are in a group of 'shooters', then collapses back on the truth: 'There is no articling with thee'. Unsurprisingly, given how he has tried to patronize God, there is also no answer.

'The Holdfast' stages a dialogue with rapid turn-taking, in which the first speaker's pious assertions of what he will do for God are undercut, repeatedly, by a second speaker who has tempted the first into these very assertions. The first speaker is told that one 'might trust in God' and courteously accepts the position, but then is told this is wrong and that all he can do is 'confesse, that nothing is our own'. Thus, the first speaker (with commendable patience) does 'confesse' this, but then is told that 'to have naught is ours, not to confesse' this. The theology of 'faith alone' is difficult enough to comprehend without being tied up in knots by a linguistic torturer, and the first speaker is left silent and 'amaz'd'. It takes a friend (presumably not the 'one' who had been speaking to him before) to pack up the problem with the seeming paradox that 'all things were more ours by being his'.

Irritation at the way one person hogs the conversation is targeted in 'The Collar', 'Time', and 'Love Unknown'. In 'The Collar', thirty-two lines of 'fierce and wilde' rhetorical questions and answers by the self are briskly cut off by a single dismissive epithet from God, '*Childe*'. When a speaker meets Time on the road (the usual place for a Protestant dialogue), he starts by insulting him ('slack thing, said I'), a rebuke courteously turned aside by Time, who makes a self-deprecatory joke about his scythe being more than sharp enough for most people's taste. The speaker, however, then takes twenty lines to offer platitudinous instruction on the godly functions of Time (turning, Schoenfeldt jokes, a potentially significant meeting into 'a progressively tedious social encounter').[76] At first pretending to be interested, 'Thus farre Time heard me patiently:/ Then chafing', he makes a sharper quip about how the speaker 'doth not crave lesse time, but more'. The same structure appears in the three fourteen-line anecdotes in 'Love Unknown' about the way the speaker's heart has been abused. He appears to fear that his listener is drifting off, given the amount of arm-tugging that goes on: he invites his 'Deare Friend' to sit down (a usual invitation in a Protestant dialogue), then gives him pointers throughout (mostly in parentheses) about what response would be welcome: 'the tale is long and sad', causing 'faintings', '(I sigh to say)', 'the very wringing yet/ Enforceth tears', 'But you shall heare', '(I sigh to tell)', '(do you understand?)',

---

[76] Schoenfeldt, 'Humor in *The Temple*', 60.

128 CONVERSING

'(I sigh to speak)', and 'Deare, could my heart not break'. The listener at first simply gives a half-line key to interpret the episodes (gratefully accepted by the speaker with the repeated phrase 'Indeed 'tis true'), but eventually cuts off the whining with a mild but firm rebuke: '*Truly, Friend,/ For ought I heare, your Master shows to you/ More favour then you wot of*'.

Even more of a concern to Herbert than being robustly contradicted or rebuked is being ignored as someone not worth correcting. Prayer poems are usually monologues, which directly address a listener but either do not pause for an answer from the addressee, or do so merely briefly and formally: thus, though they familiarly address God as 'thee', poems such as 'The Reprisall' and 'The Sinner' are not conversational. Sometimes, then, and rather desperately, Herbert tries sketching out what a conversational God might say. To the covey of talkative temptations in 'The Quip', God is asked to 'Speak not at large, say, I am thine,/ And then they have their answer home'). In 'The Odour', it is merely suggested that God utter 'My servant' in response to Herbert's repeated phrase 'My Master'. Other poems try harder to provoke a conversation out of a mono-logue, pointing out where God is not doing his part. Herbert is panic-stricken in 'Deniall' at being blanked (as Perkins and Reyner recommended is done to people of neither capacity nor will to reform): 'When my devotions could not pierce/ Thy silent eares;/ Then was my heart broken'. His thoughts speak out against this silent treatment, 'crying night and day,/ *Come, come, my God, O come,/* But no hearing'. Eventually, Herbert joins his thoughts in reproaching God: 'O that thou shouldst give dust a tongue/ To crie to thee/ And then not hear it crying! all day long/ ... no hearing'. Likewise, in 'Longing', Herbert's 'cries/ ... ascend' until his throat is 'hoarse', and he repeatedly begs for God to 'be not now/ ... dead' in refusing to listen to his own creation: 'Lord heare! *Shall he that made the eare,/ Not heare?*' He cannot believe God means to be so cruel: 'how can it be,/ That thou art grown/ Thus hard to me?' For Morgan, when interviewers do not respond to an interviewee's answer to their ques-tions it feels like a cruel practical joke, and this is what happens in 'Longing', when God's silence lets Herbert run down, reconsidering and back-tracking.[77] Silence is dangerous in 'A Parodie', when 'sinne doth rave,/ And falsely boast' of God's absence so that Herbert is brought to 'half beleeve,/ That Sinne says true'.

Bearing out the subtitle of *The Temple* (*Private Ejaculations*), when Herbert is uncertain of the acceptability of what he would want to say, he reduces his own part in the conversation to a minimal tag, as in 'The Forerunners' ('*Thou art still my God*, is all that ye/ Perhaps with more embellishment can say'), 'Jor-dan' 1 ('Nor let them punish me with losse of ryme/ Who plainly say, My God,

---

[77] Morgan, *Turn-Taking*, 138.

My King'), and 'Church-musick' ('We both together .../ ... say sometimes, *God help poore Kings*'). In 'A true Hymne', Herbert's heart 'Somewhat ... fain would say,/ And still it runneth mutt'ring up and down/ With onely this, *My joy, my life, my crown*'. These are defensive tactics, moving from an elaborated code of language (that used by those of high rank, which demands attention from the listener in being explicit, abstract, and independent of context to convey meaning) to the restricted code used by lower rank people (one which uses concrete words, and implies much of its meaning through the context of the discussion).

There has been much critical discussion about the sincerity of these ejaculations, but courtesy advice may suggest something new about why Herbert should resort to such code-switching: the sense of what would be appropriate speech from a servant. Herbert often refers to this role: he 'used in his ordinarie speech, when he made mention of the blessed name of our Lord and Saviour Jesus Christ, to adde, *My Master*' (presumably also startling his interlocutors with his shift in register), and in 'The Odour' the same phrase repeatedly comes into his mind.[78] In 'Affliction' 1 he threatens to 'change the service, and go seek/ Some other master out'. In turn, Herbert is served by his abilities ('Thousands of notions in my brain did runne,/ Off'ring their service', 'Jordan' 2), though since 'All my attendants are at strife,/ Quitting their place/ Unto my face' he suggests a change of master; they should 'Enter thy pay,/ And day by day/ Labour thy praise' ('Affliction' 4). Creation also serves: 'The starres have us to bed;/ Night draws the curtain, which the sunne withdraws', and 'More servants wait on Man,/ Then he'l take notice of', so let us, 'as the world serves us, ... serve thee' ('Man').

Servants are not interlocutors of equal standing to their masters, not one of a group whose members should save each other's face. Commentators argued that a servant should 'obey and to be in subjection, ... have no will of his owne, nor power over him selfe, but wholly ... reseigne him selfe to the will of his Master', as Thomas Fosset (minister at Ladbroke, Warwickshire) puts it.[79] William Basse talks of the serving man as an 'instrument', his role to 't'attempt with dutie, readines .../ ... not as he would, but as he shall,/ To grudge at nothing, to accept of all'. Basse is resentful about this: 'whatsoever thing belongs to you,/ That danger, trouble, paines, attention asks,/ We are your servants, and it is our tasks'.[80] So, he thinks, servants may look humble in 'acts exterior' but

---

[78] Herbert, *Works*, ed. Hutchinson, 4.

[79] T. Fosset, *The Servants Dutie ... For the Instruction, Not Only of Servants, but of Masters and Mistresses* (1613), 22. See also B. P., *The Prentises Practise in Godlinesse* (1608), 41–44.

[80] Basse, *Serving-mans Defence*, A4v, B2v, D3v.

be proud in 'private thoughts', separating themselves from their working role. The master-servant relationship of the period shows both a micro-resistance to being governed and a mirror image, a fear of being served by the less-than-willing.[81] As Della Casa says, only someone of standing in a conversation has the social credit to offer the courtesy of putting another first. Any conscious courtesy by a servant would be an implicit claim to equal status. Thus, the best servant is neither spoken to nor speaks: God merely looks 'on a servant, who did know his eye/ Better than you know me', and the servant 'instantly' acts ('Love Unknown').

Schoenfeldt speaks of the doctrinal and pastoral benefits of uttering 'affable laughter at human foibles', a natural result of contrasting divine and earthly viewpoints (following Paul's injunction to be 'fools for Christ's sake', 1 Corinthians 10). Herbert's humour, he says, is 'generous, gentle, and self-directed, emerging from deep sympathy with the speakers of the poems', so the reader laughs with them, not at them.[82] This is not, however, the humour of 'The Pulley', the only time God shows himself whole-heartedly and lengthily conversable—and that is because he is talking to himself. Midway through creating the world, God considers which blessings to give man: 'Let us (said he) poure on him all we can', and proceeds to do so. Then he suddenly pauses, 'For if I should (said he)' give man rest as well, man would 'rest in Nature, not the God of Nature'. So God tetra-puns his way to a solution ('let him keep the rest,/ But keep them with repining restlessnesse'), and adds a sardonic coda to amuse himself ('If goodnesse leade him not, yet wearinesse/ May tosse him to my breast'). This daring poem locates the moment of creation in an aggressive joke which the Trinity tells itself. A much more conventional register for divine speech would be that of 'The Sacrifice', where Christ's speech is based on the reproaches of the Good Friday liturgy. Early modern theologians debated whether Christ ever laughed, and no other poet shows God with a sense of humour, let alone showing the divinity making sarcastic cracks at another's expense, against all the canons of civility.

But then, being mocked is the point. Herbert shows how his desire to save God's face is absurdly and impertinently imputing his own (social) grace to God. The comic handling of his energetic repairs to conversations with God in which he is rebuked, blanked, and patronized is a nudge to his readers to stop thinking they can nudge God in their speech with him.

---

[81] E. Rivlin, *The Aesthetics of Service in Early Modern England* (Evanston: Northwestern University Press, 2012), 12–18.

[82] M. Schoenfeldt, 'George Herbert's Divine Comedy: Humor in *The Temple*', *GHJ*, 29/1–2 (2005–2006), 45–46.

5
Listing

The dialogue, the catechism, and the sermon are commonly recognized as characteristic Protestant genres, but not the list. They are seen as dramatic and interactive; it is not. Yet this apparently modest and transparent device structures much religious discourse in the period, including Herbert's poems. It is a triumph of strong persuasion disguised as neutral administration. This chapter looks first at the affordances of the list, and then at its three uses as a nudge in early modern practical theology, in making the reader think, feel, and act. Finally, the chapter turns to how Herbert's lists undermine the precision and certainty offered by the form. In his poems, doubt ends up being a mark of saving grace in his list-makers.

1 Lists and Cognitive Niches

Getting observations down on paper was valued not just as a matter of creating a record; the activity was held to help writers grasp the specific quality of what was before them. For instance, since there are so many aspects to assessing the quality of goods, teaching 'the theorique of this mysterious part of Commerce must needs come short', says Husband of the Levant Company and an influential mercantile writer, Lewes Roberts. Therefore the trader should take every opportunity to take 'patterns, and samples ... thereby so to imprint the very Idea thereof in a mans minde', 'and what he hath thus learned and gained, to take order never to forget, by committing the same to writing'. 'The use and custome of noting in this manner, will make a man ... more skilfull and readie in this knowledge ... than he that taketh onely a bare, idle, and superficiall view'. Recording such observations means 'graving deeper impressions in a mans mind', and will 'inforce him will he, nill he, to a more considerate and judicious observation, and marking thereof; when as he hath thus absolutely tyed himself to a necessitie of setting downe every commoditie, and each particular circumstance'.[1] Just so in the professions. The Kentish lawyer William

---

[1] L. Roberts, *The Merchants Mappe of Commerce* (1638), 41, 45.

George Herbert and the Business of Practical Piety. Ceri Sullivan, Oxford University Press.
© Ceri Sullivan (2024). DOI: 10.1093/9780198906841.003.0005

132 LISTING

Lambarde tells of how, newly appointed a justice of the peace, he tried to train himself with legal digests but soon found he needed to go back to the primary materials, the statutes and books of precedents. Thus, '(mistrusting the slippernesse of mine owne memorie) I did upon a seconde reading plot the matter with my penne, and made (as it were) a Module thereof in a small booke, wherein I brought together stuffe of ech kinde, sorted in heapes, and layed readie to be wrought and framed'.[2] Orderly, minute, and accurate noting at the moment of observation helps Roberts and Lambarde to think clearly about their material.

This is how historians of the book approach lists, as facilitating devices designed to ensure readers follow a text's arguments closely, or, alternatively, to let them use its content in ways not anticipated by the author. In the first case, research has followed Walter J. Ong's influential thesis that, with the widespread increase in literacy of the sixteenth century, writing restructured consciousness. Ong argues that the tendency of the medieval culture to aid memory with aggregative aural patterns gave way to a later written culture, in which textual space is used both to store information and to think analytically about it. He traces the influence of the sixteenth-century dialectician Peter Ramus, who advised dealing with a subject by dichotomizing it, then dividing each result, again and again, until its logic or facts are reduced to their most basic elements. Such branch diagrams produce class logic in space, as invention (the first part of rhetoric) is aided by arrangement (the second part).[3] Rowan Tomlinson finds the period's academic interest in lists arises from the desire, which lay behind new concepts of science, to encompass all the observable elements of an object. Cataloguing its parts was a way of building thorough knowledge about it, piece by piece.[4] Elizabeth Tebeaux shows how the technique of dividing a topic and listing its parts was not confined to academic treatises but reached down to popular how-to books. Teaching skills ranging from book-keeping to the care of horses, the precise order and activities of processes are recorded in lists of concrete nouns, set out in a parallel syntax of subject-verb-object to preserve the step-by-step nature of face-to-face instruction.[5]

---

[2] W. Lambarde, *Eirenarcha: or of the Office of the Justices of Peace* (1579; 1581), aiiv.

[3] W. J. Ong, *Orality and Literacy: The Technologizing of the Word*, ed. J. Hartley (1982; London: Routledge, 2012), 77–78, 96–99, 119–123; W. J. Ong, *Ramus, Method, and the Decay of Dialogue: From the Art of Discourse to the Art of Reason* (1958; Cambridge, MA: Harvard University Press, 1983), 307–318.

[4] R. Tomlinson, 'Thinking with Lists in French Vernacular Writing, 1548–1596', DPhil. Oxford (2008), 8 ff.

[5] E. Tebeaux, *The Emergence of a Tradition: Technical Writing in the English Renaissance, 1475–1640* (Amityville: Baywood, 1997), 35–90, 175–236; E. Tebeaux, 'Pillaging the Tombs of Non-Canonical

1 LISTS AND COGNITIVE NICHES   133

Such lists use the physical environment of a page to produce understanding. Early modern readers were skilled at interpreting words whose meaning was cocreated by the medium they were written in (as in the cases, say, of shape poetry, graphic dance, and emblems). Printers were equally skilled in using the authority of a list to anchor readers' eyes, and hence attention, towards particular interpretations of content. The impression that a list is giving the essential information is in part created by how its layout provides a narrative structure: valued units are placed high and to the left of the page, blank space surrounds certain words to privilege them, non-alphanumeric symbols point up an area, font distinguishes certain words from other parts of the page (for instance, by typeface, size, or depth of ink), and so on.[6] This is the list as enforcer of interpretation, the bullying impulse behind today's managerial bullet points.

Yet the early modern list could also be made to work in the opposite direction: it could yield material which could be used independently of its compiler's aim. Ann Blair, Neil Rhodes, and Jonathan Sawday have traced the efflorescence of methods to manage information in response to the burgeoning of print. Sub-headings, branch diagrams, marginal or footnoted citations and summaries, contents pages or tables, indices, and running heads developed to store, sort, select, and summarize material.[7] Though all these devices are presented as comprehensive lists, they also allow readers to find their own ways to repurpose content by skipping parts of the text and recombining other parts. Matthew Brown notes the way popular devotional texts encourage their readers to leaf to and fro for the content needed for a particular situation, aiding this with copious indices, subtitles, marginalia, and cross-references. These readers are active and independent, producing meaning from the text discontinuously; they do not rely on a linear development of a topic by the author.[8] William Eamon describes how, when random collections are made into how-to texts by sorting devices, readers gain real and accessible power.[9] Personal and printed commonplace books provide further machinery to select, sort,

---

Texts: Technical Writing and the Evolution of English Style', *Journal of Business and Technical Communication*, 18 (2004), 165–177, 171–178, 181–185; E. Tebeaux, 'Technical Writing and the Development of the English Paragraph, 1473–1700', *Journal of Technical Writing and Communication*, 41 (2011), 229–235, 242–246.

[6] G. Kress and T. van Leeuwen, *Reading Images: The Grammar of Visual Design* (London: Routledge, 1996), 39–40, 43–61, 79–107.

[7] Ann Blair, *Too Much to Know: Managing Scholarly Information before the Modern Age* (New Haven: Yale University Press, 2010), 3–4, 49–52, 117–172; N. Rhodes and J. Sawday, eds., *The Renaissance Computer: Knowledge Technology in the First Age of Print* (London: Routledge, 2000), 1–16.

[8] M. P. Brown, 'The Thick Style: Steady Sellers, Textual Aesthetics, and Early Modern Devotional Reading', *PMLA*, 121/1 (2006), 71–75.

[9] W. Eamon, *Science and the Secrets of Nature: Books of Secrets in Medieval and Early Modern Culture* (Princeton: Princeton University Press, 1994), 4, 125.

134 LISTING

and re-sort material garnered from reading, creating collections of proofs which are organized by heads. Such a notebook may 'be properly read as a stage in its compiler's production of a future work', says Ann Moss.[10] This is the list as anthology, where ideas are registered as discrete units which can be manipulated spatially to produce new ideas, along the lines of today's mind maps.

The most well known of the pious activities at Little Gidding was the production of gospel 'Harmonies' (one of which Herbert owned). The process involved cutting up printed bibles into units based on events in the life of Christ, then reorganizing these elements, taken from all four gospels, into a continuous prose list (a procedure which the compilers called the 'Composition'). There was no disrespect in doing so, Adam Smyth argues, since the purposeful reading habits of the period saw texts as already a miscellany of pieces ready to be turned into a new composition.[11] Indeed, Whitney Trettien argues that harmony-making produced a 'maker-space', designing a 'speculative future for devotional thinking' by 'distributing variance across the entire assemblage of parts, up to and including the human reader who activates the system'.[12]

There is, Robert Belknap notes, a natural instinct to classify, catalogue, and rank. The mind looks for ways to reduce the disorder it perceives in a collection of disparate items by finding ways to arrange these, either by discerning or by imposing a pattern.[13] Practical lists make the inchoate graspable—definite, ordered, inclusive, and transparent—so can represent situations whose essence or boundaries are unclear but which have at least some properties that can be captured.[14]

However, there are less neutral approaches to the form. Geoffrey C. Bowker and Susan Leigh Star argue that users of lists can be dangerously unaware of the social and moral order sustained by categories which have resulted from now-forgotten political choices. Lists may record what was previously thought significant in a flow of tasks, actions, and roles, but which may not match

---

[10] A. Moss, *Printed Commonplace-Books and the Structuring of Renaissance Thought* (Oxford: Clarendon Press, 1996), vii.

[11] A. Smyth, '"Shreds of holinesse": George Herbert, Little Gidding, and Cutting Up Texts in Early Modern England', *English Literary Renaissance*, 42 (2012), 460–467. Jon Ferrar, however, arguably felt uneasy about the process. See P. Badir, 'Fixing Affections: Nicholas and John Ferrar, and the Books of Little Gidding', *English Literary Renaissance*, 49 (2019), 390–422.

[12] W. Trettien, *Cut/Copy/Paste: Fragments from a History of Patchwork* (Minneapolis: University of Minnesota Press, 2022), 29, 37, 59.

[13] R. Belknap, *The List: The Uses and Pleasures of Cataloguing* (New Haven: Yale University Press, 2004), 5.

[14] U. Eco, *The Infinity of Lists: From Homer to Joyce*, trans. A. McEwen (London: MacLehose, 2009), 15.

1 LISTS AND COGNITIVE NICHES   135

current needs. Since their divisions are ubiquitous and interwoven into other systems, both material and conceptual, it usually takes considerable institutional or social authority, as well as a cumbersome bureaucratic effort, to recognize the insufficiency of old classifications and replace them with new ones, or to reclassify items whose group identity has already been assigned, or to put usefulness above precision in that classification.[15] Per Ledin and David Machin show how listing can turn complex processes and social relations into abstracts, which can then be fragmented and manipulated out of context by the unscrupulous. Bullet-pointed and numbered lists and tables present their content as logical, factually correct, properly ordered, and complete, giving a powerful tool to legitimize what is said. The form implies that it will present all the fundamental, essentially technical details of a particular social practice, hiding any bias in the way it categorizes, includes, omits, and ranks components.[16]

Yet a more egalitarian digital form has recently come to the fore, whose assumptions are transparent and whose classifications are easily shared and altered: the listicle, a genre which can help appreciate the reading-for-writing approach of the early modern period. In this portmanteau medium, each heading has appended to it a comment or short article. The listicle's layout facilitates an F-shaped reading process: first the header words (down the list), then across to further material, so readers are free to engage or disengage at will, depending on the depth of detail they want. Bram Vijgen, studying listicles on Buzzfeed, thinks it is popular because it is easily recognized as dealing with content in simple, rapidly read units which can be altered and readily shared again. Titles are focused on a single topic and stated concisely (usually in around nine words), giving the impression that its material will be easy to master. They often include the number of items in the listicle (generally between five and twenty-five), helping the reader to assess the time it would take to read, and so decide if it is worth doing so. The most prominent nouns in titles of listicles ('things', 'reasons', 'signs', and 'ways') indicate readers will get facts; the most prominent adjectives ('best', 'worst', 'awesome', and 'greatest') advertise that these will be the essence of a topic.[17] The ideal listicle, then, has a format which makes clear the underlying concept that brings together apparently diverse

---

[15] G. C. Bowker and S. Leigh Star, *Sorting Things Out: Classification and Its Consequences* (Cambridge, MA: M. I. T. Press, 1999), 2–3, 5–6, 35–46.

[16] P. Ledin and D. Machin, 'How Lists, Bullet Points, and Tables Recontextualize Social Practice: A Multimodal Study of Management Language in Swedish Universities', *Critical Discourse Studies*, 12 (2015), 463–481.

[17] B. Vijgen, 'The Listicle: An Exploring Research on an Interesting Shareable New Media Phenomenon', *Studia Universitatis Babes-Bolyai-Ephemerides*, 59 (2014), 103–122.

examples, allowing the collection to be developed further by readers. Even if they do not add new material, readers are encouraged to be active in hunting down and across the list, perhaps clicking through to other pages. There is, of course, a downside: as this delta spreads, content may be overlooked in the pleasure of following up the branches—what Thaler and Sunstein call sludging! Surfing through units or pages may prove to be more immediately rewarding than pausing to interrogate their content, creating a conceptually wide but thin experience.[18]

Both the print and the digital revolutions, then, have given rise to new ways of thinking about lists: as authoritative (forming users' opinions and actions), and the converse, as open-ended (encouraging users to share, apply, and amend their content). Closed lists tend to be used by results-driven readers, who are researching into a specific topic. Open lists tend to be used by habitual readers of the genre, who enjoy grazing across a wide variety of topics. The following section argues that Protestant writers use both qualities of the list to create a cognitive page-based niche for their readers, where the textual environment facilitates or impedes different sorts of mental acts.

2 Devotional Lists to Reason with, to Delight, and to Move

By the 1590s practical theologians, abandoning the hope of moving the national church closer to their views, were seeking to reach its members at the personal and local levels. One tactic was to produce profuse schematic directions for piety. These, Bozeman argues, direct the reader through three stages of activity: an investigation and attempt to transform the self by using internalized and emotional exhortation, then a methodical approach to an analysis of the results of this, followed by repeated pious exercises to regulate behaviour and provide assurance. There is a candidly pragmatic orientation to such advice, coming from Greenham, Perkins, Rogers, and the like. They extract from the Bible the ideal outlines of a regenerate life, clarify them, and arrange them as rules for living.[19]

The godly requirement to search one's heart diligently, precisely, and comprehensively makes the list an obvious finding aid for all three activities, and for all shades of Protestantism. Thus, although list-making was parodied as a zealot's activity by Ben Jonson (in such precisionist figures as Zeal-of-the-Land Busy, dividing 'the state of the question' on the morality of eating 'pig' at a fair),

---

[18] J. Brockman, ed., *Is the Internet Changing the Way You Think? The Net's Impact on Our Minds and Future* (New York: Harper Perennial, 2011), 2–4, 19–20, 70–72, 80–82, 98–100.

[19] Bozeman, *Precisianist Strain*, 74–83.

2 DEVOTIONAL LISTS TO REASON WITH, TO DELIGHT, AND TO MOVE   137

an establishment figure like the dean of St Paul's, John Donne, selects the genre to deal with the soteriological and moral issues raised by his illness (sorting them into twenty-three groups of three repeating structures, of meditation, expostulation, and prayer).[20] To give a sense of how ubiquitous the list is in Protestant writing, this section of the chapter draws on twenty-two texts which between them were, according to the English Short-Title Catalogue, issued nearly 200 times between 1590 and 1639 (a startling quantity, given most texts were published only once). All bar three appear in Ian Green's catalogue of religious 'steady sellers', that is, books printed at least five times over a generation (thirty years).[21] Their titles characteristically imply that the reader will meet division and order within, dwelling on their 'marks', 'rules', 'directions', 'collection', 'catalogue', and 'steps'. There is no particular sectarian leaning evident in the sample: some authors cited here are conformists, some reformers. They use three sorts of list: the rational, the affective, and the motivational.

The first type of catalogue intends to instruct its readers by explicating the principal biblical or theological positions on a topic, then concluding on their consequences. John Rechtien argues that the use of the binaries of Ramist logic in printed religious texts 'popularised, even democratised, logic through the pedagogical simplicity of spatial mnemonic organisation', which was 'applied to compel the rational assent of a popular audience'. In lists appearing in such texts, the analytical commonplaces of rhetoric (questions to be asked of the subject of a speech to compile material, such as the causes and effects of an issue) are combined with the spatial element of memory systems.[22]

For instance, Robert Bolton, rector of Broughton, Northamptonshire, analyses the opening of Psalm 1 (about the qualities of the elect man) as though the psalm itself is a list:

This happie man is here described unto us by many arguments.

1. First, are laid downe his markes, and properties; negative, and affirmative, in the first two verses.
2. Secondly, his happinesse is livelily set out by a similitude, in the third verse ...

---

[20] B. Jonson, *Bartholomew Fair* (1614), ed. E. A. Horsman (London: Methuen, 1960), 1.6.56; J. Donne, *Devotions upon Emergent Occasions, and Severall Steps in my Sicknes: Digested into 1. Meditations upon our Humane Condition. 2. Expostulations, and Debatements with God. 3. Prayers, upon the Severall Occasions* (1624).

[21] Green, *Print and Protestantism*, 173–182, 591–672.

[22] J. Rechtien, 'Logic in Puritan Sermons in the Late Sixteenth Century and Plain Style', *Style*, 13/3 (1979), 239, 241; J. Rechtien, 'The Visual Memory of William Perkins and the End of Theological Dialogue', *Journal of the American Academy of Religion*, 45/1 (1977), 69–99.

138 LISTING

The negative properties in the first verse are three ... amplified with a threefold gradation in the persons, actions, and objects of the actions ...

The second verse containing his imploiment in pietie, seemeth to answer in opposition, the three negatives, with three affirmatives.[23]

By cataloguing the argumentation as well as the content of each part of the psalm, Bolton points out that no individual unit is aimless; each segment contains a precise mental activity: the reader is to follow how it sets out to assert, oppose, exemplify, and so on. Bolton wants his readers to think with (not merely about) the psalm's list. The influential theologian William Ames, professor at the University of Franeker, gives his lists in catechetical form when reasoning about the conscience:

Quest. What is to bee done when the conscience is scrupulous?
Answ. For the understanding of this question, wee must consider;

1. That a Scruple is a feare of the minde ...
2. Every feare is not properly a Scruple ...
5. A Scrupulous conscience differs from a Doubtfull one ...

These things being set downe, it is answered to the question. 1. (God being instantly called unto for grace) one must ... remoove these scruples ... [by] reason ... 2. It helpeth much (if it may be conveniently) that the thinking upon those things be shunned, from which scruples may rise.[24]

The ruthless clarity of these lists nudges their readers away from being comfortably woolly about where they stand.

Such lists characteristically use virtuoso printing techniques to facilitate an F-shaped reading, pulling the attention first to the top left of the page, then to the drop-down units of the list, and finally to the explication of each point, with sub-headings, indents, missed lines, numbering, marginalia, colons and dashes before sub-units, and variable types and sizes of font. This sort of framing discourages readers from losing themselves in a flow of words. Instead, they are to navigate alertly down and across the places of the argument, in the sequence intended by the author. Going against this purpose by reordering another person's material may threaten an underlying thesis. Dudley Digges is amused at how he can defeat his opponent this way:

---

[23] R. Bolton, *A Discourse About the State of True Happinesse* (1611), 2–3.
[24] W. Ames, *Conscience with the Power and Cases Thereof* (1639), 19–20 (not in Green).

2 DEVOTIONAL LISTS TO REASON WITH, TO DELIGHT, AND TO MOVE   139

now Sir, imagine you were the Reader to bee satisfied, and you shall see, how while the froth of his [the opponent's] Meander floud and such like following fuming stuffe evaporates it selfe ... I will extract all his Objections, which now like folded sheepe, or as raw Souldiers in a rout, stand faces everie way, but I will put them in aray, in order Sir, and yet defeat them, fairely as I goe.[25]

When lists are nested, one within another, readers are expected to remember the structure of sub-divisions, so they can move up and down through the layers of argumentation. For instance, the bestselling devotional manual by Lewis Bayly (which went through forty-four editions before 1639) asks its readers to keep in mind a five-layer structure in its discussion of how to approach the eucharist worthily. Bayly starts with three divisions relating to time (preparation for communion, its reception, and after), divides the first of these into three (one of which is the value of the sacrament), divides this one into three (one of which is the parts of the sacrament), divides this one into three (one of which is heavenly grace), and, finally, divides this one into two.[26] Then he goes back up to the final division to take the second line of argument. Then he climbs back to the penultimate division, to take the second of the three parts, and so on.

The reader must navigate the delta of these sub-sections, and it is hard not to conclude that some of the mental energy expended in reading them was absorbed by the necessary virtuoso mind-mapping of their terrain, rather than in assessing the validity of their arguments. The 1593 edition of Henry Peacham's rhetoric manual (which had a godly aim too, taking most of its examples from the Bible) argues that the scheme of numbering then defining parts of a discussion, eutrepismus, is 'profitable and pleasant' because it lets an author include large amounts of varied material in an orderly way. However, Peacham also offers a 'caution' for each: 'it is verie behovefull to take heed that when the parts be numbred in generall, they be not forgotten in the particular prosecution: as he that promised to expound the twelve articles of the Creed and after could remember but nine'. Peacham offers similar cautions about making the handling of a subject 'absurd' by dividing it too often, when he covers partition and enumeration.[27] This concern lies behind the criticism in Herbert's *Country Parson* of those preachers who so crumble a Bible verse

---

[25] D. Digges, *The Defence of Trade* (1615), 16.
[26] Bayly, *Practise of Pietie*, 664 ff.
[27] H. Peacham, *The Garden of Eloquence* (1577; 1593), 124–126, 129–130; Tomlinson, 'Thinking with Lists', 23–24.

140   LISTING

into parts that its main points cannot be either discerned or plainly applied to the business of living a godly life.[28]

Listeners valued numbering when trying to follow complex material: ease of access nudges a reader into following the argument and recalling it later.[29] The proposition that there is a link between Protestantism and increased literacy might be extended to include increased numeracy, given the way believers habitually used numbering to think about their faith. The Geneva Bible (1560) was the first to divide its chapters into numbered verses (as 'most profitable for memorie'), giving the text the appearance of a numbered list.[30] As Arnold Hunt has argued, note-taking at sermons encouraged the ability to grasp the structure of a discourse by visualizing its contents as though laid out sequentially on a page.[31] Mid-seventeenth-century Oxford students, noting down sermons delivered at the university church to repeat the substance later to their tutors, numbered lists of points to fix the structures in their minds. For instance, two individual students at the same sermon at Oxford leaned heavily on numbers when trying to capture what was said, even retaining a unit's number when they could not gather or remember its content:

Dr Wilkins of Wadham

Text in ye 2 Tit. 10 ve. that they may adorn ye gospell of our Saviour in all things. in ye ep 3 parts
1 about ye ordaining of bishops.
2 concerning ye particular duties of men in their
3 ye duties of [deleted: 'comon's] xtians in genrall.
I have pitchd upon a text wch is rould under ye 2d dutie.
1 wt tis to adorne,
2 wt
3 wt by do
1 to adorne. is to set a thing of wch is [deleted 'is']
1 removing blemishes, they myt avoyd bad actions.
2 by addition of adornment.

---

[28] Herbert, *Country Parson*, 235.
[29] Thaler and Sunstein, *Nudge*, 96–99.
[30] E. Tribble, *Margins and Marginality: The Printed Page in Early Modern England* (Charlottesville: University Press of Virginia, 1993), 32, 35, 40.
[31] A. Hunt, *The Art of Hearing: English Preachers and their Audiences, 1590–1640* (Cambridge: Cambridge University Press, 2010), 97–99.

2 DEVOTIONAL LISTS TO REASON WITH, TO DELIGHT, AND TO MOVE   141

And the second student's notes:

Dr. Wilkins

Tit. 2.10.
That ye may adorne ye doc: of Gd our Saviour in all things.
St Paul having by his preaching ld a found of Xian faith in Crete he reputes
Tit: to be his dputy & to yt end writes this epistle to him.
1. concerning episcopacy
2. touching ye dutyes of family
3. touching all dutyes of all sorts of people.
The text is in ye 2nd pt: wr he exhorting all sorts degrees & condicons of men
speaks here to servants. to be subject to yr masters.
There are but 3 terms in ye text yt seem to need explication
1. Adorne. wch sig: to set a thing off to the best show. yt it may appear lovely.
1. a removall of blemishes
2. and a supaddition of ornaments.[32]

Learning to listen and learning to list were, for these students, skills acquired hand in hand. The habit continued when reading such material: manuscript marginalia on printed religious texts sometimes repeat the latter's numbers, not (or not just) their logical divisions and sub-headings. For instance, in the Huntington Library copy of Perkins's best-selling discussion of the marks of salvation, manuscript notes on the contrasting ways in which the reprobate and the elect hear the word of God retain Perkins's figures, even when his content is not noted: '8 speciall notes how ye elect receive ye word of god', 'two thinges to be observed of a christian', 'Ye first thinge', 'Ye second thing'.[33]

Lists, however, are not merely instruments to think with, they are also devices to arouse or control feelings. The second type of list, the meditative one, is antithetical in purpose to the closed list of reasons. In the meditative list a reader can linger on—or skip—any of its items, according to the zeal or boredom encouraged by each. Charlotte Clutterbuck argues that poems praising God's presence in the world are frequently ejaculatory, or at least fairly

---

[32] C. Sullivan, 'The Art of Listening in the Seventeenth Century', *Modern Philology*, 104 (2006), 63–65.

[33] W. Perkins, *A Treatise Tending unto a Declaration Whether a Man be in the Estate of Damnation or in the Estate of Grace* (1590), 24–26.

142 LISTING

short, to stay in the moment of celebration.[34] This is not how the meditation lists appear, but it is, to some extent, how they can be used. Each entry is complete in itself, so need not be read in a particular order, or even at all. Readers are thus encouraged to lose themselves in the flow of units in the catalogue, or to wander from them into other topics which have pricked their hearts to turn to God. Unlike the argumentative lists, the mise-en-page of lists for meditating on is generally unobtrusive, with no visual prompts to march a reader's thoughts through a series of regimented moves. Take, for instance, the way John Andrewes, one-time minister of Berwick Basset, Wiltshire, praises the elect man. By contrast to what Bolton does, Andrewes speaks largely and uninterruptedly of how

> hee rejoyceth in forgiving them that hurt him; and loveth them that hate him; and rendreth good for evill, he dispiseth none, but loveth all, and is not rash in words, but reasonable, not hasty but seasonable, not grievous, but gracious, not provoking, but appeasing, not offensive, but to good purpose: Sober in censuring, faithfull in answering, milde in reprooving, carefull in defending.[35]

Such litanies are based on what Umberto Eco calls 'a poetics of the "etcetera"' rather than a desire for completeness, their form suggesting the many things not (yet) included in them. He thinks the lists of unstoppable 'numeration (and enumeration)' give an 'uneasy pleasure, which makes us feel the greatness of our subjectivity, capable of wishing for something we cannot have', after the end of what could have been an endless list.[36] Tracing an oral influence in popular prose of the period, Sandra Clark argues that 'the wandering, digressive, non-organic structures of many pamphlets, the easy movement through a series of scarcely-connected devices reaching a conclusion in no way related to the beginning', their 'loose conversational flow and disregard for formal unity', could 'perplex and irritate a reader accustomed to closely organised structures'.[37] Such irritation could indeed arise in those, then and now, who are reading a text to get to the point, but not in those reading it for the meditative experience of reading.

There is no beginning or end to the goodness of God, so itemization can flow on endlessly, readers occasionally dipping in for what appeals to them

---

[34] C. Clutterbuck, *Encounters with God in Medieval and Early Modern Poetry* (Aldershot: Ashgate, 2005), 15.

[35] J. Andrewes, *The Converted Mans New Birth ... With an Excellent Marke, to Know the Childe of God* (1629), 34–35.

[36] Eco, *Lists*, 8, 10, 15–18.

[37] S. Clark, *The Elizabethan Pamphleteers: Popular Moralistic Pamphlets, 1580–1640* (London: Athlone Press, 1983), 243–245.

2 DEVOTIONAL LISTS TO REASON WITH, TO DELIGHT, AND TO MOVE 143

most. When Nicholas Breton, a popular poet and devotional writer, surveys the manifold signs of God's care for creation, he runs to one creature a line for around eighty stanzas. Readers can choose to linger on how God humbles the proud:

> The Lyon first is fearefull of the Bee,
> The Elephant doth dread the little mouse,
> A crowing Cocke the Dragon may not see,
> The stoutest Eagle subject to the louse.

Or they can reflect on how God gives all creatures a home:

> Within the depth the fish their holes doe keepe,
> And in the rocks the Conny makes his house,
> Into the earth the crawling wormes doe creepe,
> And hollowe rocks are harbour for the mouse.[38]

Each unit in such lists has the potential to generate devotion, but their compilers do not insist that this be felt at every step. Their lists emphasize helpless awe at God's sublimity, rather than trying to prove a framework for a human to comprehend it. Unlike the reasoning lists, which appeal to the eye, the meditative lists appeal to the ear. They are structured by sound, not numeration or hypotaxis: parallels in schemes or syntax suggest thematic ties between apparently heterodox items. Andrewes, for instance, uses antithesis (love/hate, good/evil, none/all), isocolon (not/but, adjective-verb, the elision of 'he'), homeoteleuton ('censuring ... answering ... reproving ... defending'), rhyme ('reasonable ... seasonable'), and repetition ('them ... him'). Breton repeats (sometimes in reverse) a syntactical pattern of subject-verb-object.

The third type of list, a prompt to action, draws out the human consequences of catalogues which argue or praise to nudge their readers into changing their usual behaviour. For instance, Robert Bolton's list on how to recognize a besetting sin uses anaphora and numbered units, after a sub-heading, to cue readers to tick off each item:

2. Thou mayst discover it by such markes as these:
   1. It is that, which thy truest friends, thine own conscience, and the finger of God in the Ministerie, many times finds out ...
   2. It is that, which if it breake out into act ...
   3. That which thou are lothest to leave ...[39]

---

[38] N. Breton, *A Solemne Passion of the Soules Love* (1598), A3r, A2v.
[39] R. Bolton, *Some Generall Directions for a Comfortable Walking with God* (1626), 36.

144   LISTING

Lists of marks, promises, and signs characteristically urge readers to treat them not as descriptions but as 'to do' notes. Stephen Denison, the curate of St Katharine Cree, London, preaching at the funeral of the godly Elizabeth Juxon, describes how she habitually conducted a written examination of herself for marks of salvation. He summarizes her list of such signs (preserving the format of the list, he says, by noting each separate item in 'small letters for distinction'), and urges his readers to take it 'not as a bare report or commendation of the partie deceased; but duly observe every marke ... and ... examine whether thou findest these signes in thy selfe or no'.[40] Lists about the marks of salvation nudge their readers towards a perceptual order which points to a particular decision or conclusion to act on.[41]

Such lists often appear in self-scrutiny before communion, which is usually organized around the ten commandments or the seven petitions of the Lord's Prayer. John Dod and Robert Cleaver reduce all the sins a reader could possibly commit into eighteen leaves of numbered heads. For instance, those against the first commandment are:

1. Aetheisme, which is, when men either thinke there is no God, or live as if there were no God.
2. Idolatry: which is, the having of a false god.
3. Ignorance ...

A 'no' to any of these header words lets one move on down the list; a doubt requires a pause (registered by 'which is') to test the appended definition against one's conscience. The 1629 edition of A. F.'s collection of 104 (numbered) promises made by God to his elect is organized by a double layer of repetition ('The IV. Legacy/ If thou despaire', 'When thou ... When thou ... When thou', 'The V. Legacy/ If thou findest Sinne a heavy burden ... If ... If ... '). The 1631 edition helps readers still further by providing concluding 'Tables for the right and ready finding out of any Promise in this Booke, for the comfortable supplie of present necessitie: the number shewes the page, where the Promise (wee would have) is to bee found'. The book's index is ordered in the same way: 'If wee .../ If thou .../ When thou'.[42] Richard Bernard compiles numbered lists of ways to sanctify each moment of the day: six 'to dos' while dressing, four while washing, five while brushing one's clothes, four

[40] S. Denison, *The Monument or Tombe-stone: or, a Sermon Preached at Laurence Pountnies Church in London ... at the Funerall of Mrs. Elizabeth Juxon* (1620), 83–84.
[41] On the morality associated with order, see Douglas, *Purity and Danger*, 140–172.
[42] A. F., *A Collection of Certaine Promises Out of the Word of God* (1629), 6–8; A. F., *The Saints Legacies, or a Collection of Certaine Promises Out of the Word of God* (1631), I11r ff.

2 DEVOTIONAL LISTS TO REASON WITH, TO DELIGHT, AND TO MOVE   145

when glancing at a mirror before leaving the bedchamber, and so on.[43] The section on practical divinity in a popular anthology of writings (the best of the best) by Rogers, Perkins, Greenham, Miles Mosse, and George Webbe combines alphabetized and numbered double-layered sub-sections in laying out its advice:

> A Threefold Alphabet of rules concerning CHRISTIAN practise.
>
> A
>
> 1. Awake with GOD in the morning, and before all things give him your first fruits and calves of your lips, 1. in Confession of sinnes: 2. Petition of necessaries for body and soule. 3 Thankefulnesse for mercies receiued, especially your late preservation, rest, and protection of you and yours.
> 2. Account it not enough that your selfe serve GOD, unlesse you see all in your charge doe the same.
> 3. Arme your selfe against whatsoeuer the day may bring forth ...
>
> B
>
> 1. Beware of occasions of sinne, and wisely inure your selfe in subduing the least, that at length the greater may be foiled ...[44]

Numbering or alphabetizing the list tends to increase the speed of movement the reader goes down it, but these lists also indicate a contrasting pace of reading: the fast move down the page is contrasted with an occasional and slower move across, to gather further information.[45]

The device of the list does not appear in Ian Green's magisterial coverage of the principal genres and sub-genres in religious writing, but some of those genres he discusses rely on one of the three types of list, especially those of popular theology, comfortable words, and godly directions for life. Their classification could be seen in terms of the Horatian aims for literature, that it should teach, delight, and move its readers, or in terms of the three branches of classical rhetoric (judicial, demonstrative, and deliberative), which appealed to the reason, the emotions, and the will, respectively. When some authors want to do all three (often sequentially), they cycle between, or combine, the different types of list. Bayly, for instance, states the theology of the attributes

---

[43] Bernard, *Weekes Worke*, 38 ff.
[44] R. Rogers [et al.], *A Garden of Spirituall Flowers* (1609; 1613), second signature series, A2r–v.
[45] On differing speeds, see Tomlinson, 'Thinking with Lists', 23, 25.

of the divine essence (concisely, in sub-sectioned numbered lists), provides meditations on the 'seaven sanctified thoughts, and mournfull sighes of a sicke man' (in amplified lists of feelings about, and prayers on, death), and gives 'Rules to be observed in singing of Psalmes' (short lists of stage directions: '2. Remember to sing Davids Psalmes with Davids spirit ... 4. As you sing uncover your heads').[46] Clement Cotton, drawing on his secretarial skills as a compiler of biblical concordances, catalogues the twenty-three terrors of a sinful heart. He describes each fear individually and emotionally, and then rebuts it with a reasoned list based on the phrase 'None but Christ':

> 1. Fall.
> *I am fallen in Adam, I am falne, I am fallen, Oh! Who shall raise mee?*
> None but Christ, who as hee is set for thy uprising, Lke 2.34. so is hee perfectly able to keep thee, that thou fall not againe, from thy own stedfastnesse, Jud. 24.
>
> 2. Guilt.
> *By my fall I have ...*

Cotton concludes by showing, in intermittent soliloquy, how this accumulated evidence finally changes the will of the speaker, so he comes to feel and act as one who is saved:

> here the afflicted began a little to pause: and having received much refreshing, and good satisfaction from those several answers which a good conscience hitherto framed to his severall demands and doubtings: ceased from further objecting: and began thus to be a little cheared and revived.
> Well then, I finde and feele, to my no litle joy, and contentment, that there is None indeed but Christ ...
> And then, after some further pantings, and breathings (faith having put, as it were, a new life into him) he brake foorth into this passion, of admiration and thankfulnesse.
> And it is true indeed, O thou lover of men![47]

Such a list is an emotion-script of what to feel when, which offers the reader a strong incentive to move through its different sections to gain the assurance of grace.

---

[46] Bayly, *Pietie*, 52 ff., 942 ff., 464–465 ff. See also J. Dyke, *Good Conscience: or a Treatise Shewing the Nature, Meanes, Marks, Benefit, and Necessitie Thereof* (1626), 10 ff.

[47] C. Cotton, *None But Christ, None But Christ Intimating that in Him ... is to be Found, the Full and Absolute Cure of Mans Misery* (1629), A12r–v, B11v–12r.

2 DEVOTIONAL LISTS TO REASON WITH, TO DELIGHT, AND TO MOVE   147

Lists are especially useful in the case of the most pressing of all decisions, how *'euery man may cleerely see, whether he shall be saued or damned'*, as the subtitle of the best-selling dialogue by Arthur Dent put it.[48] It was not a matter of mere curiosity: all needed to feel sure on this point. Martin Luther argued that only the Holy Spirit could produce faith that one was saved, but that one should live in hope that assurance would be granted to those who desired it. Jean Calvin, by contrast, thought that since saving grace was only offered to a few, then uncertainty was probably an indication one lacked faith. For both, doubt was an evil, being either a lack of trust in God or a sign of damnation. It was to be rooted out as an act of piety, concludes Susan Schreiner.[49]

The pre-eminent maker of devotional lists to eradicate doubt was Nicholas Byfield, vicar of Isleworth, Middlesex, with best-sellers on the infallible signs of a blessed man ('The signs particularly expounded; and first of povertie of spirit ... by properties, or by effect. Gods poor have eight properties. First they are sensible ... of their own wants'), a companion volume on the indications of an evil man ('thirty signes of an open wicked man ... thirteen signes of an Hypocrit'), rules for things to be listed when reading scripture ('Places that in reading I found sensible comfort in./ Places that in the reading of them I found did rebuke corruption in my nature or practise', and even the catch-all 'Miscellanea or places I would faine remember but know not to what head to referre them'), and a collection of biblical verses on when and how to be assured that one is saved ('Seven principles concerning Gods providence .../ Eleven things admirable in Gods providence .../ Foure sorts of men reproved .../ Eight uses for instruction') (see Figure 5.1).[50]

Byfield often uses numbers to stop readers being so sunk by fear and confusion that they lose heart:

> First, it is proved by eight apparant Arguments, that [being
>   freed of the fear of death] may bee attained to ...
> Secondly, it is shewed by fifteene considerations, how shame-
>   full ... it is for a Christian to bee afraid to die ...
> Thirdly, the way how this feare may bee removed, is shewed ...

---

[48] On making incentives transparent, see Thaler and Sunstein, *Nudge*, 99–102.

[49] S. Schreiner, *Are You Alone Wise? The Search for Certainty in the Early Modern Era* (Oxford: Oxford University Press, 2010), 75.

[50] N. Byfield, *The Signes, or an Essay Concerning the Assurance of Gods Love and Mans Salvation* (1614), 20; N. Byfield, *The Signes of the Wicked Man* (1619), A6r–v; N. Byfield, *The Beginning of the Doctrine of Christ. Or a Catalogue of Sinnes Shewing how a Christian May Finde Out the Evil, He Must Take Notice of* (1619), later repeatedly republished as *The Marrow of the Oracles of God*; N. Byfield, *Directions for the Private Reading of the Scriptures* (1618), [118 ff.] (not in Green); N. Byfield, *The Paterne of Wholsome Words, or a Collection of Such Truths are of Necessity to be Believed* (1618), A2r.

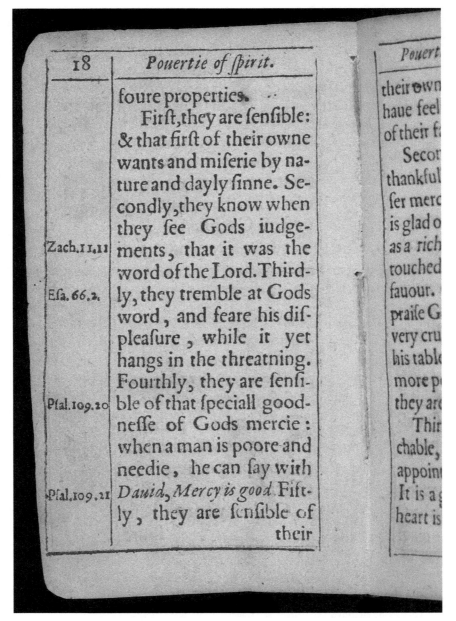

Figure 5.1 Nicholas Byfield, *The Signes, or An Essay Concerning the Assurance of Gods Love, and Mans Salvation* (1617), Bodleian Library, University of Oxford, Vet A2 f413 (1), 18.

2 DEVOTIONAL LISTS TO REASON WITH, TO DELIGHT, AND TO MOVE   149

> Two waies of Cure ...
> Seventeen Priviledges of a Christian in death ...
> Eight aggravations of Gods corrections in this life ...
> Eight apparant miseries from the world ...
> Fifteen manifest defects and blemishes ...[51]

His contents pages mix the styles of technical catalogue and self-help manual, promoting an interactive reading with section titles which (like his preface) tell readers what rational or emotional states of mind or heart (being prepared, ruled, persuaded, relieved, and so on) will result from applying each unit to their own circumstances. Such prompting should become a self-fulfilling prophecy:

> The persons whom those Treatises concerne, pag. 11. 12
> Incouragement to the study of those things, p. 13. to 18
> Generall directions by way of preparation, p. 18. to 22 ...
> The rules that shew distinctly what men must doe about their
>   sins. p. 22 to 59
> Motiues to perswade to the care of these rules. pag. 23. 24
> Three rules of preparation. pag. 24. 25. 26
> Foure things deliuer vs from all sinnes past. p. 27
> About the gathering of the Catalogue of sins. p. 27. to 35.[52]

Peter Kaufman shows how Protestants consciously adopted reformed attitudes they had read and heard about, then repeatedly referred to these pre-prepared approaches until they were engrained as second nature.[53] This is the intention behind Byfield's lists. He frequently states that his aim is to make things clear so that readers can take action. It might, he thinks, be more intellectually respectable to read the original authorities behind his treatises, but his work provides the most 'distinct digesting' of the principal points in salvation; thus 'things are made more plaine, and so more easy'. Curating the options offered helps a reader attend to each item more thoroughly.[54] In searching the conscience, for instance, Byfield's lists aim to take the strain off the penitent's memory: 'look upon the Catalogue ... so thou maist observe, what faults thou couldst not finde, or remember by thy private examination, and withall see in

---

[51] N. Byfield, *The Cure of the Feare of Death* (1618), A8r–9v (not in Green).
[52] Byfield, *Beginning*, A7r–v.
[53] Kaufman, *Prayer, Despair*, 32–36.
[54] Byfield, *Beginning*, 12, 13, 30–32, 41–42, 44, 47. On curating options, see Thaler and Sunstein, *Nudge*, 97–98.

150   LISTING

what phrase or order to digest thy sins'. Byfield urges a 'good enough' approach to working down the list, to make it seem doable: 'cheerefully endure this triall of thy selfe, and take heed thou do it not cursorily, but take time enough, and so thou maist, if thou wilt only take one of the Chapters, or two of them, as they lye in the Catalogue, and no more in a day'. The perfect should not be the enemy of the good. If readers feel their sins to be 'innumerable, and so cannot be gathered into a Catalogue', then they are simply to tick them off under one of his general headings. Precision should not overwhelm substance.[55] This measured, low-key, practical approach frees the reader from the 'perplexities of an unquiet hart'. Thus, Byfield advises, in going down the list be as 'earnest as thou canst, and when that is done, goe cheerfully about the works of thy calling. Hang not downe thy head like a bulrush'. Moreover, he balances pains with gains. Readers can compile their own 'distinct catalogue of promises' by God to hear the repentant, as a 'treasure' against future anxiety. After giving a few examples of such comfortable assurances, Byfield recommends that they make 'a full Catalogue, and write out the words verbatim, & learne them without book', so they are readily available in daily life.

Such advice was heeded. Richard Rogers, for instance, repeatedly lists life choices to 'season' his heart: twelve 'perswasions' to be content even if his ministry were to be suspended (numbered, and each item starting with 'seeing', to bullet point it further), five ways to carry 'my selfe in a wise manner towards all sortes with whom I have to deal, as winninge them backe againe' (numbered), an unnumbered list of the disadvantages which would accrue if his wife were to die in childbirth, ending with a depressed note that the list was unfinished ('these are some').[56] Wallington tried to discern God's will in the chaos of daily life by writing about events, giving him some distance and hence objectivity, then clarifying their significance further by using the conventional categories of the Protestant process of salvation. 'Conformity, not originality, was the hallmark of the disciplined life', David Booy and Paul Seaver argue of such categorization.[57] In 1654 Wallington listed forty-nine of his works (some multi-volumed). Of these, at least nineteen were themselves lists: 'places' of scripture, 'day books' of sins, 'examples' of punishments and of mercies, collections of 'marks' of salvation, and so on. The earliest of his six surviving notebooks, for example, is divided into two: a personal introduction (a nineteen-page list of Wallington's particular sins, followed by an

---

[55] On this danger, see Bowker and Star, *Categories*, 24–26.
[56] Knappen, ed., *Puritan Diaries*, 90–92, 87, 74.
[57] 'Introduction', in Wallington, *Notebooks*, ed. Booy, 13; P. Seaver, *Wallington's World: A Puritan Artisan in Seventeenth-century London* (London: Methuen, 1985), 182–185.

2 DEVOTIONAL LISTS TO REASON WITH, TO DELIGHT, AND TO MOVE   151

eleven-page list of seventy-seven 'resolutions' or 'covenants' he had made to guide his life), and then about 350 pages of impersonal reflections on spiritual concerns, again often appearing as lists. These include a catalogue of God's promises, collections of proofs of a living faith, seven ways natural man is miserable, eight motions towards sin, twenty marks of a child of God (another list gives sixteen signs), eight remedies against sorrow, six ways to pray correctly, and five ways to show love to an enemy.[58]

Godly reading and writing are discussed by a range of early modern historians as technologies of the self. Of spiritual diaries, Tom Webster argues that, 'unlike other facets of the godly discipline, [such as] fasting and prayer, meetings for sermon repetition, solitary meditation and self-examination', journals produce a 'material site for the self'.[59] Narveson shows how, when reading, the godly expected to do so pen in hand, excerpting and listing their proofs, and sharing their work with family, friends, or parishioners as guides for life.[60] Ryrie goes further: godly writing was also done for its own sake as a way to fill the writer's time with the presence of God's word (and done, indeed, on a heroic scale in some cases). 'Writing felt like the perfect medium in which to consummate Protestantism's love affair with the bible, and Protestants did so with dizzying ingenuity and persistence'.[61] Brown shows how popular devotional texts were navigated by hand as well as eye; readers valued 'the non-linear cross-referencing of passages, handled tactilely and experienced aurally, as contrasted with the conventional image of literacy defined by the silent, solitary, linear consumption of written texts'.[62] Lori Anne Ferrell argues that in books on how to be saved, readers were choreographed in manipulating the pages: following up diagrams with their fingers, cutting out paper tools and unfolding tables, each time releasing a burst of kinetic energy which gave them the sense that they were able to deal with the ideas while doing the paper-work. Reading was a physical act, and Protestants, so often thought of as aurally inclined people of the Word, could also be seen as tactile people of the physical page.[63]

However, lists have not hitherto been included among these writing technologies, either as a way for the reader to reform herself or, in a less

---

[58] Seaver, *Wallington's World*, 199–208.
[59] T. Webster, 'Writing to Redundancy: Approaches to Spiritual Journals and Early Modern Spirituality', *The Historical Journal*, 39/1 (1996), 40.
[60] Narveson, *Bible Readers and Lay Writers*, 1–13.
[61] Ryrie, *Being Protestant*, 302.
[62] Brown, 'The Thick Style', 69.
[63] L. A. Ferrell, 'How-to Books, Protestant Kinetics, and the Art of Theology', *Huntington Library Quarterly*, 71/4 (2008), 591–606.

152 LISTING

obviously instrumental way, for her to bathe in the experience of the Word. The genre should be added: some lists recount their compiler's life from God's perspective, framing lived experience in a different way, others allow their compilers and readers to lose themselves in the pleasure of rewriting scripture. Far from being an *écriture grise*, Protestants found themselves in lists, coming to a sense of what they could be as they classified and categorized parts of their selves, whether those were qualities, sins, or marks.[64] Then they used the device to form an exoskeleton around the flagging will, giving clarity and pleasure to their activity. The list is a nudge put together when feeling zeal, in anticipation of cooler moments, knowing that decisions vary according to states of arousal.[65]

3 Herbert's 'Done' and 'To Do' Lists

Critical approaches to Herbert relish his sociable qualities (as a courtier, a minister, or a musician) and his meditative moments (of agony, content, or ecstasy); Herbert the bureaucrat is a less appealing image. Readers have debated how he picks up contemporary religious genres, particularly cate-chisms and case casuistry.[66] They have also commented on his shape poems (such as 'The Altar' and 'Easter-wings'), on his spiritual play with different typefaces (as in 'Anagram of the Virgin Marie' and 'Coloss. 3.3'), and even on the differing spaces which printers included between his words to point up the processes of spiritual fracture and regeneration.[67] They have not, however, noticed his purposeful use of lists as an expression of his wider commitment to an intelligible and practical style of communication in his ministry, and as part of a serious spiritual playfulness, where words are treated as 'dense

---

[64] As is argued of forms. See L. Gowing, 'Girls on Forms: Apprenticing Young Women in Seventeenth-century London', *Journal of British Studies*, 55/3 (2016), 447–473.

[65] On the difference between decision-making in hot/aroused and cold/passive states, see Thaler and Sunstein, *Nudge*, 41–42.

[66] For instance, Fish, *Temple*, 19–25; C. Wells Slights, *The Casuistical Tradition in Shakespeare, Donne, Herbert, and Milton* (Princeton: Princeton University Press, 1981), 183–246; Hodgkins, *Authority, Church, and Society*, 2–3, 11, 110–120; K. Narveson, 'Herbert and Early Stuart Psalm Culture: Beyond Translation and Meditation', in C. Hodgkins, ed., *George Herbert's Pastoral: New Essays on the Poet and Priest of Bemerton* (Newark: University of Delaware Press, 2010), 221–228.

[67] For instance, F. Cruickshank and G. Kuchar, 'Broken Altars: The Work of Form in George Herbert's *Temple*', *Christianity and Literature*, 66/1 (2016), 24–38; S. Swanner, 'The Beauty of Ho(me)liness: the Unhandsome Sacramentality of Almost-shape Poems in George Herbert's *The Temple*', *Studies in Philology*, 115 (2018), 544–579; G. Bloomfield, 'Herbert the Space Man: Scenes of Printing and Spaces of Reading in *The Temple*', *ELH*, 87/1 (2020), 1–38; Summers, *George Herbert*, 92–93.

3 HERBERT'S 'DONE' AND 'TO DO' LISTS   153

textual objects', as Tomlinson says of lists, there to absorb readers' attention to good effect.[68]

The meditative form appears in 'Prayer' 1, 'The H. Scriptures 1', 'The Quidditie', 'Providence', and 'Constancie', whose echoes of lists in secular love poems (such as blazons) have been widely noted. Belknap argues of such poetry that 'the stacked lines of a verse provide virtual ledger entries in which the poet can itemise, registering and elaborating a certain number of items per line'. While partial completion may come at the end of each line, there is the possibility of many further lines to come, and 'though without bounds in principle, the list has a load limit of what it can skilfully hold'. Thus, Belknap says, genres which are tightly limited as to length (like the sonnet) may be selected for lists in order to impose an arbitrary but much needed cut-off.[69]

Herbert, however, does not employ such limits. Indeed, these five poems go out of their way to refuse to imply a conclusion or hierarchy about what they are presenting. Their opening lines provide concise headers: 'shall I write,/ And not of thee', 'My God, a verse is not … ', 'Prayer the Churches banquet … ', 'Oh Book! infinite sweetnesse … ', and 'Who is the honest man?' However, the implication of these blunt openings—that a plain description or argument will follow—is not then substantiated. Instead, the poems go on to accumulate epithets (either positive or negative), or provide a series of examples which have roughly the same emphasis or theme, but which are not linked together in an explicit argument. The beginning of each new unit of content in three of the poems ('The Quidditie', 'Providence', and 'Constancie') is bullet-pointed by grammatically related words, often placed at the start of a line or a phrase, encouraging an F-shaped direction of reading (as in listicles). 'The Quidditie' uses 'not', 'nor', 'never', and 'no'. The eleven introductory stanzas of 'Providence' repeat 'all' ten times. 'Constancie' is structured by the repetition, at the start of seven stanzas and the mid-point of a further three, of 'who', 'whose', or 'whom': 'Who is the honest man?', 'Whom neither force nor fawning', 'Whose honestie is not', 'Who rides his sure and even trot', and so on.

Such syntactic tissue does not suggest which comments are more or less important, or indicate the shape of an implied argument. 'The H. Scriptures 1' groups disconcertingly secular and varied uses for its addressee (in medicine, cosmetics, and accounting). The register in 'The Quidditie' of what poetry is not (not a crown, not gossip about the stables, not commercial news, and so on) has the same basic area of interest (what one might assume are

---

[68] Tomlinson, 'Thinking with Lists', 35.
[69] Belknap, *List*, 15, 31, 32–33.

154 LISTING

the courtier's pursuits), but no conclusion. Herbert's conceits about prayer (grouped around the topics of searching for it, struggling in it, and being refreshed by God's love) are presented as discrete miniature riddles for the reader to solve: it is a measure of 'Angels age' (perhaps because angels express creation's praise of God, first voiced when first made), for instance, or a vision of 'man well drest' (perhaps because prayer arises out of grace which is given to cover the sinner). 'Constancie' brings together diverse circumstances in which its hero stays true to his principles (who gives all their dues, regardless of positive or negative pressure; who does not blindly follow the world's opinion; who weighs up the circumstances calmly, and so on), but develops none of them.

Reading Herbert's praise poems side by side with such Protestant devotional works as Nicholas Breton's suggests a celebratory reason for compiling such potentially endless lists. Rather than a reader thinking that every unit has to be read in full—and, consequently, feeling anxious and even depressed about the number of lines still to get through—Herbert offers a series of instances which can be sampled, until striking one that arouses zeal. Pausing on any of these units becomes a private moment of blessing and praise. In prompting the reader to skip-read, such poems offer both the psychological pleasure of choice and a theological point: all or any of these instances can show God's plenitude and spontaneity, and there could be many more.

Angus Vine argues that early modern readers used the random aspect of commonplace books to think creatively, rather than their ordering aspect. They were seen not just as stores of content (collected haphazardly but then rationally indexed for retrieval), but also as miscellanies which had the advantage of bringing material together in a heterogeneous way. The resulting contrasts could point to new lines of enquiry and knowledge.[70] Praise poems produce such congeries, thickening each topic taken up in turn, rather than arguing their readers into a conclusion about the whole. There is thus no particular hierarchy among the items, but instead a network which connects nodes of praise in any way the reader thinks would be striking.

'Providence' provides a good example of this. God is an especially difficult object to list: one cannot anatomize him into parts, top down, nor enumerate all his qualities and deeds, bottom up. 'Providence' praises the climate, the landscape, the food chain, diurnal and seasonal changes, the water cycle, the transformation of soil to leaves to leaf-mould, and then turns to apparent antitheses, or challenges to usual practices, to show that God is never bound,

---

[70] A. Vine, *Miscellaneous Order: Manuscript Culture and the Early Modern Organization of Knowledge* (Oxford: Oxford University Press, 2019), 12–14.

even by his own conventions (glass gives light without drafts, thorn trees are harsher to handle than pear trees but make better hedges, every creature but the elephant sleeps lying down, the coconut has many surprising uses, and so on). The poem orders the world by a chant that creates new relations between what have hitherto appeared to be independent units, until they are encountered in the poem. Readers can participate if they realize they are part of this whole, one in a chain of singular instances forming the universal.[71] Creation is a synecdoche of God, not a metaphor for him, and the list is offered as a sample of how much more could be said.[72] As 'Providence' finally declares, 'Each thing that is .../ ... hath many ways in store/ To honour thee .../ ... yet this one more'.

Lists as rhetorical amplifications, showing Eco's 'poetics of the etcetera', point out how God's qualities and actions are beyond the reach of human understanding.[73] They negotiate between the sublimity of God, on one hand, and, on the other, the limited number of ways in which human understanding can be dizzily appreciative of what it knows it does not yet know about. Vanessa Steinroetter argues that writers find lists attractive because, even while they show what is present, they hint at what has been lost, erased, or abstracted, in attempts to create order.[74] Two of the five poems teasingly conclude that they can offer no definitive conclusion. Throughout, 'Prayer' 1 evades producing a main verb, and ends with the definition of prayer as undefinable: the reader will know it when she sees it, as 'something understood'. 'The Quidditie' suggests the poem will turn its negative definition of what poetry is not into a positive definition of what it is, but does not do so; poetry remains an undefined good, something 'which while I use/ I am with thee'. Such occupatio emphasizes the known unknowns of devotion.

Herbert also writes the opposite sort of list: clear arguments for or against a position. Six poems of this type show careful reflection on the sorts of categories created when a topic is divided into different instances.[75] The poems' closed lists of reasons drive to a single point: readers should recategorize life events to recognize them as evidence of God's love. 'The Pearl', 'Vanitie' 1, 'The Quip', 'Unkindnesse', 'Sinne' 1, and 'Mortification' are, effectively, conversion

---

[71] J. Mason, 'Walt Whitman's Catalogues: Rhetorical Means for Two Journeys in "Song of Myself"', *American Literature*, 45 (1973), 38, 43–45.

[72] On lists as registers of a sample of God's properties, see Eco, *Lists*, 50, 133–134.

[73] K. Murphy, '"No Things but in Thoughts": Traherne's Poetic Realism', in E. S. Dodd and C. Gorman, eds., *Thomas Traherne and Seventeenth-Century Thought* (Cambridge: Cambridge University Press, 2016), 48–52.

[74] V. Steinroetter, '"Reading the List": Casuality Lists and Civil War Poetry', *ESQ: A Journal of the American Renaissance*, 59 (2013), 53.

[75] On taxonomies, see Blair, *Too Much to Know*, 132 ff.

156   LISTING

narratives.[76] As with lists of praise, the topic is usually declared in the first few lines: what an ambitious person should know, or the likely collusion between different temptations, or the ways to treat a friend, or the preventatives to sinning, or the events which prefigure death. Words or phrases are repeated, with some slight variation at the start of each stanza ('First ... Then ... Then ... Then ...' in 'The Pearl', or 'I know the wayes of ...' in 'The Quip'), or by different topics dealt with in parallel syntax ('The fleet Astronomer .../ The nimble Diver .../ The subtil Chymick ...' of 'Vanitie' 1). The conclusions of the units in the argumentative lists are also marked out by refrains, such as 'I would not/ could not/ cannot use a friend, as I use Thee' ('Unkindnesse'), 'But thou shalt answer, Lord, for me' ('The Quip'), and 'Yet I love thee' ('The Pearl'). Such lists have readers nodding along, with mounting satisfaction, towards the increasingly familiar end of each stanza.

Their clarity of sound and of organizing principle tends to dull any deep interrogation of their content. Thus, it comes as a shock when, at the end of each of these six poems, Herbert abruptly reverses its line of argument away from an expected outcome. The moment is marked by the logical dis-connectives of 'yet' and 'but'. For instance, though a catalogue of parents, schoolmasters, ministers, afflictions, Bible verses, promises of salvation, shame, guilt, and angels has been accumulated in 'Sinne' 1, 'Yet .../ One cunning bosome-sinne blows quite away' these defences. In 'The Pearl', the list which Herbert compiles of disciplines he is expert in but willing to subordinate to his love of God does not end in self-congratulation, but with a sober realization that 'Yet ... not my groveling wit,/ But thy silk twist let down from heav'n .../ Did both conduct and teach me'. Committed research by astronomers, divers, and chemists goes on in 'Vanitie' 1, before the poem concludes that each 'searchest round/ To finde out death, but misses life at hand'. The speaker of the 'The Quip', having repeatedly asked God to answer freely on his behalf, suddenly changes direction and tells God what to say ('Yet .../ Speak not at large, say, I am thine').

Such reversals have long engaged critics. For Fish they provide catechetical moments when a reader, having been invited to make an interpretation too soon, is then challenged and the conclusion reinstated in a deeper or more accurate way. For Raphael Lyne they are new stages in an ongoing process of discovering the truth. For Sophie Read they are corrections in a drama of doubt, where the poet illustrates how to amend his understanding (though

---

[76] Herbert argues that the dislocated questions of catechisms produce attention but not zeal, *Country Parson*, 257.

3 HERBERT'S 'DONE' AND 'TO DO' LISTS   157

without actually performing this, which would entail rubbing out the old poems entirely).[77]

However, remembering Bowker and Star's warning about how lists invisibly replicate a social and moral order, and how much effort it takes to redo categories or redirect items, the abrupt turns in Herbert's lists can be read as pointing up the repeated efforts needed to rethink faulty categories. The original classifications behind the lists, embedded in a particular cultural or theological context, turn out to be inadequate. Such 'reformed' writing tests the usual epistemological categories, exposing their worldly bias; in effect, 'yet' and 'but' are the bullet points which start God's reclassifications. Thus, in 'Unkindnesse', the speaker's list of his repeated and laudable efforts to help a friend are reversed into a self-reproach for not acting so by God. The poem's opening stanza appears at first to be a prayer to behave well to friends, then turns tail:

> Lord, make me coy and tend to offend:
> In friendship, first I think, if that agree,
> Which I intend,
> Unto my friends intent and end.
> I would not use a friend, as I use thee.

Three subsequent stanzas list the virtues of his behaviour towards his friends, virtues which are turned on their head as markers of sinfulness when not extended to God (care for a friend's credit points up his contrasting blasphemy; money is loaned to a friend, not the poor; a friend is helped to a proper place, not God). As the speaker realizes this, each stanza ends with a refrain whose principal change is an ever-less conditional (and ever-more damning) modal verb: 'I would not use a friend, as I use Thee', becomes 'I could not use a friend, as I use thee', becomes 'I cannot use a friend, as I use Thee', becomes 'Nor would I use a friend, as I use Thee'. The studied artlessness of this list accumulates material for the final overwhelming revelation that something quite other has been proved than how well the speaker treats his friends: *'Yet use I not my foes, as I use thee'*.

The third form of list Herbert uses, the action list, aims to flip the reader from a state of high anxiety and low agency to the opposite state. The affordances of such lists guard against entropy, changing the behaviour of those who use them. Lyne, taking a theory of mind approach to ask how believers

---

[77] Fish, *Living Temple*, 26–29, 32–34, 38–39; R. Lyne, 'Reading for Evidence of Faith in Herbert's Poems', *Review of English Studies*, 71 (2020), 78–83; S. Read, *Eucharist and the Poetic Imagination in Early Modern England* (Cambridge: Cambridge University Press, 2013), 102–104.

158   LISTING

could interrogate themselves for reliable signs of salvation, points out that 'the believer was meant to be highly receptive to the meaning of nuances in their thought processes, but also robustly practical in moulding these processes'.[78] He mentions spiritual autobiography and meditation as two practical methods to reform the self. Lists, I would argue, are a third, where Smyth's history of shredded books meets Lyne's cognitive literary study.

Before the reader enters the body of *The Temple*, 'The Church-porch' has already recommended making such action charts: 'Summe up at night, what thou hast done by day;/ And in the morning, what thou hast to do'. As John E. Booty argues, much of 'The Church-porch' echoes catalogues used to examine the conscience when preparing to take communion, voiced in brisk segments of two or three lines (as also in 'Charms and Knots').[79] Helen Wilcox notes how early readers were impressed with the action-oriented advice of 'The Church-porch'.[80] For instance, the 184 lines from 'The Church-porch' cited by a 1662 pamphlet *The Way to be Rich* all endorse career-enhancing qualities like effort, self-control, and thrift.[81] The back of the first edition of *The Temple* provides an alphabetical index of the titles of the poems, rather than a table of contents. Given the relatively unenigmatic quality of many of these ('Prayer', 'The Priesthood', 'Providence'), there was some chance that the reader could use the collection as a spiritual directory of advice on how to act or think, to be consulted as occasion arose. By the 1656 edition, a tenth of the pages have been devoted to a table of topics referred to by the poems, to act as prompts in digesting and applying the contents, such as 'Beauty, how to be accounted of ... It is one of the Worlds baits ... It raiseth wit ... True Beauty where ... '.[82]

Modern readers, however, are more attracted by the lists of what cannot be done, thus voicing the theological complexities of *sola fide*. 'Love Unknown', 'The Thanksgiving', and 'The Holdfast' are registers of concrete actions, either of what God has done to the speaker (in the first poem, his heart is scrubbed, boiled, and pricked), or what the speaker intends to do in return for God (in the other two poems he will weep blood, submit to be scourged, sing hymns, give alms, be celibate or dedicate his family to God; obey God's laws, trust in God, admit that trust comes from God). Such realistic details are a list-maker's

[78] Lyne, 'Evidence of Faith', 80.
[79] J. E. Booty, 'George Herbert: *The Temple* and *The Book of Common Prayer*', *Mosaic*, 12 (1979), 78–79.
[80] Herbert, *Poems*, ed. Wilcox, 48–49.
[81] R. Anselment, 'Seventeenth-Century Adaptations of "The Church-porch"', *GHJ*, 5/1–2 (1981–1982), 66–68.
[82] Herbert, *Temple* (1656), I2r.

3 HERBERT'S 'DONE' AND 'TO DO' LISTS   159

mode of self-regulation, encouraging the will to resolve on actions which are small enough and clear enough to be credibly doable.[83]

As with the other types of list, the points in these three poems are divided off by repeated words ('Shall I weep blood .../ Shall I be scourged .../ Shall I then sing .../ If thou does give me wealth .../ If thou dost give me honour ... ' of 'The Thanksgiving'), or refrains ('Your heart was foul/hard/dull, I fear', 'Indeed, 'tis true', 'I sigh to say/tell/speak' of 'Love Unknown'), or parallel syntax ('I will do' [verb], 'Then will I' [verb]') of 'The Holdfast'). Belknap notes how such lists join and separate their individual units with these conjunctions and repetitions, each item having meaning in itself and also taking meaning from its position in the whole.[84] Such structures should give their speakers (and readers) the momentum to undergo the process of being organized, as their compilers pose as street-level bureaucrats, accommodating an ideal form to a real-life situation. As, too, in the case of self-contracts, these to-do lists offer the excitement of making some clear resolutions to structure a new life (though the need for them also hints that there is a fear that there may be some backsliding in the future).

In 'The Method', for instance, a fault-detection system prompts action when the speaker finds that he cannot contact God directly: 'There is some rub, some discontent,/ Which cools his will'. First, the speaker assesses the other party's receiving equipment, and finds all is well: God 'could' and 'would' help (he has the power and the love to do so), on his side. The tone is dispassionate: this is simply a situation whose parts need analysis, followed by action. Then the speaker turns to his own register (the 'book' of his heart), finding a two-part list of technical reasons for the problems. 'What do I see/ Written above there?' and 'But stay! what's there?' The glitches turn out to be careless prayer and ignoring a godly motion, with the same obvious result in each case (why should God bother, if the person praying does not). The analysis is ticked off in each case by the same rhetorical question of 'And should Gods eare' be open. The poem concludes briskly with the equally obvious and necessary action: 'Then once more pray:/ Down with thy knees, up with thy voice'.

David Leverenz suggests Protestants sought to make themselves into obsessive compulsives (the contrary impulse to how we deal with this mental health problem). They constantly ordered experience into a proper pattern. Ambivalent or complex situations were tidied up into binary opposites, rather than being left to provoke a painful state of doubt. There were typical expressions

---

[83] D. Birke, 'The World is Not Enough: Lists as Encounters with the "Real" in the Eighteenth-Century Novel', *Style*, 50 (2016), 303–306.
[84] Belknap, *List*, 15.

160   LISTING

of this desire for clarity: a preoccupation with what 'should' happen, much compulsive ordering, a fear of dirt, a pleasure in rigid order, a ready recourse to external authorities, and a zeal for exact distinctions. A literature of polarization, repetition, and reversal emerged, in forms which defended against guilt, inadequacy, and resentment. Relentless self-observation and categorization along such binaries were expressed in catalogues of personal sinfulness. Zealous writers, Leverenz observes, might be witty when they found providential meaning in new interpretations of scripture, but they were rarely willing to be humorous by maintaining two views of a situation at once.[85]

Herbert, however, is exceptionally able at trying for certainty while admitting a state of doubt—and seeing the comedy in doing so. In 'Affliction' (1), for instance, he carefully itemizes, in writing, the terms of his engagement in the service of God: 'When first thou didst entice to thee my heart .../ So many joyes I writ down for my part', then equally carefully lists their failure, as health, friends, and work all give out. He is left in doubt, to 'reade, and sigh, and wish I were a tree' (an off-the-wall suggestion which laughs at his own perplexity). Sometimes, poems undercut the speaker's enthusiastic 'to do' lists with God's sardonic assurance that the items have already been ticked off. The reversals may not even be held over to the end of the poems, but come at the end of each proposed action. In 'Love Unknown', the speaker keeps offering his heart in good faith, and is horrified and bewildered about its apparent mistreatment, until a friend briefly points out the lesson of each stage. In 'The Holdfast', the speaker tries to respond in kind to each instance of God's goodness, but his assurance gives way to mounting alarm as each of his suggestions is immediately prevented, so he stands 'amaz'd'. In 'The Thanksgiving', a programme of sixteen separate actions (reported halfway through to be an attempt to 'Copie' Christ's own list) is let run down of its own accord, uninterrupted, as the speaker counters each idea himself. Moreover, the monologue points up the speaker's dwindling confidence that his brainstorming will ever work: for 'thy passion—But of that anon,/ When with the other I have done', and 'Then for thy passion—I will do for that—/ Alas, my God, I know not what'.

The double vision of the doctrine of faith alone is both a problem and its solution, producing genial self-mockery, Strier points out, as when 'A true Hymne' says 'if th'heart be moved' but can only sigh 'O, could I love! and stops: God writeth, Loved'.[86] However, what appreciating the presence of pragmatic lists of such poems as 'The Holdfast', 'Love Unknown', and 'The

---

[85] Leverenz, *Puritan Feeling*, 3–18.
[86] Strier, *Love Known*, 66–73.

Thanksgiving' does is point out how the poems' humour comes not just from the sophisticated irony arising from prevenient grace (which makes it clear that the speakers' actions are irrelevant), but also from a sort of clowning. The would-be worker *keeps* taking an eager run-up to an action or clarification, and *keeps* being tripped up by some tart note that 'to have nought is ours, not to confesse/ That we have nought'. Henri Bergson argued that onlookers laugh when a person shows themselves to be inflexible in thinking or acting, as the graceful energy of animate beings drains away, leaving them mere material, rigid or mechanical.[87] In the case of Herbert's 'action' poems, caricatural figures compile what turn out to be pointless lists of actions to remove doubt about their situation. By contrast, their concluding—reformed—souls know 'not what' to do or 'wot'. Being thus 'amaz'd' and 'much troubled', rather than clear about what they can do or understand themselves, becomes their distinguishing mark of grace. Such a bureaucratic approach to creating a saved self (self-regulation by authoritative listing) tries to make salvation thinkable and actionable, to cope with a situation in which readers could feel overwhelmed and inadequate. Occluding the awe-inspiring facts of *sola fide* and predestination, such lists give something, at least, that could be ticked off, even if the last item on the list would be the 'etcetera' of waiting for God's grace to complete the actions to make them valid.

It is, as Eva von Contzen says, 'remarkable that such a simple formal element [as the list] can elicit ... feelings of control and security (the world is in order) or, on the contrary, insecurity and fear (of that which we cannot grasp, in size and number)'.[88] The ubiquitous lists in Herbert's poems—there variously to expand on divine plenitude, redefine life events, or bring an action to mind—create powerful nudges, all the more so for appearing so unassuming.

[87] H. Bergson, *Laughter: An Essay on the Meaning of the Comic*, trans. C. Brereton and F. Rothwell (1911; New York: Dover Publications, 2013), 13–14, 21–25, 31–32, 89–90.

[88] E. von Contzen, 'Experience, Affect, and Literary Lists', *Partial Answers: Journal of Literature and the History of Ideas*, 16/2 (2018), 324.

6

Working to a Conclusion

1 The Duty to Endure Work

At Little Gidding the Chief is contemptuous of fictions starring noble heroes who show a 'hatred & contempt of Laborious Imployments, which hath cut the sinews of industry & brought in Idlenes as the Perfection of a brave spirit So that theres no shame … like to the Earning of a mans bread by the work of his hands'.[1] The Affectionate at first is equally as austere about the need for 'continual Imployment' in order to leave no time for 'Envy, Pride, vanitee, wrath, malice, and all other fleshly lusts and desires'. But she then adds a surprisingly positive note: work can be personally enjoyable because in doing it 'theres exercize of Invention, of Composition, of Order, and of all the other excellent operations of the Soule, and the Beauty, and Pleasure, and other good effects that arise from these Imployments. And herein lies our delight, not in the things themselves'.[2]

This seems like a startlingly original sidestep away from the impasse created by the doctrine of *sola fide*: God's grace inspires all good work, so the absence of good works can be a sign of a depraved soul, yet any effort to perform these without this grace would be irrelevant or even impious. Article 13 of the Thirty-nine Articles, 'Of Works before Justification', terrifyingly declares that

> works done before the grace of Christ, and the Inspiration of his Spirit, are not pleasant to God, forasmuch as they spring not of faith in Jesus Christ, neither do they make men meet to receive grace, or (as the School-authors say) deserve grace of congruity: yea, rather, for that they are not done as God hath willed and commanded them to be done, we doubt not but they have the nature of sin.

By thinking of work as an affective rather than instrumental activity, one which produces pleasure and creativity rather than goods and services, the

---

[1] Williams, ed., *Conversations*, 92.
[2] Sharland, ed., *Little Gidding*, 134, 169.

George Herbert and the Business of Practical Piety. Ceri Sullivan, Oxford University Press.
© Ceri Sullivan (2024). DOI: 10.1093/9780198906841.003.0006

Affectionate edges herself into a position to work from, without falling into the heresy of supererogation. In fact, there is a precedent for her approach, though not one which tends to get acknowledged by our own, largely dour, commentary about representations of work in early modern fiction.

This chapter looks first at how the Affectionate's second argument echoes advice in practical theology and in secular occupational manuals on the necessity of nudging oneself into engaging in work whole-heartedly. Both groups of texts are keen to show their readers how to do the emotional work to make a task enjoyable. Such a celebratory tone is worth dwelling on as it is in stark contrast to the way early modern representations of work are usually considered by today's literary critics, variously aghast at the implications of Article 13 and the inequities of the labour market. This more positive context (including that of the secular texts, which Herbert scholarship mostly overlooks) makes it clearer why, although Herbert dismisses the 'worky-daies' as 'the back-part' where 'the burden of the week' lies, 'Making the whole to stoup and bow' ('Sunday'), he is at his happiest when busiest. He sounds irritated as much as anxious when kept idle, as he repeatedly tries to nudge God to choose to work through him.

Calvin distinguishes between the categories of the general vocation (that of all Christians, to follow Christ's commands) and the particular vocation (that of each individual Christian, to work in the particular office in which God has placed them). He presents the particular vocation as a corollary of election: a situation in life assigned by God, which may only be changed at the direct and clear prompting of the Spirit. Each person, says Calvin, is given a 'sentry post so that he may not heedlessly wander about throughout life'.[3] Early modern divinity reflects this approach: labours are duties exacted both by reason and by scriptural law. Results are granted or denied solely at God's discretion. The first sermon on good works in the second Book of Homilies (1563) starts with reasons to do them: to obey God's command to perform them, to show oneself justified, and to encourage others in them. The homily against idleness in the same book points out that God's will on the matter is shown both in scriptural injunctions to work and in 'the nature of man', which makes it necessary to labour for oneself and for others.[4] 'God loveth adverbs better than adjectives', says William Loe (pastor of the English company of

---

[3] J. Calvin, *Institutes of the Christian Religion* (1559), ed. J. T. McNeill, trans. F. L. Battles, 2 vols. (London: SCM Press, 1960), 2.724.

[4] J. Griffiths, ed., *The Two Books of Homilies Appointed to be Read in Churches* (Oxford: Clarendon Press, 1859), 280, 516.

164   WORKING TO A CONCLUSION

Merchant Adventurers at Hamburg).[5] For Robert Bagnall (minister at Hutton, Somerset) God requires 'painfull labour in … [one's] vocation'. 'Husbandmen, Artificers, Trades-men, and all other workemen of occupation and labourers whatsoever are Stewards, and ought trustily, and not deceitfully; diligently, and not idly labour and take paine early and late'.[6] Work is a punishment, as the godly surveyor John Norden points out: humanity is marked with Genesis's 'Motto or Poesy of our shame: "With the sweat of thy face thou shalt eat thy bread, all the days of thy life"'.[7]

Adriano Tilgher has pithily characterized the figure of the labourer in such texts—working in the world but not of it—as an 'anchorite of the marketplace'.[8] Of course, it was often difficult to keep up this high-minded determination to convert time to good use. Though Wallington, for instance, was clear that his occupation of wood turner was his calling, he frequently felt 'murmuring and discontent' with how doing it interrupted his formal devotions. He strove to be 'diligent, faithful, and cheerful' at his job, yet 'Many times … I have gone down to my shop with these thoughts and holy resolutions: now will I go about earthly things with an heavenly inside', but 'when I come down, all this is forgot … and I begin to be a dead man again'.[9]

There were a number of negative remedies to ensure a worker engaged with this painful duty. Occasional meditations could bookend spells of work, isolated and allocated in a form of mental accounting as devout moments created from small fragments of leisure.[10] Prayers could be said before the day's work, as a commitment strategy. Those published for servants and apprentices often confess a temptation to perform mere 'eie-service' (working only when supervised) or evasion, so ask to be made enthusiastic, to work with a 'cheereful wilingnes'. 'Take sloth from my fingers, and drowsinesse from the lids of mine eye; whether I rise early, or lie downe late, so gladly let me doe it, as if my prentiship were to bee consumed in thy seruice', petitions Thomas Dekker's apprentice, while Norden's servant dwells on his duty to work 'cheerefully and

---

[5] W. Loe, *The Merchant Reall* (1620), 25.

[6] R. Bagnall, *The Stewards Last Account* (1622), 28–29. See also W. Holbrooke, *A Sermon Preached Before the Antient Company of Black-smiths in S. Marie Magdalens Church in London* (1612), 15 ff; Bernard, *Weekes Worke*, 95.

[7] J. Norden, *The Surveyor's Dialogue (1618): A Critical Edition*, ed. M. Netzloff (Farnham: Ashgate, 2010), 7, quoting Genesis 3.9 and citing the doctrine of *sola fide*.

[8] A. Tilgher, *Work: What It Has Meant to Men Through the Ages*, trans. D. C. Fisher (London: George Harrap, 1931), 57.

[9] Seaver, *Wallington's World*, 124–125.

[10] M-L. Coolahan, 'Redeeming Parcels of Time: Aesthetics and Practice of Occasional Meditation', *The Seventeenth Century*, 22 (2007), 124–125, 127. On mental accounting, see Thaler and Sunstein, *Nudge*, 49–52.

hartily'.[11] I. C.'s servant asks for grace 'faithfully to execute' his masters' commands: 'let mee neuer entertaine a thought to wrong them, but deale truely and vprightly in whatsoeuer they shall commit to my charge ... let me be studious and diligent to dispatch what they shall appoint mee to do.'[12] Another tactic was to consider the alternative choices. A collection of precepts purporting to be by Sir William Cecil focuses on disagreeable affect: 'continuall ease, as it is more dangerous, is more wearisome then labour, and it is no freedome to live licentiously, nor pleasure to live without some paine'.[13] Bagnall warns about the danger of taking the route of idleness: Satan, like a crab, 'when he seeth the Oyster lye gaping against the Sunne-beames, privily stealeth upon him, and putteth a pibble into the mouth of the Oyster, and so getteth out the fish, and leaveth nothing behind him but the shell'.[14] Appealing to the observer effect was another effective nudge.[15] Abraham Jackson addresses apprentices who think 'the thing commanded [by their master] be not agreeable to their birth or breeding, [and] will either not doe it at all; or if they doe, it will be so unseasonably, and in so ill a manner, as it would have beene better they had never meddled with it'. He recommends that they 'imagine that [they] see every where written in capital letters, *CAVE, DEUS VIDET*'.[16]

2 A Duty to Enjoy Work?

Early modern practical divinity, however, does not discuss work solely in terms of the pincer formed by Article 13 on one side and divine commands on the other ('damned if you do and damned if you don't'). Although the curse put on Adam makes work a duty, the original functions of work in Eden are still seen as a possibility: as a pleasant and wholesome discipline, and as an expression of divine activity in creation. Workers are primed with concrete images of how God himself undertook human work. For instance, Donne, Norden, Loe, and William Holbrooke (curate of St Andrew Hubbard, London) speak of how God was, at various times, a leather-worker (clothing Adam), a shipwright

---

[11] T. Dekker, *Foure Birds of Noahs Arke* (1609), first page series, 9, 11; J. Norden, *A Pensive Soules Delight Or, the Devout Mans Helpe* (1615), 276, 279. See also Habermann, *The Princes Prayers*, 346–351, 367–372.

[12] I. C., *The Ever-burning Lamps of Pietie and Devotion ... Heavenly Prayers* (1619), 142–144.

[13] W. Cecil, *Directions for the Well Ordering ... of a Mans Life* (1636), 21–22. On how loss aversion influences judgements, see Thaler and Sunstein, *Nudge*, 34, 85, 122–123.

[14] Bagnall, *Account*, 28–29.

[15] On the spotlight effect, see Thaler and Sunstein, *Nudge*, 60–62.

[16] Jackson, *Pious Prentice*, 74, A12r.

166 WORKING TO A CONCLUSION

(teaching Noah), and a carpenter (apprenticed to Joseph).[17] Christ's parables give authority for valuing secular as well as devotional toil, thinks Daniel Price (rector of Wiston, Sussex), citing the husbandman who prunes and dresses his vines, the labourer worthy of his hire, the builder who puts in foundations, the farmer sowing grain, the fishermen casting nets, the merchant valuing a pearl, and so on.[18] Loe finds this encouraging: 'were I a marchant, & did see, & heare Christ resembling his kingdome to my vocation. I should conceive veary highe thoughts of it'.[19] Work is proverbially described as an opportunity to cooperate with providence: 'when the Marriners see a tempest approching, first they call uppon God, that they may arrive safelie in the Haven, then they take in their sayles, and do what is to be done: so we must rely upon the divine providence, but so, that wee also use our own labour and industry'.[20] There is talk of enjoying appropriate remuneration: Immanuel Bourne (preacher at St Christopher-le-Stocks, London) inspires merchants with the thought that they 'performe that service which is acceptable to God, and may expect with joyfulnesse a blessing from him', such as being able both to provide for their families and to be more widely charitable (see Figure 6.1).[21]

Workers are eager to find themselves eager to work, for, as Article 12 ('Of good works') says, such works are 'pleasing and acceptable to God in Christ, and do spring out necessarily of a true and lively faith, insomuch that by them a lively faith may be as evidently known as a tree discerned by its fruit'.[22] The 'Sermon of Good Works Annexed unto Faith' in the first Book of Homilies (1559) describes the difference between these works and those done without faith as a matter of liveliness and deadness: the latter are 'dead before God', are like a 'picture graven or painted' which is only a 'dead representation of the thing itself ... without life or any manner of moving', and are 'but shadows and shews of lively and good things'. It cites Chrysostom on how those people 'which glister and shine in good works without faith in God be like dead men, which have godly and precious tombs'.[23]

---

[17] J. Donne, *A Sermon ... to the Honourable Company of the Virginian Plantation* (1622), 2–3; Loe, *Merchant Reall*, 22–23; Holbrooke, *Black-smiths*, 16; Norden, *Surveyor's Dialogue*, 8; A. Williams, *The Common Expositor: An Account of the Commentaries on Genesis, 1527–1633* (Chapel Hill: University of North Carolina Press, 1948), 109–111. On priming, see Thaler and Sunstein, *Nudge*, 69–73.

[18] D. Price, *The Marchant. A Sermon Preached at Paules Cross ... the Day Before Bartholomew Fair* (1608), A2r.

[19] Loe, *Merchant Reall*, A2v.

[20] F. Meres, 'Labour', in *Palladis tamia. Wits Treasury being the Second Part of Wits Common Wealth* (1598), Y3r–Y4v.

[21] I. Bourne, *The Godly Mans Guide* (1620), 28. See also Calvin, *Institutes*, 1.821.

[22] B. Cummings, ed., *The Book of Common Prayer. The Texts of 1549, 1559, and 1662* (Oxford: Oxford University Press, 2011), 677.

[23] *Homilies*, 48, 51–52.

2 A DUTY TO ENJOY WORK? 167

Figure 6.1 John Parkinson, *Paradisi in sole paradisus terrestris. A Garden of all Sorts of Pleasant Flowers ... with A Kitchen garden ... and An Orchard* (1656), Bodleian Library, University of Oxford, R2.10 Med, title page.

168   WORKING TO A CONCLUSION

The focus is on affect: feeling lively, joyful, cheerful, hopeful, acceptable, and fiery is a sign of faith. Noticing such a sign in oneself will naturally create yet more pleasing feelings, a virtuously cheerful circle discussed in Martin Luther's *Treatise of Good Works*. The first good work is faith in Christ. After securing this, then it becomes possible, as Ecclesiastes 9.7 says, to do all other works gladly, 'to eat thy bread with joy and drink thy wine with a cheerful heart: for God now accepteth thy works'. 'This faythe dothe brynge with her charyte & peace, so doth she joy and hope'. 'In this fayth, al works be made lyke and equall', and in doing them 'it is delyte and pleasure ... to please God well', whereas works without faith cause one to feel 'payne, doubtfulness, indygnacyon and sorowe ... werynesse and labour'.[24] Luther's popular commentary on Galatians (published in English eight times between 1575 and 1644) takes up the topic. It caricatures Catholics as noisily indignant about how 'a husband, a wife, a Prince, a governour, a master, a scholer ... an hireling or drudge bearing sackes, ... a wench sweeping the house, ... be accepted as better and more worthy before God' than those who rely on formal acts of devotion to save them.[25] By contrast, the truly godly soul expresses its faith in Christ in all secular occupations, and such faith produces laudable joy: 'God loueth not heauines and doulfulnes of spirite: he hateth vncomfortable doctrine, heauy and sorowfull cogitations, and loueth chearfull hearts ... The heart inwardly reioyceth through faith in Christ ... and outwardly it expresseth this ioy with wordes and gestures'.[26] Gustaf Wingren argues this turns a job into an ethical agent, one which can call out laudable qualities in its holder, regardless of the latter's initial interest or personal characteristics, if engaged in fully.[27] A vocation becomes a cognitive environment which creates a godly worker, among its other products.

Even while ostensibly advising their readers to enter into a particular vocation in a mood of resignation to the will of God, moderate English divines retain the idea of taking pleasure in doing the work. Admittedly, Perkins dismisses 'mens owne fancies' in finding special jobs to do as 'will-worship, whereby men thrust upon God their own inventions for his service'. He also brushes aside 'papist' arguments about there being only certain types of works

---

[24] M. Luther, *A Propre Treatyse of Good Works* (1520), trans. anon (1535), biiiv–bivr, bvv, bvir.
[25] M. Luther, *A Commentarie ... Upon the Epistle of S. Paul to the Galathians* [sic], trans. anon. (1575), 142v.
[26] Luther, *Galathians*, 261v. A spirit of joy could be a proof of salvation. See A. Potkay, 'Spenser, Donne, and the Theology of Joy', *Studies in English Literature, 1500–1900*, 46/1 (2006), 43–66.
[27] G. Wingren, *Luther on Vocation* (1957), trans. C. Rasmussen (Eugene, Oregon: Wipf and Stock, 2004), 6–9.

which could be accounted as good: 'the building of Churches, and Hospitals, the mending of high waies, giving of large alms, etc' (the tasks listed in Herbert's 'The Thanksgiving').[28] Nor does Perkins dispute the impossibility of doing enough to earn salvation. In a lengthy concluding passage in his treatise on the vocation, he takes up the metaphor of accounting: blessings and gifts are billed as receipts, sins as expenses, and good works are the balance, to be paid over to God at the 'triall of every mans worke' at death. However, he concludes, we will never be able to give 'an even reckoning with God' without using Christ as 'suretie'. Only then can 'we have assurance in our consciences, that the bookes in heaven are cancelled, and that God is content to account of Christ his satisfaction, as a paiment for our sins.'[29]

Yet despite these warnings, Perkins also considers that the particularities of an individual's tastes, abilities, and situation should be taken into account. There is a humanist slant to this assumption that work completes and corrects nature.[30] Since enjoying a job is a sign that 'that is his calling; because he liketh it best, and is everie way the fittest for it', Perkins suggests giving children toy tools to discern their bent by seeing what they like playing with.[31] He also dwells on the comfortable assurance of faith which good words provide: 'this is one of the chiefest uses of good works, that by them, not as by causes, but as by effects of predestination and Faith, both we, and also our neighbours, are certified of our election.'[32]

In 1630 John Preston, master of Emmanuel College, Cambridge, delivered eighteen sermons on the topic of good works, amplifying Perkins's positive slant. Preston endorses a pleasurable zeal in approaching jobs, not 'as a hard taske, whereof you could willingly be excused', but with a 'heart inflamed to walke in them, as a loving wife, that needes not to be bidden to doe this, or that, but if the doing of it may advantage her Husband, it will be a greater griefe to her to let them lye undone, than to labour to doe them'. The regenerate soul 'is ready ... to every good worke, it is nimble and ready to goe about them'. Each person will then act with 'naturalnesse and readinesse', 'as the fire is carried upwards, and not as stones are carried upwards with the force of another' 'readilie and chearfullie', with a 'burning desire in your hearts, longing

---

[28] W. Perkins, *A Godly and Learned Exposition of Christs Sermon in the Mount* (1608), 59, 60, 63.
[29] Perkins, *Vocations*, 119 ff.
[30] Tilgher, *Work*, 72–78, citing comments by Tommaso Campanella, Giordano Bruno, Marsilio Ficino, and Leon Battista Alberti. See also I. M. Veldman, 'Representations of Labour in Late Sixteenth-Century Netherlandish Prints: The Secularization of the Work Ethic', in J. Ehmer and C. Lis, eds., *The Idea of Work in Europe from Antiquity to Modern Times* (London: Ashgate, 2009), 149–175.
[31] Perkins, *Vocations*, 41–42.
[32] W. Perkins, *A Case of Conscience the Greatest Taht* [sic] *There Ever Was, How a Man May Know, Whether He Be the Son of God or No* (1592), 68.

after' good works. The very desire to act allows its possessor to feel comfortably assured of justification: 'there is an aptness in it to doe good workes, so that now a man delighteth in the Law of God ... he desires nothing more then to be employed in it'. We are made fit to labour by God: 'he is the workeman, we are the materials, as the clay, and the wood, that he takes into his hands ... it is Gods worke to cast us into a new Mould'. Our good works show we have 'not a dead, liveless, workelesse faith, but a powerfull, energeticall faith, a faith that is stirring and active, a faith that is effectuall'. Even 'the very ordinary workes of our Calling, ordinary things to men, ordinary service from day to day, if it come from faith ... are good workes indeed'.

Preston builds to the same conclusion as does the Affectionate in Little Gidding: working should be an enjoyable activity. 'What is it that a man serves for in all his labour under the Sunne? What is it that he desires but pleasure, comfort and contentment? Now, my brethren, this consists in doing, in working, for all pleasure followeth upon operation, and further than there is working there is no delight'. 'Even as light followeth the flame, so pleasure and contentment followeth action'. Moreover, 'the beauty in good works' is evident: 'how goodly a sight is it when a man looks into the husbandry, to see the vine full of clusters, to see the furrowes full of corne, to see the trees laden with fruite; when we looke upon men, it is the goodliest sight we can behold in Gods husbandry, to see men full of actions and good workes'.[33]

On the secular side, too, imaginative effort is put into priming labourers (regardless of what job they do) with positive images. Workers do not always feel engaged or disposed to engage with others, and 'It cannot but bee distastfull to any man, comming into a Shop, when he sees a man stand as if hee were drown'd in flegme and puddle; having no other testimony of his being awake, than that his eyes are open', Scott reminds the trader.[34] So, as in the practical divinity, a second order of work is recognized, of working at being enthusiastic at work.[35] Browne advises the factor to remember the incentive: 'If either of goodwill or necessity thou must doe a thing, see thou do it gladly & cheerfully: for so shall thy gift be well accepted, & thy labour and cost neuer a whit the more'.[36] Thomas Powell's book about how to choose occupations for children recommends that their dispositions be studied, since they will take delight in

---

[33] J. Preston, *The Breast-plate of Faith and Love ... As They Are Expressed in Good Workes* (1630), 24, 40, 60, 71, 84, 95, 128–129, 205, 206, 207.

[34] Scott, *Citizen*, 85, 127–128.

[35] On emotional labour at work, see A. R. Hochschild, *The Managed Heart: Commercialization of Human Feeling* (1983; Berkeley: University of California Press, 2012), 1–40.

[36] Browne, *Avizo*, 62. On incentives, see Thaler and Sunstein, *Nudge*, 99–102.

2 A DUTY TO ENJOY WORK? 171

what they do best, and vice versa (as Perkins had done).[37] Fitzherbert wants the farmer to marry his job: 'sith then thou art in such large chaines bound unto the Earths bridall, close not the closets of thine eyes with sloth'; 'when thou seekest to plant thine affection immovelesse uppon husbandry, and ... the Earths profitable beautie, first learne her nature and disposition'; to 'wooe with the best discretion' keep 'enamored' of the Earth, in order to receive from her 'wombe a well-pleasing living'.[38]

Literary critics who find a prevailing heroic register in early modern fictions about merchants and craftsmen largely consider that this comes from a social reluctance to value trade on its own terms, causing writers to reach for features of the romance instead.[39] One might instead argue, following Thorstein Veblen, that work is in essence a heroic effort to impose an individual's will onto resistant or passive material, either raw materials (in low status occupations) or other people (in high status ones).[40] Early modern occupational manuals anticipate Veblen's thesis when they speak of work as a form of control over materials, information, and other people, across a range of economic sectors and job positions within each sector.

For instance, starting with extraction and manufacture, the influential Jesuit economist Giovanni Botero praises how 'Art doth contend and strive with nature' in imposing form on matter. 'Such a wealth there is in Art and Industry, that neither the mynes of Silver, nor the mynes of gold in Nova Hispania nor in Peru, can be compared with it'. He celebrates the labour and skill exerted in each stage of production of different commodities: in processing wool into cloth (carding it, picking it over, spinning it, warping it, weaving it, dyeing it, fulling it, thickening it, cutting it, then sewing it), in producing silk (a process that 'makes the very excrement of a base and baggage worme, hyghly esteemd with Princes'), in smithing (mining iron ore, scouring it, melting it, forging it, casting it, and then selling it to the many industries that require tools), and in fashioning wood ('compare Tymber with the Gallies, Galliownes, Ships ... carved Images, furnitures of house and other things without count' that are made with it).[41] A treatise on the manufacturing possibilities of the Virginian

---

[37] Powell, *Tom of All Trades*, 5–6.

[38] Fitzherbert, *Husbandrie*, 1, 2, 3.

[39] An approach dating from C. Camp, *The Artisan in Elizabethan Literature* (New York: Columbia University Press, 1924), 13–24, and L. C. Stevenson, *Praise and Paradox: Merchants and Craftsmen in Elizabethan Popular Literature* (Cambridge: Cambridge University Press, 1984), 1–8, 77–91, 107–130.

[40] T. Veblen, *The Theory of the Leisure Class: An Economic Study of Institutions* (1899), ed. M. Banta (Oxford: Oxford University Press, 2007), 8 ff., 55 ff. See also Tilgher, *Work*, 95–98, 131–139, 145–147.

[41] G. Botero, *Concerning the Causes of the Magnificencie and Greatnes of Cities* (1588), trans. R. Peterson (1606), 48–51.

172   WORKING TO A CONCLUSION

plantation, by the Keeper of Silkworms at Whitehall, John Bonoeil, ends with a personified Nature in raptures:

> What should I speake of the store of Timber, so necessary for your buildings, and other uses? for Clapboard, Pipe-staves, and other rich wood for noble services? or of the abundant store of wood, never to be spent, for your Iron workes? and for your Glass Furnaces now set up? for Pot-ashes and Sope-ashes? for boyling of Sugars? ... I cannot, I confesse, conceal the pride I take in my Virginia.

It is this which distinguishes the immigrants from the 'native Savages ... [who] know no industry, no Arts, no culture, nor no good use of this blessed Country heere, but are ... an unprofitable burthen onely of the earth' (and so, Bonoeil concludes blandly, can be deemed merely another natural resource ready for exploitation, as 'naturally borne slaves').[42]

Turning from making to trading, a merchant and Husband of the Levant Company, Lewis Roberts, sees a poetry in such work. Of the merchant's expertise, he comments that

> his art may be compared to the Poets, whose excellency must consist in a cursory judgement in all sciences, and to be learned in all professions, the difference being that the Merchants skill must be reall, solid and substantiall, and the Poets may be fained and poeticall.

The trader's 'skill and inspection must be such, that it extend it selfe from the commodities belonging to the meanest artificer, to the commodities belonging to the most eminent shop-keeper', continues Roberts, reaching from a 'low and close Cellerage' to the 'high and airy warehouses'. 'With the fisherman', for instance, 'he must dive into the deep and know all sorts of merchantable fish, as ling, codde, haberdine, herings, pilchards, salmon, eeles, how caught and how preserved, and the proper season for the same'. 'Neither is it sufficient that a Merchant doe know how to preserve his wares and Commodities in their first splendor, goodnesse, and vertue, but ... [his] skill must extend, if possible, to give ... [them] new vigour, life, strength, and beautie'.[43] This is what London's annual Lord Mayor's show impressed on its viewers, with its wagons of task-scapes full of vigorous and expert activity, not just displays of the products of

---

[42] J. Bonoeil, *His Majesties Gracious Letter to the Earle of South-Hampton, Treasurer, and to the Councell and Company of Virginia* (1622), 83–84, 85–86.
[43] L. Roberts, *The Merchants Mappe of Commerce* (1638), 42–44.

2 A DUTY TO ENJOY WORK? 173

such industry.[44] In 1614 the Drapers staged a hill of clothing with shepherds, carders, spinners, and weavers working on it (a device copied in 1620 by the Haberdashers); in 1617 the Grocers featured workers gathering and bagging spices; in 1618 the Blacksmiths showed Mulcibar and Cyclops at forges, 'nimble and dexterious youths, such as to the continuall fall of their Hammers, in sweet Musicall voyces, and delicate variety of pleasing changes; doe out-weare their work merrily, accounting no toyle tedious'; in 1619 the Skinners set out a wilderness full of furry beasts, waiting to be trapped.[45]

A similar and popular priming image is of the interdependent community of labour. Markham praises how 'the labour of the Husbandman giveth liberty to all vocations, Arts, misteries, and trades, to follow their severall functions, with peace and industry'; this job is 'the great Nerve and Sinew which holdeth together all the joints of a Monarchie'.[46] John Browne, a Bristol merchant, writes celebratory verses on the mutuality of occupations around the clothing trade: the merchant buying material from the clothier, the clothier the services of the spinners, weavers, and shears-men, they the raw materials to work on from farmers, who in turn use labourers, bargemen, and carters, who also transport cloth to the merchants, who hire sailors to export it and to import goods, that are sold to all these workers by grocers, vintners, and mercers.[47] Gerard Malynes, the prolific economic writer, describes a royal banquet honouring representatives of the six principal classes of occupation (church ministers, noblemen, magistrates, merchants, artificers, and husbandmen), each of whom summarizes for the king 'in one only word ... the propertie of his profession or calling' in providing for the country.[48] Holbrooke lauds the work of the Company of Blacksmiths as underpinning most other industries (albeit less 'sweet and pleasant', and one, moreover, which makes its workers' less 'beautifull and fashionable'!).[49]

Mastery over information flows was valued as a core quality in the professions. The surveyor Thomas Clay, tracing the functions of an estate

---

[44] T. Hill, *Pageantry and Power: A Cultural History of the Early Modern Lord Mayor's Show, 1585–1639* (Manchester: Manchester University Press, 2011), 288–294; K. Northway, '"To kindle an industrious desire": The Poetry of Work in Lord Mayors' Shows', *Comparative Drama*, 41/2 (2007), 167–192.

[45] A. Munday, *Himatia-poleos the Triumphs of Old Drapery* (1614), 7; T. Middleton, *The Triumphs of Honor and Industry* (1617), A4v; A. Munday, *Sidero-thriambos, or Steele and Iron Triumphing* (1618), A4v–B1r; T. Middleton, *Triumphs of Love and Antiquity* (1619), B1v–B2r; J. Squire, *Tes irenes trophaea. Or, the Tryumphs of Peace* (1620), B3r–v.

[46] Markham, *Husbandman*, A3r.

[47] I. B. [J. Browne], *The Marchants Avizo. Very Necessarie for Their Sonnes and Seruants, When They First Send Them Beyond the Seas* (1589), A3r–v.

[48] G. Malynes, *Consuetudo, vel lex mercatoria, or the Ancient Law-merchant* (1622), 62.

[49] Holbrooke, *Black-smiths*, 38.

174 WORKING TO A CONCLUSION

management team, asks these 'officers of order' to see themselves as parts standing in for the whole, acting not on their own behalf (as 'natural' men), but as synecdoches of a system. The auditor of an estate, for instance, 'representeth the Lord his owne person' in being the end point of records from all other divisions; 'in his office, as in a maine stream or River, the effects of all the other, as the branches therof, doe concurre and are made manifest'.[50] These officers note down all details to give clarity and proof. The surveyor, for example, is to 'set downe and distinguish in his ... Bookes, the particular lands' of the estates, 'entering each ... orderly and severally', 'expressing the same orderly', so he can regulate the information streams, finding 'the errors which he may commit in platting of grounds, or casting up the contents, and amend the same, as also to prove the truth of his worke, and to give a reason thereof'. The household steward is 'to call to Accompt weekely, or at the most monethly, all the inferior Offices of expence', keeping 'faire and orderly Bookes ... entering in the same each particular, in his due and convenient place and under his proper title, that all things may appeare without confusion'. His auditor examines all records to ensure facts 'evidently appeare upon every occasion without confusion'.[51] There is strict control over the population of transactions. The merchant adventurer John Carpenter works with an ever-ready pen:

in the Memoriall, or Waste booke, must be written, daily, whatsoever passeth concerning Merchandizing ... without omission of any thing. In which booke any may write that is of Capacity, observing in their entries, the yeere, moneth, day, name, and Sir-name of the Merchant, the place of his dwelling, and of what faculty hee is: the kinde, quantity, and quality of the Wares bought, or received, sold, shipped, or delivered; the price, weight, measure, and Colour, the number, and marke; the Contract in buying and selling, be it for ready money or time, or in barter, and for what Accounts.[52]

The arduous dedication needed to acquire such knowledge is lauded. The Northampton physician John Cotta speaks of how his peers

most continually converseth with nature ... [and] dependeth upon the perpetuall study, view, & observation of nature, and the continual consultation

---

[50] T. Clay, *The Well Ordering, Disposing and Governing of an Honorable Estate or Revennue Briefely Describing the Duties of Divers Officers Therein* (1619), [38], 6. See also G. E. Aylmer, 'From Office-Holding to Civil Service: The Genesis of Modern Bureaucracy', *Transactions of the Royal Historical Society*, 30 (1980), 91–108; C. Sullivan, *Literature in the Public Service: Sublime Bureaucracy* (Basingstoke: Palgrave Macmillan, 2013), 12–19.

[51] Clay, *Estate*, 7, [9], 37, [38].

[52] J. Carpenter, *The Exact and Perfect Keeping Merchants Bookes of Accounts* (1632), 5.

with Nature in every action. For it is requisite in a competent Physition, that he be truly able & fully furnished to be unto nature a governor & moderator to preserve her, to conserve her, ... to dispose & guide her in her best and rightest way.[53]

He devotes to his profession 'long dayes and time carefully spent, indefatigable studie, paines and meditation, restlesse vigilance, a cleare eye of understanding, and sincere affection'.[54] John Fitzherbert makes a mock-modest 'protestation' that while he cannot assert his advice on husbandry is the best possible, it is the result of over forty years managing an estate.[55] 'If a workeman of any trade, or mistery, cannot give directions how, and in what manner, the tooles wherewith he worketh should be made or fashioned, doubtless hee shall never worke well with them, nor know when they are in temper and when out', says Gervase Markham, for 'a plough is to a Husbandman like an Instrument in the hand of a Musitian, which if it be out of tune can never make good Musicke'.[56] The London spice garbellers assert that their expertise relies on 'a habit of working according to right, reason, and mechanicall or a handicraft, the full knowledge thereof was partlie gotten by use ... and partly by instructions and reason'.[57] By contrast, those who do not value such experience are satirized. The surveyor Aaron Rathborne dismisses those who try to do-it-themselves,

> who having but once observed a Surveyor, by looking over his shoulder, how and in what manner he directs his sights, and drawes his lines thereon; they presently apprehend the businesse ... and within small time after, you shall heare them tell you wonders, and what rare feats they can performe.[58]

Wye Saltonstall's lawyer's clerk is another would-be, who wants to skip the hard part of getting mastery; he 'would fain read Littleton if he might have a comment on him, otherwise hee's too obscure, and dotes much on Wests Symboliography for teaching him the forme of an acquittance'.[59]

---

[53] J. Cotta, *A Short Discourse of the Unobserved Dangers ... of Ignorant and Unconsiderate Practisers of Physicke in England* (1612), 118. On the value placed on applied knowledge, see E. Ash, *Power, Knowledge, and Expertise in Elizabethan England* (Baltimore: Johns Hopkins University Press, 2004), 1–18.

[54] Cotta, *Physicke*, 120.

[55] Fitzherbert, *Husandrie*, 198–199.

[56] G. Markham, *The English Husbandman* (1613), B1v, C1v.

[57] 'Divers Grocers of London', *The Bad Garbelling of Spices, Used in these Daies* (1592), 3.

[58] A. Rathborne, *The Surveyor in Foure Bookes* (1616), A5v. See also Norden, *Surveyor's Dialogue*, 8–9.

[59] Preferring William West's primer of documents to Sir Thomas Littleton's thorough legal discussions from first principles. See W. Saltonstall, *Picturæ loquentes: or Pictures Drawne Forth in Characters* (1631), D4r.

Veblen speaks of the higher forms of work as an imposition of one's will over other people, as well as over material items. Occupational manuals suggest a variety of ways to encourage the right attitude. The German humanist Conrad Heresbach advises an estate's Bailiff to give employees priming images of the work to be done, and 'himselfe go lustily before [coworkers, so] ... they follow ... lustily with a courage, as if he were their captaine in a skirmish', and to 'use sundry devises to cheere them up in their labor, [such as] sometime to helpe him that fainteth, to take his toole out of his hand, & labour lustily before him'. 'We must remember that servants be men: besides, such good looking to, will breed a greater good will & dutie'.[60] In *The Country Parson* likewise, Herbert criticizes those who 'think, that servants for their money are as other things that they buy, even as a piece of wood, which they may cut, or hack, or throw into the fire, and so they pay them their wages, all is well'.[61] A master who comes home at night and checks whether his dogs have been fed but not his servants deserves the latter to be mere 'men-pleasers', for 'feare and fashion-sake' only pretending to work, argues Fosset.[62]

Thomas Deloney's popular biographies of the master clothier John Winchcombe ('Jack') of Newbury and shoemaker Simon Eyre of London provide models for how excellent masters can generate commitment among their work force. Eyre 'set many journey-men and prentises to work, who followed their businesse with great delight, which quite excludeth all wearinesse; for when servants do sit at their worke like Dromedaries, then their minds are never lightly upon their businesse'.[63] They sing at work like the cobblers in ballads, who warble of how 'We set our stitches just and straight .../ And doe our work without deceite'.[64] As apprentice and as master, Jack of Newbury is 'well knowne in all his countery for his good fellowship' as much as his skill and diligence.[65] His visitors are struck by the pay and on-site facilities for workers (Jack employs a butcher, a brewer, a baker, and four cooks), but even more by the cheerful *esprit de corps* of each functional group (quill-makers, carders, spinners and weavers), each with their own song and in-jokes.[66]

Managing upwards uses similar emotional intelligence to get a superior to engage. Francis Bacon suggests using distractions when an unpopular decision

---

[60] C. Heresbach, *The Whole Art of Husbandry*, trans. B. Googe (1577; 1657), 23, 24.
[61] Herbert, *Country Parson*, 265.
[62] Fosset, *Servants Dutie*, 44
[63] T. Deloney, *The Works*, ed. F. O. Mann (Oxford: Clarendon Press, 1912), 110.
[64] *Round Boyes Indeed. Or the Shoomakers Holy-day* (c.1632). See also *A Merry New Catch of All Trades* (c.1620); Camp, *Artisan*, 47–85.
[65] Deloney, *Works*, 3–4. Working hard and drinking hard were admired and interlinked aspects of artisan identity. See M. Hailwood, 'Sociability, Work, and Labouring Identity in Seventeenth-Century England', *Cultural and Social History*, 8/1 (2011), 9–29.
[66] Deloney, *Works*, 21, 31–32.

has to be made, bouncing superiors into answers before they are ready, pretending good will to projects to be foiled secretly, breaking off mid-sentence to elicit questions on a matter, suggesting an opinion is generally thought, burying difficult matter in a sub-clause, using lightweight colleagues to break bad news, arranging to be surprised into declaring an opinion, circulating ideas on the grapevine, suggesting plans by saying they are not to be thought of, winding to a point, and so on.[67] Robert Beale (clerk of the Privy Council) and Nicholas Faunt (clerk of the signet) give similar advice on recognizing and managing superiors' emotions (though never 'exceedinge the boundes of your calling and dutie'). For instance, Beale counsels that 'when her highness signeth, it shalbe good to entertaine her with some relacion or speech whereat she may take some pleasure.'[68]

The cheerful encouragement to work, in both religious and secular texts, needs to be kept in mind because most literary commentary is dispiritingly suspicious about whether anything good ever came out of the early modern workplace. Characteristically, representations of professionals (such as lawyers, officials, great merchants, secretaries, courtiers, and actors) are castigated for fighting for precedence, fictions about workers offering personal services (such as soldiers, servants, hosts, housewives, and whores) are read as focusing on their remnants of personal agency, and the dire effects of structural shifts in the economy (the move from feudal to wage labour and globalization) are exposed.[69]

3 Herbert Keeps Busy

In terms of tone, commentary on Herbert's poems about work is no exception to this gloomy critique, as it anxiously debates who (God? Herbert?) is producing what (ministerial good works? A godly self?), and rarely considers

---

[67] Bacon, 'Of Counsell', 'Of Cunning', in *Essayes*, 63–68, 69–73.

[68] R. Beale, 'A Treatise of the Office of a Councellor and Principall Secretarie to her Majestie', in C. Read, *Mr. Secretary Walsingham and the Policy of Queen Elizabeth*, 3 vols. (Oxford: Clarendon Press, 1925), 1.438–439, 441; 'Nicholas Faunt's Discourse Touching the Office of Principal Secretary of Estate, &c. 1592', ed. C. Hughes, *English Historical Review*, 20 (1905), 499–508. See also Sullivan, *Public Service*, 28–38.

[69] On professionals, see E. Gieskes, *Representing the Professions: Administration, Law, and Theater in Early Modern England* (Newark: University of Delaware Press, 2006); J. Winston, *Lawyers at Play: Literature, Law, and Politics at the Early Modern Inns of Court, 1558–1581* (Oxford: Oxford University Press, 2016). On servants, see M. Thornton Burnett, *Masters and Servants in English Renaissance Drama and Culture: Authority and Obedience* (London: Macmillan, 1997); Rivlin, *Aesthetics of Service*. On economic structural shifts, see M. M. Dowd and N. Korda, 'Working Subjects', in M. M. Dowd and N. Korda, eds., *Working Subjects in Early Modern English Drama* (Farnham: Ashgate, 2011), 2–6; M. Kendrick, *At Work in the Early Modern English Theater: Valuing Labour* (Madison: Fairleigh Dickinson University Press, 2015); T. Rutter, *Work and Play on the Shakespearean Stage* (Cambridge: Cambridge University Press, 2008).

178 WORKING TO A CONCLUSION

the secular context of advice on work. There is a long and rather austere tradition of debating whether Herbert displays a rigorously Calvinist approach to the calling or whether he finds space for cooperation with grace. The consensus is that while the poems show prevenient grace as necessary to desire to do good, such grace is not irresistible; the human will can consent or not to act on this God-given desire. Robert B. Shaw, Diana Benet, Marion Singleton, Russell Hillier, and Robert Kilgore are amongst those who argue that Herbert's poems show a doubt-ridden search for his own calling, first at court and then in the ministry, and discern in his poems the frustration or even affliction of never feeling fully assured of his usefulness to God, more or less alleviated by intermittent moments of understanding that this focus on his own activity is mistaken.[70] Cristina Malcolmson argues that Herbert tries to combine the period's 'dominant belief of innate quality in the ... gentleman, and the emerging ideology of achievement and merit', by presenting both the work and the self as the godly results of God's labour. In *The Country Parson*, for instance, the chapter on 'The Parson Preaching' talks of the 'mountaine of fire' needed to move parishioners who are 'thick, and heavy' in spirit, yet in 'The Windows' God's grace does the work, in shining through the preacher.[71] For Anthony Low and Julianne Sandberg, Herbert puts 'interior husbandry' above a georgic spirit of working for the common good (Protestantism, Low adds wittily, is not in itself a sufficient motive for a Protestant work ethic).[72] Sandberg concludes that 'work for its own sake does not exist in Herbert's world; rather, his is one in which the fruit of production defines the quality of both the labour and the labourer'.[73] A few commentators ask how Herbert registers the experience (as opposed to the soteriology) of work, but anxiety is still at the heart of these studies. Anne-Marie Miller Blaise argues that he follows medical advice about making work a remedy for melancholy (here caused by despair over election).[74] Gene Veith contrasts a Lutheran sacramental approach to work (also

---

[70] R. B. Shaw, *The Call of God: The Theme of Vocation in the Poetry of Donne and Herbert* (Cambridge, MA: Cowley Publications, 1981), 11–21, 71–107; D. Benet, *Secretary of Praise: The Poetic Vocation of George Herbert* (Columbia: University of Missouri Press, 1984), 20–25, 100–132; Hillier, 'Good of Works', 3–26; M. W. Singleton, *God's Courtier: Configuring a Different Grace in George Herbert's Temple* (Cambridge: Cambridge University Press, 1987), 118–142; R. Kilgore, 'From "Employment" (1) to "Grace": George Herbert's Restructuring of Work', *GHJ*, 35/1–2 (2011–2012), 72–81.

[71] Herbert, *Country Parson*, 233; Malcolmson, *Heart-Work*, 5–25, 138–142. See also D. M. Friedman, 'Donne, Herbert, and Vocation', *GHJ*, 18/1–3 (1994–1995), 133–158.

[72] A. Low, *The Georgic Revolution* (Princeton: Princeton University Press, 1985), 89–98.

[73] J. Sandberg, 'The Georgic Mode and "Poor Labours" of George Herbert', *Renaissance Studies*, 30/2 (2016), 223.

[74] A-M. Miller Blaise, 'George Herbert's Distemper: An Honest Shepherd's Remedy for Melancholy', *GHJ*, 30/1–2 (2006–2007), 74–77.

present in early writings by Calvin), in which God acts through humanity's work, with later Calvinist reasoning about how labour should be a repeated act of submission to God's will, and failure to do this is a sin.[75] *The Country Parson*, Veith argues, approaches the calling as what God requires, not what God performs. This belief adds greatly to the duties of a minister, and Herbert's poems worry about not living up to this ideal.

Since these commentaries largely focus on the theological implications of unemployment, rather than Herbert's relish for the concrete activities of work, his unsubtle hints and nudges to get God working—so Herbert can work also—can get overlooked. It is true that *The Country Parson* gives the standard four reasons which practical divinity offers for labouring in a vocation. God gives everyone 'two great Instruments ... as ingagements of working': the reason and the hands, and 'Every gift or ability is a talent to be accounted for, and to be improved to our Masters Advantage'. Working in one's calling prevents sinful or vain activity. Income earned can be distributed to help others. Finally, 'it is a debt to our Countrey to have a Calling, and it concerns the Commonwealth, that none should be idle, but all busied'. Thus, Herbert rebukes the 'great and national sin' of 'Idleness', either 'in having no calling' or 'in walking carelessly in our calling'. Thus, too, 'diligence' is one of the three principal qualities to be looked for in a servant. Herbert also offers the three standard cautions against anyone 'thinking that their own labour is the cause of their thriving, as if it were in their own hands to thrive, or not to thrive', against labouring 'profanely' in 'never raising ... thoughts to God, nor sanctifying ... labour with daily prayer', and against not observing the sabbath.[76]

That said though, the register of hearty enjoyment in which *The Country Parson* (itself, as Ronald Cooley shows, an occupational manual with aspirations to extend the minister's expertise in medicine and law, as well as pastoral work) speaks of putting effort into a job is also worth noticing, though often passed over:

> The Country Parson, as soon as he awakes on Sunday morning, presently falls to work, and seems to himselfe so as a Market-man is, when the Market day comes, or a shopkeeper, when customers use to come in. His thoughts are full of making the best of the day, and contriving it to his best gaines.[77]

---

[75] G. B. Veith, '"Brittle crazy glass": George Herbert, Vocation, and the Theology of Presence', in C. Hodgkins, ed., *George Herbert's Pastoral: New Essays on the Poet and Priest of Bemerton* (Newark: University of Delaware Press, 2010), 52–71.

[76] Herbert, *Country Parson*, 240, 247–248, 274.

[77] Herbert, *Country Parson*, 235; R. W. Cooley, 'George Herbert's *Country Parson* and the Enclosure of Professional Fields', *GHJ*, 19 (1995–1996), 1–25.

180   WORKING TO A CONCLUSION

Like Donne, Loe, Holbrooke, and Norden, Herbert offers God as the prime example of a labourer. Each household is expected to imitate the 'wonderfull providence and thrift of the great householder of the world', who has 'provided Creatures' to use what is too small or too dirty for man's use, such as poultry to peck up scattered crumbs and pigs to eat swill, 'growing themselves fit for his table'. After all, 'even in Paradise man had a calling'. Like Perkins and Scott, Herbert advises that when the Parson chooses the 'calling' of each of his children, he 'turnes his care to fit all their dispositions' (as long, of course, as their taste is not for 'vain trades ... unbefitting their Fathers calling, such as are tavernes for men, and lace-making for women; because these trades, for the most part, serve but the vices and vanities of the world').[78]

There is little soul searching about how to choose a calling; the issue is not what to do but how to do it. Herbert dwells again and again on how 'fit imployment is never wanting to those that seek it'. He gives two detailed examples: the spiritual and physical tasks which await the married householder (first those concerning his own family and affairs, then those of the village or parish, and then those of the country) and the work (and training for work) which is suitable for a single gentleman. The latter, if heir to a property, has a particularly arduous programme sketched out for him: he is to understudy the current owner's activities, and consider innovations elsewhere; he is to read books of law (including the statutes) and attend the sessions and assizes; he is to go to court; he is to travel across the country to survey its political and economic state; he is to endeavour to become a Member of Parliament (and an active one at that, sitting on committees). And 'when none of these occasions call him abroad, every morning that hee is at home hee must either ride the Great Horse or exercise some of his Military gestures'. As for any younger brother, he is to study law, then mathematics (especially that relating to navigation and fortification, which is 'usefull to all Countreys')—or, indeed, anything else, as long as he keeps busy:

> if the young Gallant think these courses dull, and phlegmatick, where can he busie himself better, then in those new Plantations, and discoveryes, which are not only a noble, but also as they may be handled, a religious imployment? Or let him travel into Germany, and France, and observing the Artifices, and Manufactures there, transplant them hither, as divers have done lately, to our Countrey's advantage.[79]

---

[78] Herbert, *Country Parson*, 239–241.
[79] Herbert, *Country Parson*, 276–278.

This register is also reflected in the proverbs which Herbert collects about work, which praise diligence: 'He that staies does the business', 'Not a long day, but a good heart rids worke', and 'The Citizen is at his businesse before he rise'.[80]

When Herbert advises Arthur Woodnoth about a projected career change, he emphasizes how Woodnoth has already been working in his calling. Woodnoth was considering leaving the service of Herbert's stepfather, Sir John Danvers (for whom he acted as business manager), in order to be ordained. Woodnoth told Ferrar how Herbert had given him a numbered list of seven points. 'Mr Herberts reasons for Arth. Woodenoths Living with Sr. Jhon Danvers' start with the axiom that 'higher opportunities of doing good are to be preferred before lower, even where to continue in the lower is no sinn', then go on to consider the sunk costs of time, expenses, and the 'thoughts & prayers', which Woodnoth had already put into Danvers's affairs. Herbert cautions that 'to Change shewes not well', since a perceived lack of 'Constancy' damages the reputation. However, 'for any scruple of leaving your trade, throw it away. when we exhort people to continue in their vocation, it is in opposition to idlenes. work rather then doe nothing. but to chuse a higher work, as God gives me higher thoughts ... can not but be not only allowable but commendable'. Unexpectedly, though, Herbert then turns the argument on its head by assuring Woodnoth that the latter is currently doing the 'office' of a divine, in his daily work of being 'the prompter of good to Sr John'. Above all, Woodnoth is surely succeeding in this: since the outcome lies only in God's hands, for Woodnoth to try to do well is, in fact, for him to do well.[81]

Herbert's poems relish the activity of work. Non-human creation naturally and sure-footedly exerts itself as a form of praise. Stars 'Glitter, and curle, and winde', for 'That winding is their fashion/ Of adoration' ('The Starre'). 'All things are busie' in 'Employment' 1, in the sort of interdependent community of labour praised by Markham, Browne, and Maynes. They are in a chain of husbandmen who water flowers, which then make honey, which bees then collect, which then 'flie home ... laden' to their hive ('The Starre'), as bees do too in 'Praise' 1, where they 'work all day'. In 'Providence', creatures' natural operations form a community of work and praise, as when 'Sheep eat the grasse, and dung the ground for more:/ Trees after bearing drop their leaves for soil', and 'Ev'n poysons praise' God through their natural operations. Plants offer multiple products, as sources of nectar and fruit, garlands of praise,

---

[80] Herbert, *Outlandish Proverbs*, nos. 24188, 958. See also numbers 47, 67, 107, 178, 419, 560, 704, 755, 978, 1009.

[81] Blackstone, ed., *Ferrar Papers*, 267, 269, 270; Charles, *Life*, 168–170.

182 WORKING TO A CONCLUSION

shelter for birds, shade for humans, and reeds for music (trees in particular can multitask, in 'Employment' 2 and 'Affliction' 1). In 'Man', the speaker receives such services from other creatures: 'Herbs gladly cure our flesh', 'For us the windes do blow,/ The earth doth rest, heav'n move, and fountains flow', 'starres have us to bed;/ Night draws the curtain, which the sunne withdraws', and water provides 'navigation', 'drink', and the means of washing.

Human figures of workers are equally zealous at their trades. The poems' frequent references to the occupations of ministry, music-making, and courtiership may obscure the specificity and range of other jobs which Herbert mentions: road mending and public building ('The Thanksgiving', 'Giddinesse'), carpentry ('Confession'), scholarship ('Affliction' 1, 'The Church-porch', 'Vanitie' 1), husbandry ('Employment' 1, 'Grace', 'Content'), decoration ('Employment' 1), grave digging and metal working ('Grace'), spinning ('Praise' 3), carting ('Praise' 3), military activity ('Employment' 2, 'Giddinesse', 'The Church-porch'), oratory ('The Quip'), peddling ('Employment' 2), magistracy ('The Church-porch'), and so on. 'Vanitie' 1 dwells on the expertise of some of these workers: the 'fleet Astronomer' does not gaze passively awestruck on heavenly bodies, but bores and threads them, views them, walks among them, and surveys them 'as if he had design'd/ To make a purchase there'. The 'nimble Diver' does not just sink into the sea, but 'Cuts through the working waves' to fetch pearls. The 'subtil Chymick' does not just observe the elements, he strips and manipulates them, then redresses them in different forms.

Such activity is not regarded as a disagreeable duty: Herbert's speakers celebrate the activity as much as the product. When he enters God's service, Herbert finds it 'brave' and full of 'joyes', so he takes up 'the place' with 'youth and fiercenesse' ('Affliction' 1). 'The Answer' considers that to be 'eager, hot, and undertaking' in projects is vital, and 'The Church-porch' offers admonitions to plot 'where,/ And when, and how the businesse may be done'. A personified Time gets a brisk career interview to correct any potential slacking, as his job is scaled up by the poem's speaker, first from 'executioner' to 'gard'ner', and then to 'An usher to .../ ... the utmost starres'. Writing starts as a lively search for words, not a passive surrender to inspiration (even if the latter course is eventually adopted to get the strongest product): 'I sought out quaint words', 'My thoughts began to burnish, sprout, and swell', 'curling' and 'Decking the sense', as 'Thousands of notions in my brain runne'. Revision too, as Amanda Taylor points out, is vigorously undertaken.[82] The speaker is

---

[82] Amanda Taylor argues that revisions made between the Williams and Bodleian manuscripts to 'Praise' 1 and 'Employment' 1 and 2 show Herbert claiming credit for his own revisions, although disclaiming ownership of the initial inspiration to write. See '"Use alone": Usefulness and Revision in George Herbert's *The Temple*', *GHJ*, 34/1–2 (2010–2011), 92–95.

willing to delete what are not good works, not 'lively' enough, as Preston and Perkins would put it: 'I often blotted what I had begunne;/ This was not quick enough, and that was dead', says 'Jordan' 2. Naturally, evil is energetically and skilfully prosecuted: in 'Grace', the sexton 'Death is still working like a mole' to dig graves, and the blacksmith 'Sinne is still hammering my heart' to get it properly hardened. The 'Busie enquiring heart' of 'The Discharge' is quick to 'prie,/ And turn, and leer', looking 'high and low'. Even leisure is pursed vigorously: Herbert's heart is likely to 'Gad abroad at ev'ry quest and call', 'discoursing' ('Content'), and his 'soul would stirre/ And trade in courtesies and wit', as a 'quick coal/ Of mortall fire' ('Employment' 2). In short, since 'Life is a businesse' ('Employment' 2), all workers should be zealous:

> Art thou a Magistrate? then be severe:
> If studious; copie fair ...
> ... if souldier,
> Chase brave employments with a naked sword
> Throughout the world. ('The Church-porch')

Such a positive approach reflects that taken by both secular and religious advice on work, rather than the latter's admonitions about the negative aspects of toil, as a duty imposed as a post-lapsarian badge of shame or to prevent the devil finding work for idle hands to do.

Thus, moments of entropy are marked out as exceptional, and enquired into earnestly.[83] In 'Businesse', Herbert catechizes himself about whether he 'Canst be idle', contrasting this state with the way 'Rivers run and springs each one/ Know their home and get them gone', and 'Windes still work: it is their plot,/ Be the season cold, or hot'. The questioner turns to Christ's example of complete engagement: 'He so farre thy good did plot,/ That his own self he forgot'. The poem's middle four stanzas pun on 'did' and 'di'd', moving six times between the two to emphasize that Christ's dying, his concluding good work, was his ultimate undoing: 'Did he die, or did he not?', asks the speaker, to nudge himself into a feeling response. When such prompts fail, Herbert is at a loss:

> Why do I languish thus, drooping and dull,
> As if I were all earth?
> O give me quicknesse, that I may with mirth
> Praise thee brim-full. ('Dulnesse')

---

[83] On entropy in Herbert, see C. Sullivan, *The Rhetoric of the Conscience in Donne, Herbert, and Vaughan* (Oxford: Oxford University Press, 2008), 157–192.

184   WORKING TO A CONCLUSION

He stresses the unpleasant affect arising from being inactive (of feeling barren, weedy, dead, dull, damp, freezing, and flabby), rather than the soteriological implications of being unable to act. In 'The Answer', for instance, when in 'prosecutions slack and small', Herbert distastefully imagines himself to be a dripping, 'pursie and slow' cloud, not even engaged enough to give an answer as to why he is so: others 'that know the rest, know more than I'. Likewise in 'The Church-porch', 'sloth' is distastefully described as a form of 'flegme' to be coughed up, and slackness is seen as making one something which 'rots to nothing at the next great thaw'.

One possible cure, suggested by Perkins, Jackson, Preston, and the like, is to focus on the process, not the outcome, of work. 'The Elixer' asks God to teach the speaker to recognize that God is in all his creation, so 'what I do in any thing,/ To do it as for thee'. Thus, 'Who sweeps a room, as for thy laws,/ Makes that and th'action fine'. Malcolmson recalls Perkins's image of how workers may 'reape marvelous contentation in any kind of calling, though it be but to sweepe the house, or keep sheepe' to argue that Herbert reclassifies a menial physical job into a gentlemanly expression of love.[84] One might also say that the calling referred to here is not the act of sweeping itself, but the speaker's determination to convert the act into a prayer by sweeping 'as for' God. The emotional work he does is to find a 'tincture', helpfully putting it into parentheses to allow it to be detached and reused on other occasions: the 'drink me' label of '(for thy sake)'. It is the 'servant', not God, who applies this 'clause' to upgrade 'drudgerie' into the class of the 'divine'.

As the poem starts by saying, this laudable action depends on the speaker receiving an initial lesson from God ('Teach me .../ In all things thee to see'). Herbert never denies the necessity for prevenient grace, so humanity's initial energetic labour can at best be a form of preparationism, the success of whose outcome depends on God then doing his share of the work. However, the rest of the chapter will argue that the enthusiasm which the poems show for human effort is a not-so-subtle invitation to God—not just to the reader—to 'Joyn hands ... to make a man to live' ('The Church-porch'), where the 'man' here is the speaker of the poems as well as any recipient of his alms. Herbert, daringly, is nudging God to imitate his creation. This argument does not—and cannot—end up in a different place to that of other commentators on work in the poems: God's grace is always needed to make the works good. The approach does, however, recognize how Herbert expresses both irritation and forbearance at how much affective work he has to do in order to keep bearing in mind that God has every right to keep him idle. Irony rather than affliction is the register

[84] Perkins, *Vocations*, 34; Malcolmson, *Heart-Work*, 170. See also Veith, 'Vocation', 66.

taken in some of the poems on employment. God's position is acknowledged as completely right, of course ... but this is not allowed to rub out entirely a human response to this fact.

There are poems of flatly voiced agreement to wait. 'The Crosse' repeatedly reproaches God for his 'contrarieties' in prompting the speaker to 'serve' (and 'not onely I,/ But all my wealth, and familie'). Unlike other images of enjoyable work, the project of this poem turns out to be one of painful labour, subject to 'delay,/ Much wrestling, many a combate'. When complete, the speaker repeats four times, in grimly direct ways, how God has moved straight to take away the 'power to serve', 'to unbend/ All my abilities', to 'confound' all the plans, to leave designs 'bleeding on the ground'. He is left 'in all a weak disabled thing', in health, in the memory of what he expected to do, in willpower. The speaker finally reaches for a tincture to cure the problem: taking Christ's submission to God as his own, 'Thy will be done'. It is God's plan to keep the speaker unoccupied; so, the poem unsubtly implies, the outcome has to be God's, too.

Most poems are much less unyielding, though. Sometimes they simply note when God cooperates with his own creatures in further acts of creation, and when not. 'Providence' acknowledges to God that

> ... either thy *command*, or thy *permission*
> Lay hands on all: they are thy *right* and *left*.
> The first puts on with speed and expedition;
> The other curbs sinnes stealing pace and theft.
>
> Nothing escapes them both; all must appeare,
> And be dispos'd, and dress'd, and tun'd by thee.

Likewise, 'Praise' 3 admires the quality and speed resulting when God 'dost favour any action,/ It runnes, it flies:/ All things concurre to give it a perfection'. Contrariwise, when God 'dost on businesse blow,/ It hangs, it clogs', so that 'Legs are but stumps', and 'struggling hinders more'. Generally, such poems speak of how God works through his creatures (in Luther's example, using the dairymaid's hands to milk the cow). Taking this line further, 'Praise' 3 ends by stating how some creatures are permitted to put God to work, to master their calling:

> Thousands of things do thee employ
>   In ruling all
> This spacious globe: Angels must have their joy,
> Devils their rod, the sea his shore.

186   WORKING TO A CONCLUSION

There is no tone of dispute here, only a simple recognition that productivity is God's choice. This is the position of the favoured speaker of 'Even-song', who is indulgently granted both the permission and the ability to work. God gives him 'eyes, and light, and power this day,/ Both to be busie, and to play'. Admittedly (and inevitably), the outcome is mediocre: 'I ranne; but all I brought, was fome'. However, God accepts the motivation and effort behind the activity as its chief product, with a satisfied '*It doth suffice: Henceforth repose; your work is done*'. Thus, the speaker is able to look forwards to receiving the 'favour' of grace to do more business the following day, with 'new wheels' to his 'disorder'd clocks'. As Perkins says of working well in one's calling ('in a clocke, made by the arte and handy work of man, there be many wheeles, & every one hath his severall motion'), by doing so one becomes part of God's plan.[85]

Other poems, however, argue with God over his decision not to employ their speakers. 'Employment' 1 is a sweetly reasonable protest. Its first move is a gentle 'why not?', pointing out the option open to God: 'If .../ Thou wouldst extend me to some good,/ The sweetnesse and the praise were thine' still, and the remainder, mere 'room', could be left to the speaker. The poem's second move is a positive argument about the opportunity cost of leaving something 'barren to thy praise'. God is being nudged into action through fear of missing out (an argument which also appears in 'The Starre', whose speaker coaxingly says that 'Sure thou wilt joy, by gaining me' as a worker). At last, there comes an argument based on the consistency bias: since 'All things are busie', why ever would God leave Herbert alone as 'no link of thy great chain'? The same heuristic, designed to woo a response from God, appears in 'Grace'. In the latter poem, God is offered a series of images of the rest of his creation (the sun, the dew, death) at work, unlike the speaker. It would surely be inconsistent of God not to grant such grace to all, especially given the final, provocative limit case offered by the speaker, where even Sinne is allowed to work away. In the Williams manuscript version of 'Grace', this point is sharpened by an additional stanza, a thought experiment which reproaches God openly: 'What if I say thou seek'st delayes,/ Wilt thou not then my fault reprove?/ Prevent my Sinn to thine own praise'. The poem has demonstrated that God has already caused delays in sending grace to 'increase' the speaker's 'dull husbandrie'. The slowness with which God granted prevenient grace, Herbert implies, has created sin, not prevented it, in either sense of the latter word.

---

[85] Francis de Sales compares regular times for prayer and for clock winding and repair. See J. Downer, '"Disorder'd clocks": Time, Grace, and the Mechanics of the Soul in George Herbert's "Even-song"', *GHJ*, 38 (2014–2015), 41.

An equally sidling approach appears in the middle lines of 'The Thanksgiving' (ll. 15–48), which rapidly flick through twelve fantasy careers, each prefaced with a Veblerian 'I will' or 'I shall', which glories in the speaker's capacity to act. 'I will' or 'shall', says the speaker, alleviate poverty, build a chapel, play music to God's glory, and so on. Many critics find this speaker scandalously (and eventually ineffectively) competitive with Christ. Such a reading focuses on the start and end of the poem, both of which acknowledge the impossibility of recompensing Christ for the Passion, even by thanks. The middle lines of the poem, however, emphasize that Christ would have to start the gift exchange by first giving Herbert wealth, honour, family, friends, great place, musical talent, wit, and all other 'works of thy creation'. The speaker repeats conditional phrases about God's acts ('If thou dost', 'For thy', 'If thou shalt', 'If I', 'If thou hast') to warn God that if he is given further benefits, God will get them right back. The apparently rhetorical question which ushers in this list of careers, 'Shall I then sing, skipping thy dolefull storie,/ And side with thy triumphant glorie?', in fact indicates the most sensible option open to the speaker. There is no point in attempting to match the Passion, so one might as well (as practical divinity advises) focus on what one can do still on a more quotidian level.

In 'Affliction' 1, Herbert is bitterly frank about feeling that he has been crossbiased, entangled, betrayed, and made to linger, melt, and dissolve by God, when the latter refuses to put work his way. However, the poem does not focus on whether such a lack of productivity shows that Herbert is 'just' or not. Rather, it dwells on how his own reluctant resignation to the situation is a form of emotional work, undertaken for a God who will not make 'Thine own gift good, yet me from my ways taking'. After listing many ingenious ways in which God has raised the prospect of avenues of service, then cut off each, Herbert tries a jokingly eccentric 'what if' image (also used in 'Employment' 2). If being granted the productivity of a fruiting tree is too much to ask of such a crossgrained God, what if he downgrades the request into one of being allowed to provide a perch:

> Now I am here, what thou wilt do with me
>   None of my books will show.
> I reade, and sigh, and wish I were a tree;
>   For sure then I should grow
> To fruit or shade: at least some bird would trust
> Her houshold to me, and I should be just.

188 WORKING TO A CONCLUSION

'At least' prepares the way for the triple pun on 'just': justified, certainly, but as just what exactly, and even then, only just useful. The speaker then takes the moral high ground: 'Yet, though thou troublest me, I must be meek;/ In weakness must be stout'. The concluding threat to change 'service; and 'Seek/ Some other master out' is abandoned in a chiasmatic riddle ('Let me not love thee, if I love thee not'), not in self-reproach. Indeed, since the speaker desires so earnestly to serve, he is already serving, as Herbert told Woodnoth he was doing to Danvers.

It is not that Herbert doubts the theology of *sola fide*, or does not understand that his calling is to stand and wait. It is more that the speaker of his poems taps his fingers so obviously, to remind God he is still there. In 'Submission', the speaker starts with a stiffly polite occupatio, on how, *if* he had not already acknowledged God's wisdom, 'My minde would be extreamly stirr'd/ For missing my designe'. He then tries fear of missing out. This is a lost opportunity, of the sort that—were their positions were reversed—he would be holding God to account for.

> Were it not better to bestow
> Some place and power on me?
> Then should thy praises with me grow,
> And share in my degree.

The speaker, rebuking himself for regaining a human perspective briefly, tries to regroup by justifying the ways of God to God: it is a divine right to choose whether to use an instrument or not, and anyway, if the speaker were to be raised to some effective place of action, 'Perhaps great places and thy praise/ Do not so well agree'. Yet, even after a properly submissive conclusion ('I will no more advise'), he cannot resist giving God a final nudge to act, that of fairness: 'Onely do thou lend me a hand,/ Since thou hast both mine eyes'. In 'Obedience', too, after a reminder of the correct attitude to work ('Let me not think an action mine own way,/ But as they love shall sway'), the speaker ungraciously nudges God by giving him permission to act, as though the speaker had any choice in the matter ('Thou mayst as well my actions guide, as see').

In short, the amount of effort which Herbert overtly puts into prompting God to offer him the opportunity to act suggests that, since the emotional engagement (and not the goods and services produced) is the proper output then Herbert's nudges do, in fact, (his) work.

4 Conclusion: Reasons to be Cheerful

The word 'cheerful', so common in the work of practical divinity and so often used by Herbert, signals today a laudable disposition to make the best of a situation. It also, however, has the connotation of a slightly obtuse approach, one which fails to appreciate the sublimity or complexity of a situation. This was not, however, how practical predestinarians saw the quality. Commentators today focus on the anguished soteriology expressed by much early modern Protestant writing. This is undoubtably there—but so, too, are echoes of a brisk willingness to prepare the mind and heart to cooperate with grace, and to leave the result to God.

Early modern divines throw a line across the chasm between acting like God (rational, fully informed, and able to dedicate oneself wholly to what is good) and acting like a human (liable to rely on heuristics, and lacking the willpower to follow up). Edwin Hutchins calls a thinker 'a very special medium that can provide coordination among many structured media—some internal, some external, some embodied in artefacts, some in ideas, and some in social relationships'.[86] Practical divinity, while fully accepting the awesome doctrine of *sola fide*, nonetheless finds positive and incremental ways to bring these different media together, to create a space for grace to enter. It is less concerned with the result in the long run (unknowable, in any case) and more concerned with short-run nudges to the self. As Herbert's poems show, the end point is none of our business; it's God's.

---

[86] Hutchins, *Cognition in the Wild*, 316.

Bibliography

Primary Texts

Ames, W., *Conscience with the Power and Cases Thereof* (1639).

Andrewes, J., *The Converted Mans New Birth ... With an Excellent Marke, to Know the Childe of God* (1629).

Angier, J., *An Helpe to Better Hearts for Better Times* (1647).

Aubrey, J., *Brief Lives*, ed. K. Bennett, 2 vols. (Oxford: Oxford University Press, 2015).

B., I. [J. Browne], *The Marchants Avizo. Very Necessarie for Their Sonnes and Seruants, When They First Send Them Beyond the Seas* (1589).

B., I., *A Dialogue Betweene a Vertuous Gentleman and a Popish Priest* (1581).

B., R. [misattributed to Richard Brathwait], *Some Rules and Orders of the Government of the House of an Earle* (MS *c.*1605) (London: R. Triphook, 1821).

Bacon, F., *The Essayes or Counsels, Civill and Morall*, ed. M. Kiernan (Oxford: Clarendon Press, 1985).

Bagnall, R., *The Stewards Last Account* (1622).

Barrell, R., *The Spirituall Architecture. Or, the Balance of Gods Sanctuary* (1624).

Basse, W., *Sword and Buckler, or, Serving-mans Defence* (1602).

Bayly, L., *The Practise of Pietie* (1613).

Beale, R., 'A Treatise of the Office of a Councellor and Principall Secretarie to her Majestie', in C. Read, *Mr. Secretary Walsingham and the Policy of Queen Elizabeth*, 3 vols. (Oxford: Clarendon Press, 1925), 1.423–443.

Bentley, T., *The Fift Lampe of Virginitie* (1582).

Bentley, T., *The Monument of Matrones* (1582).

Bernard, R., *Ruths Recompence* (1628).

Bernard, R., *A Weekes Worke: and a Worke for Every Weeke* (1616).

Bible and Holy Scriptures, The (1560).

Blackstone, B., ed., *The Ferrar Papers* (Cambridge: Cambridge University Press, 1938).

Bolton, R., *A Discourse about the State of True Happinesse* (1611).

Bolton, R., *Some Generall Directions for a Comfortable Walking with God* (1626).

Bonoeil, J., *His Majesties Gracious Letter to the Earle of South-Hampton, Treasurer, and to the Councell and Company of Virginia* (1622).

Botero, G., *Concerning the Causes of the Magnificencie and Greatnes of Cities (1588)*, trans. R. Peterson (1606).

Bourne, I., *The Godly Mans Guide* (1620).

'Breviate Touching the Order and Governement of a Nobleman's House (1605), A', in *Archaeologia ... the Society of Antiquaries of London*, 13 (1807), 315–389.

Breton, N., *A Solemne Passion of the Soules Love* (1598).

Brinsley, J., *Ludus literarius: or, the Grammar Schoole* (1612).

Brinsley, J., *The True Watch, or a Direction for the Examination of our Spirituall Estate* (1606).

Browning, J., *Concerning Publicke-prayer ... Six Sermons* (1636).

Bullard, J. V., ed., *Constitutions and Canons Ecclesiastical, 1604, Latin and English* (London: Faith Press, 1934).

Byfield, N., *The Beginning of the Doctrine of Christ. Or a Catalogue of Sinnes Shewing how a Christian May Finde Out the Evils, He Must Take Notice of* (1619).

Byfield, N., *The Cure of the Feare of Death* (1618).

Byfield, N., *Directions for the Private Reading of the Scriptures* (1618).

BIBLIOGRAPHY 191

Byfield, N., *The Paterne of Wholsome Words, or a Collection of Such Truths are of Necessity to be Believed* (1618).

Byfield, N., *The Signes, or an Essay Concerning the Assurance of Gods Love and Mans Salvation* (1614).

Byfield, N., *The Signes of the Wicked Man* (1619).

C., I., *The Ever-burning Lamps of Pietie and Devotion ... Heavenly Prayers* (1619).

Calvin, J., *Institutes of the Christian Religion* (1559), ed. J. T. McNeill, trans. F. L. Battles, 2 vols. (London: SCM Press, 1960).

Camden, W., *Reges ... et alii in ecclesia collegiate B. Petri Westmonasterii sepulti* (1600; 1606).

Carpenter, J., *The Exact and Perfect Keeping Merchants Bookes of Accounts* (1632).

Casa, G. Della, *Galateo ... a Treatise of the Manners and Behaviours, it Behoveth a Man to Use and Eschewe, in his Familiar Conversation*, trans. R. Peterson (1576).

Cecil, W., *Directions for the Well Ordering ... of a Mans Life* (1636).

Churchyard, T., *A Discourse of the Queenes Majesties Entertainment in Suffolk and Norffolk* (1578).

Cicero, M. T., *On Duties (De officiis)*, trans. W. Miller (Cambridge, MA: Harvard University Press, 1913).

Clay, T., *The Well Ordering, Disposing and Governing of an Honorable Estate or Revennue Briefely Describing the Duties of Divers Officers Therein* (1619).

Cleaver, R., *A Godlie Forme of Householde Government* (1598).

Cleland, F., *Hero-paideia, or the Institution of a Young Noble Man* (1607).

Calendar of State Papers Domestic (1629–1631).

Calendar of State Papers Domestic (1631–1633).

Calendar of State Papers Domestic (1633–1634).

Common Prayer. The Texts of 1549, 1559, and 1662, The Book of, ed. B. Cummings (Oxford: Oxford University Press, 2011).

Cornwallis, W., *Essayes* (1600).

Cotta, J., *A Short Discourse of the Unobserved Dangers ... of Ignorant and Unconsiderate Practisers of Physicke in England* (1612).

Cotton, C., *None But Christ, None But Christ Intimating that in Him ... Is to be Found, the Full and Absolute Cure of Mans Misery* (1629).

Crashaw, W., *Londons Lamentation for Her Sinnes* (1625).

Darell, W., *A Short Discourse of the Life of Servingmen* (1578).

Day, A., *The English Secretary* (1599).

Dekker, T., *Foure Birds of Noahs Arke* (1609).

Deloney, T., *The Works*, ed. F. O. Mann (Oxford: Clarendon Press, 1912).

Denison, S., *The Monument or Tombe-stone: Or, a Sermon Preached at Laurence Pountnies Church in London ... at the Funerall of Mrs. Elizabeth Juxon* (1620).

Dent, A., *The Plaine Mans Path-way to Heaven. Where Every Man Shall Cleerly See, Whether He Shall Be Saved or Damned* (1601; 1607).

Digges, D., *The Defence of Trade* (1615).

Dod, J., and R. Cleaver, *A Brief Dialogue, Concerning Preparation for the Worthy Receiving of the Lords Supper* (1614).

Donne, J., *Devotions upon Emergent Occasions, and Severall Steps in my Sicknes: Digested into 1. Meditations upon our Humane Condition. 2. Expostulations, and Debatements with God. 3. Prayers, upon the Severall Occasions* (1624).

Donne, J., *The Poems of John Donne*, ed. R. Robbins, 2 vols. (Harlow: Pearson Longman, 2008).

Donne, J., *A Sermon ... to the Honourable Company of the Virginian Plantation* (1622).

Downame, J., *A Guide to Godlynesse* (1622; 1629).

Ducci, L., *Ars aulica, or the Courtiers Arte*, trans. [E. Blount?] (1607).

Dyke, D., *The Mystery of Selfe-deceiving* (1614).

Dyke, J., *Good Conscience: or a Treatise Shewing the Nature, Meanes, Marks, Benefit, and Necessitie Thereof* (1626).

East India Company, The Lawes or Standing Orders of (1621).

192 BIBLIOGRAPHY

English Broadside Ballad Archive (https://ebba.english.ucsb.edu/).

Erasmus, D., *The Civilite of Childehode*, trans. T. Paynell (1560).

F., A., *A Collection of Certaine Promises Out of the Word of God* (1631).

F., A., *The Saints Legacies, or a Collection of Certaine Promises Out of the Word of God* (1631).

Faret, N., *The Honest Man: or the Art to Please in Court*, trans. E. Grimeston (1632).

Fasti Ecclesiae Anglicanae 1541–1857. Volume 9: Lincoln Diocese (1999) (http://www.british-history.ac.uk/report.aspx?compid=35195).

Faunt, N., 'Nicholas Faunt's Discourse Touching the Office of Principal Secretary of Estate, &c. 1592', ed. C. Hughes, *English Historical Review*, 20 (1905), 499–508.

Fincham, K., ed., *Visitation Articles and Injunctions of the Early Stuart Church*, 2 vols. (Woodbridge: Church of England Record Society and Boydell Press, 1994–1998).

Fitzherbert, J., *Booke of Husbandrie* (1523), rev. J. R. (1598).

Fleming, G., *Magnificence Exemplified: and, the Repaire of Saint Pauls Exhorted Unto* (1634).

Fosset, T., *The Servants Dutie ... For the Instruction, Not Only of Servants, but of Masters and Mistresses* (1613).

Foxe, J., *Acts and Monuments Online* (1583 edition) (https://www.dhi.ac.uk/foxe/index.php?realm=text&edition=1583&gototype=).

Gifford, G., *A Briefe Discourse of Certaine Points of the Religion, which is Among the Common Sort of Christians, which May Bee Termed the Countrie Divinitie* (1581; 1582).

Gouge, W., *Of Domesticall Duties* (1622).

Gouge, W., *The Whole-armor of God* (1619).

Greenham, R., 'Practical Divinity': The Works and Life of Revd Richard Greenham, eds. K. L. Parker and E. J. Carlson (Aldershot: Ashgate, 1998).

Griffith, G., *Bethel: or, a Forme for Families* (1633).

Guazzo, S., *The Civile Conversation* (1574; trans. G. Pettie, 1581).

Habermann, J., *The Princes Prayers*, trans. anon. (1610).

Harvey, C., *Schola Cordis, or the Heart of It Selfe Gone Away from God* (1647).

Harvey, C., *The Synagogue, or the Shadow of The Temple* (1640).

Harvey, C., *The Synagogue, or the Shadow of The Temple* (1679).

Herbert, G., *A Priest to the Temple, or, The Country Parson* (1652), in *The Works of George Herbert*, ed. F. E. Hutchinson,, (Oxford: Clarendon Press, 1941).

Herbert, G., *The Complete Poetry*, ed. J. Drury and V. Moul, trans. V. Moul (London: Penguin, 2015).

Herbert, G., *The English Poems of George Herbert*, ed. H. Wilcox (Cambridge: Cambridge University Press, 2007).

Herbert, G., *Herbert's Remains*, ed. B. Oley (1652).

Herbert, G., *The Temple* (1656).

Herbert, G., 'Oration ... [at the] Return from Spain of ... Prince Charles' (1623), trans. C. Freis and G. Miller, *GHJ*, 41/1–2 (2017–2018), 10–33.

Herbert, G., *Outlandish Proverbs, Selected by Mr. G. H.* (1640), in F. E. Hutchinson, ed., *The Works of George Herbert* (Oxford: Clarendon Press, 1941).

Herbert, G., *The Temple* (1633).

Herbert, G., *The Temple: A Diplomatic Edition of the Bodleian Manuscript (Tanner 307)*, ed. M. Di Cesare (Binghamton: Medieval and Renaissance Texts and Studies, 1995).

Herbert, G., *The Williams Manuscript of George Herbert's Poems: a Facsimile Reproduction*, intro. A. Charles (Delmar: Scholars' Facsimiles and Reprints, 1977).

Heresbach, C., *The Whole Art of Husbandry*, trans. B. Googe (1577; 1657).

Hieron, S., *The Preachers Plea, or, a Treatise in Forme of a Plain Dialogue, Making Known the Worth and Necessary Use of Preaching* (1604).

Holbrooke, W., *A Sermon Preached Before the Antient Company of Black-smiths in S. Marie Magdalens Church in London* (1612).

Homilies Appointed to be Read in Churches, The Two Books of, ed. J. Griffiths (Oxford: Clarendon Press, 1859).

Hooker, R., *Of the Lawes of Ecclesiasticall Politie* (1593).

BIBLIOGRAPHY   193

Hoole, C., *The Petty-schoole, Shewing a Way to Teach Little Children to Read English* (1659).
'Housewife, The Description of a Bad' (1699).
Hunnis, W., *Seven Sobs of a Sorrowfull Soule for Sinne* (1583).
Jackson, A., *The Pious Prentice* (1640).
Jonson, B., *Bartholomew Fair* (1614), ed. E. A. Horsman (London: Methuen, 1960).
Knappen, M. M., ed., *Two Elizabethan Puritan Diaries, by Richard Rogers and Samuel Ward* (Chicago: American Society of Church History, 1933).
Lambarde, W., *Eirenarcha: Or of the Office of the Justices of Peace* (1579; 1581).
Larkin, J. F., ed. *Stuart Royal Proclamations*, 2 vols. (Oxford: Clarendon Press, 1983).
Le Muet, P., *The Art of Fair Building*, trans. anon (1670).
Lemnius, L., 'A Dutch Physician', in W. B. Rye, trans. and ed., *England as Seen by Foreigners ... The Journals of the Two Dukes of Wirtemberg in 1592 and 1610* (London: John Russell Smith, 1865).
Leybourn, W., *A Platform for Purchasers, Guide for Builders, Mate for Measurers* (1668).
Loe, W., *The Merchant Reall* (1620).
'London, Divers Grocers of', *The Bad Garbelling of Spices, Used in these Daies* (1592).
[*London, The Manner of Crying Things in*] (c.1640).
London, the Corporation of, *The Lawes of the Market* (1595).
Luther, M., *A Commentarie ... Upon the Epistle of S. Paul to the Galathians* [sic] (1535), trans. anon. (1575).
Luther, M., *A Propre Treatyse of Good Works* (1520), trans. anon (1535).
Malynes, G., *Consuetudo, vel lex mercatoria, or the Ancient Law-merchant* (1622).
Markham, G., *Countrey Contentments: or, the English Huswife* (1623).
Markham, G., *The English Husbandman* (1613).
Meres, F., *Palladis tamia: Wits Treasury being the Second Part of Wits Common Wealth* (1598).
Merry New Catch of All Trades, A (c.1620).
Middleton, T., *The Triumphs of Honor and Industry* (1617).
Middleton, T., *Triumphs of Love and Antiquity* (1619).
Mirrour of Complements ... to Converse with Persons of Worth and Quality, The (1635).
Montaigne, M. de, *The Essayes* (1580–88), trans. J. Florio (1603; 1613).
Munday, A., *Himatia-poleos the Triumphs of Old Drapery* (1614).
Munday, A., *Sidero-thriambos, or Steele and Iron Triumphing* (1618).
Norden, J., *A Pensive Soules Delight. Or, The Devout Mans Helpe* (1615).
Norden, J., *The Surveyor's Dialogue (1618): A Critical Edition*, ed. M. Netzloff (Farnham: Ashgate, 2010).
P., B., *The Prentises Practise in Godlinesse* (1608).
P., S., *The City and Country Purchaser and Builder* (1667).
Page, S., *A Sermon Preached at the Funerall of ... S. Richard Loveson* (1605).
Patrides, C. A., ed., *George Herbert: The Critical Heritage* (London: Routledge and Kegan Paul, 1983).
Peacham, H., *The Garden of Eloquence* (1577; 1593).
Perkins, W., *A Case of Conscience the Greatest Taht* [sic] *There Ever Was, How a Man May Know, Whether He Be the Son of God or No* (1592).
Perkins, W., *A Direction for the Government of the Tongue* (1593).
Perkins, W., *A Discourse of Conscience* (1596).
Perkins, W., *A Godly and Learned Exposition of Christs Sermon in the Mount* (1608).
Perkins, W., *A Treatise Tending unto a Declaration Whether a Man be in the Estate of Damnation or in the Estate of Grace* (1590).
Perkins, W., *A Treatise of the Vocations, or, Callings of Men* (1603).
Playfere, T., *The Pathway to Perfection* (1593).
Playfere, T., *The Sicke-mans Couch* (1604).
Powell, T., *Tom of All Trades. Or the Plain Way to Preferment ... in All Professions, Trades, Arts, and Mysteries* (1631).

194 BIBLIOGRAPHY

Preston, J., *The Breast-plate of Faith and Love ... As They Are Expressed in Good Workes* (1630).

Price, D., *The Marchant. A Sermon Preached at Paules Cross ... the Day Before Bartholomew Fair* (1608).

Profitable Booke Declaring Dyvers Approoved Remedies, to Take Out Spottes and Staines, in Silkes, Velvets, Linnnen [sic] and Woollen Clothes, A, trans. L. Mascall (1583).

Quintilian, M. F., *The Education of the Orator (Institutio oratoria)*, trans. D. A. Russell, 5 vols. (Cambridge: Harvard University Press, 2001).

R., S., *The Courte of Civile Courtesie* (1577).

Rathborne, A., *The Surveyor in Foure Bookes* (1616).

Reyner, E., *Rules for the Government of the Tongue* (1656).

Robarts, F., *Gods Holy House and Service* (1639).

Roberts, L., *The Merchants Mappe of Commerce* (1638).

Rogers, R., et al., *A Garden of Spirituall Flowers* (1609; 1613).

Rogers, R., *Seven Treatises, Containing Such Direction as is Gathered Out of the Holie Scriptures* (1603).

Round Boyes Indeed. Or the Shoomakers Holy-day (c.1632).

Ruscelli, G., *The Seconde Part of the Secretes of Master Alexis of Piemont*, trans. W. Warde (1560).

Sales, F. de, *An Introduction to a Devout Life* (1609), trans. J. Yakesley (1613).

Saltonstall, W., *Picturæ loquentes: or Pictures Drawne Forth in Characters* (1631).

Scott, W., *An Essay of Drapery. Or, the Compleate Citizen. Trading Justly. Pleasingly. Profitably* (1635).

Sharland, E. Cruwys, ed., *The Story Books of Little Gidding. Being the Religious Dialogues Recited in the Great Room, 1631-2* (London: Seely and Co., 1899).

Skinner, R., *A Sermon Preached Before the King at White-Hall* (1634).

Sorocold, T., *Supplications of Saints: a Booke of Prayers* (1612).

Squire, J., *Tes irenes trophaea. Or, the Tryumphs of Peace* (1620).

'State Trials in the Reign of Charles the First, A.D. 1627–1640', in *Cobbett's Complete Collection of State Trials*, 33 vols. (1809–1812), vol. 3.

Swan, J., *Profano-mastix. Or, a Briefe and Necessarie Direction Concerning the Respects which Wee Owe to God, and his House* (1639).

T., R., *De templis: a Treatise of Temples* (1638).

Tasso, T., *The Housholders Philosophie ... the True Oeconomia and Forme of Housekeeping*, trans. T. K. (1588).

Tilley, M. P., ed., *A Dictionary of the Proverbs in England in the Sixteenth and Seventeenth Centuries* (Ann Arbor: University of Michigan Press, 1950).

Virginia, A Declaration of the State of the Colonie and Affaires in (1620).

Vaughan, H., *Silex scintillans: Sacred Poems and Private Ejaculations* (1655).

Waldstein, Z., *The Diary of Baron Waldstein: A Traveller in Elizabethan England*, ed. and trans. G. W. Groos (London: Thames and Hudson, 1981).

Wallington, N., *The Notebooks of Nehemiah Wallington, 1618–1654. A Selection*, ed. D. Booy (Aldershot: Ashgate, 2007).

Walton, I., *The Complete Angler and The Lives of ... Herbert*, ed. A. W. Pollard (London: Macmillan, 1901).

Webbe, G., *The Araignement of an Unruly Tongue* (1619).

Weever, J., *Ancient Funerall Monuments within the United Monarchie of Great Britaine, Ireland, and the Islands Adjacent* (1631).

Williams, A. M., ed., *Conversations at Little Gidding ... Dialogues by Members of the Ferrar Family* (Cambridge: Cambridge University Press, 1970).

Woolley, H., *The Gentlewomans Companion* (1673).

Xenophons Treatise of House Holde, trans. G. Hervet (1532; 1573).

Youths Behaviour, or Decency in Conversation Amongst Men, trans. F. Hawkins (1646).

Secondary Texts

Albrecht, R., '"The Pulley": Rundles, Ropes, and Ladders in John Wilkins, Ramon Lull, and George Herbert', *GHJ*, 30/1–2 (2006–2007), 1–18.

Anderson, M., *The Renaissance Extended Mind* (Basingstoke: Palgrave Macmillan, 2015).

Anselment, R., 'Seventeenth-Century Adaptations of "The Church-porch"', *GHJ*, 5/1–2 (1981–1982), 63–69.

Ash, E., *Power, Knowledge, and Expertise in Elizabethan England* (Baltimore: Johns Hopkins University Press, 2004).

Ashenburg, K., *Clean: An Unsanitized History of Washing* (2007; London: Profile Books, 2008).

Aylmer, G. E., 'From Office-Holding to Civil Service: The Genesis of Modern Bureaucracy', *Transactions of the Royal Historical Society*, 30 (1980), 91–108.

Badir, P., 'Fixing Affections: Nicholas and John Ferrar, and the Books of Little Gidding', *English Literary Renaissance*, 49 (2019), 390–422.

Baldwin, T. W., *William Shakspere's Small Latine and Lesse Greeke*, 2 vols. (Urbana: University of Illinois Press, 1944).

Bawcutt, N. W., ed., *The Control and Censorship of Caroline Drama. The Records of Sir Henry Herbert, Master of the Revels, 1623–73* (Oxford: Clarendon Press, 1996).

Behavioural Insights Team (https://www.gov.uk/government/organisations/behavioural-insights-team).

Belknap, R., *The List: The Uses and Pleasures of Cataloguing* (New Haven: Yale University Press, 2004).

Benet, D., *Secretary of Praise: The Poetic Vocation of George Herbert* (Columbia: University of Missouri Press, 1984).

Bergson, H., *Laughter: An Essay on the Meaning of the Comic*, trans. C. Brereton and F. Rothwell (1911; New York: Dover Publications, 2013).

Birke, D., 'The World is Not Enough: Lists as Encounters with the "Real" in the Eighteenth-century Novel', *Style*, 50 (2016), 297–308.

Blair, A., *Too Much to Know: Managing Scholarly Information before the Modern Age* (New Haven: Yale University Press, 2010).

Blaise, A-M. Miller, 'George Herbert's Distemper: An Honest Shepherd's Remedy for Melancholy', *GHJ*, 30/1–2 (2006–2007), 59–82.

Bloch, C., *Spelling the Word: George Herbert and the Bible* (Berkeley: University of California Press, 1985).

Bloomfield, G., 'Herbert the Space Man: Scenes of Printing and Spaces of Reading in *The Temple*', *ELH*, 87/1 (2020), 1–38.

Blum, B., *The Self-Help Compulsion: Searching for Advice in Modern Literature* (New York: Columbia University Press, 2020).

Booty, J. E., 'George Herbert: *The Temple* and *The Book of Common Prayer*', *Mosaic*, 12 (1979), 75–90.

Bowker, G. C., and S. Leigh Star, *Sorting Things Out: Classification and its Consequences* (Cambridge, MA: M. I. T. Press, 1999).

Bozeman, T. D., *The Precisianist Strain: Disciplinary Religion and Antinomian Backlash in Puritanism to 1638* (Chapel Hill: University of North Carolina Press, 2004).

Brockman, J., ed., *Is the Internet Changing the Way You Think? The Net's Impact on our Minds and Future* (New York: Harper Perennial, 2011).

Brown, K., *Foul Bodies: Cleanliness in Early America* (New Haven: Yale University Press, 2009).

Brown, M. P., 'The Thick Style: Steady Sellers, Textual Aesthetics, and Early Modern Devotional Reading', *PMLA*, 121/1 (2006), 67–87.

Brown, P., and S. Levinson, *Politeness: Some Universals in Language Usage* (Cambridge: Cambridge University Press, 1987).

Brown, W. S., and B. D. Strawn, 'Beyond the Isolated Self: Extended Mind and Spirituality', *Theology and Science*, 15/4 (2017), 411–423.

Brown, W. S., and B. D. Strawn, *The Physical Nature of Christian Life: Neuroscience, Psychology, and the Church* (Cambridge: Cambridge University Press, 2012).

196   BIBLIOGRAPHY

Bryson, A., *From Courtesy to Civility: Changing Codes of Conduct in Early Modern England* (Oxford: Clarendon Press, 1998).

Burke, P., *The Art of Conversation* (Cambridge: Polity Press, 1993).

Burnett, M. Thornton, *Masters and Servants in English Renaissance Drama and Culture: Authority and Obedience* (London: Macmillan, 1997).

Cahn, S., *Industry of Devotion. The Transformation of Women's Work in England, 1500–1660* (New York: Columbia University Press, 1987).

Cambers, A., *Godly Reading: Print, Manuscript and Puritanism in England, 1580–1720* (Cambridge: Cambridge University Press, 2011).

Cambers, A., 'Reading, the Godly, and Self-Writing in England, circa 1580–1720', *Journal of British Studies*, 46 (2007), 796–825.

Camp, C., *The Artisan in Elizabethan Literature* (New York: Columbia University Press, 1924).

Charles, A. M., *A Life of George Herbert* (Ithaca: Cornell University Press, 1977).

Chenovick, C., '"A balsome for both the hemispheres": Tears as Medicine in Herbert's *Temple* and Seventeenth-century Preaching', *ELH*, 84/3 (2017), 559–590.

Clark, A., and D. Chalmers, 'The Extended Mind', *Analysis*, 58/1 (1998), 7–19.

Clark, S., *The Elizabethan Pamphleteers: Popular Moralistic Pamphlets, 1580–1640* (London: Athlone Press, 1983).

Clutterbuck, C., *Encounters with God in Medieval and Early Modern Poetry* (Aldershot: Ashgate, 2005).

Cocke, T., and P. Kidson, *Salisbury Cathedral: Perspectives on the Architectural History*, Royal Commission on the Historical Monuments of England (London: H. M. S. O., 1993).

Cohen, C. Lloyd, *God's Caress: the Psychology of Puritan Religious Experience* (New York: Oxford University Press, 1986).

Cohen, W. A., 'Introduction: Locating Filth', in W. A. Cohen and R. Johnson, eds., *Filth: Dirt, Disgust, and Modern Life* (Minneapolis: University of Minnesota Press, 2004), vii–xxxvii.

Collinson, P., 'Shepherds, Sheepdogs, and Hirelings: The Pastoral Ministry in Post-Reformation England', in W. J. Sheils and D. Wood, eds., *The Ministry: Clerical and Lay* (Oxford: Basil Blackwell, 1989), 185–220.

Contzen, E. von, 'Experience, Affect, and Literary Lists', *Partial Answers: Journal of Literature and the History of Ideas*, 16/2 (2018), 315–327.

Coolahan, M-L., 'Redeeming Parcels of Time: Aesthetics and Practice of Occasional Meditation', *The Seventeenth Century*, 22 (2007), 124–143.

Cooley, R. W., '*Full of all knowledg': George Herbert's Country Parson and Early Modern Social Discourse* (Toronto: University of Toronto Press, 2003).

Cooley, R. W., 'George Herbert's *Country Parson* and the Enclosure of Professional Fields', *GHJ*, 19 (1995–1996), 1–25.

Cooper, T., ' "Wise as serpents": The Form and Setting of Public Worship at Little Gidding in the 1630s', in N. Mears and A. Ryrie, eds., *Worship and the Parish Church in Early Modern Britain* (Farnham: Ashgate, 2013), 197–220.

Coster, W., and A. Spicer, 'Introduction: The Dimensions of Sacred Space in Reformation Europe', in W. Coster and A. Spicer, eds., *Sacred Space in Early Modern Europe* (Cambridge: Cambridge University Press, 2005), 1–16.

Cowen, P., *A Guide to Stained Glass in Britain* (London: Michael Joseph, 1985).

Cox, V., *The Renaissance Dialogue: Literary Dialogue in its Social and Political Contexts, Castiglione to Galileo* (Cambridge: Cambridge University Press, 1992).

Craig, J., 'Bodies at Prayer in Early Modern England', in N. Mears and A. Ryrie, eds., *Worship and the Parish Church in Early Modern Britain* (Farnham: Ashgate, 2013), 173–196.

Cruickshank, F., and G. Kuchar, 'Broken Altars: The Work of Form in George Herbert's *Temple*', *Christianity and Literature*, 66/1 (2016), 24–38.

Davidson, C., 'George Herbert and Stained Glass Windows', *GHJ*, 12/1 (1988), 29–39.

Davidson, C., *A Woman's Work is Never Done: a History of Housework in the British Isles, 1650–1950* (London: Chatto and Windus, 1982).

BIBLIOGRAPHY 197

Dawson, B., 'The Life of the Mind: George Herbert, Early Modern Meditation, and Materialist Cognition', *ELH*, 86/4 (2019), 895–918.

Deakins, R., 'The Tudor Prose Dialogue: Genre and Anti-Genre', *Studies in English Literature, 1500–1900*, 20 (1980), 5–23.

Deitch, J., ' "Dialoguewise": Discovering Alterity in Elizabethan Dialogues', in H. Ostovich, M.V. Silcox, and G. Roebuck, eds., *Other Voices, Other Views: Expanding the Canon in English Renaissance Studies* (Newark: University of Delaware Press, 1999), 46–73.

Dixon, L., *Practical Predestinarians in England, c. 1590–1640* (Farnham: Ashgate, 2014).

Doelman, J., *King James I and the Religious Culture of England* (Woodbridge: D. S. Brewer, 2000).

Douglas, M., *Purity and Danger: An Analysis of the Concept of Pollution and Taboo* (1966; London: Routledge, 2002).

Dowd, M. M., *Women's Work in Early Modern English Literature and Culture* (Basingstoke: Palgrave Macmillan, 2009).

Dowd, M. M., and N. Korda, eds., *Working Subjects in Early Modern English Drama* (Farnham: Ashgate, 2011).

Downer, J., ' "Disorder'd clocks": Time, Grace, and the Mechanics of the Soul in George Herbert's "Even-Song" ', *GHJ*, 38/1–2 (2014–2015), 41–53.

Durkheim, E., *The Elementary Forms of the Religious Life* (1912), trans. J. W. Swain (1915; London: George Allen and Unwin, 1976).

Dyck, P., 'Approaching the Table: Invitation and the Structure of Herbert's "The Church" ', *GHJ*, 35/1–2 (2011–2012), 45–54.

Dyck, P., 'Locating the Word: The Textual Church and George Herbert's *Temple*', in ed. D. W. Doerksen and C. Hodgkins, eds., *Centered on the Word: Literature, Scripture, and the Tudor-Stuart Middle Way* (Newark: University of Delaware Press, 2004), 224–244.

Eamon, W., *Science and the Secrets of Nature: Books of Secrets in Medieval and Early Modern Culture* (Princeton: Princeton University Press, 1994).

Eco, U., *The Infinity of Lists: from Homer to Joyce*, trans. A. McEwen (London: MacLehose, 2009).

Ehrenreich, B., 'Maid to Order', *The Guardian*, 20 August 2000 (https://www.theguardian.com/theobserver/2000/aug/20/features.magazine37).

Elliot, A. J., and M. A. Maier, 'Color-in-Context Theory', *Advances in Experimental Social Psychology*, 45 (2012), 61–126.

Elliot, A. J., and M. A. Maier, 'Color Psychology: Effects of Perceiving Color on Psychological Functioning in Humans', *Annual Review of Psychology*, 65/1 (2014), 95–120.

Ferrell, L. A., 'How-To Books, Protestant Kinetics, and the Art of Theology', *Huntington Library Quarterly*, 71/4 (2008), 591–606.

Ferry, A., 'Titles in George Herbert's "little Book" ', *English Literary Renaissance*, 23/2 (1993), 314–344.

Fish, S. E., *The Living Temple: George Herbert and Catechizing* (Berkeley: University of California Press, 1978).

Fish, S. E., *Self-consuming Artifacts: the Experience of Seventeenth-century Literature* (1972; Berkeley: University of California Press, 1974).

Fitzgerald, W., *Spiritual Modalities: Prayer as Rhetoric and Performance* (University Park, PA: Penn State University Press, 2012).

Fourth Report of the Royal Commission on Historical Manuscripts 1 (London: H. M. S. O., 1874).

Fore, K., ' "Blest be the architect": Church-building in Foxe, Spenser, Lanyer, and Herbert', PhD Columbia (2017).

Friedman, D. M., 'Donne, Herbert, and Vocation', *GHJ*, 18/1–2 (1994–1995), 133–158.

Furey, C., *Poetic Relations: Intimacy and Faith in the English Reformation* (Chicago: Chicago University Press, 2017).

Gaston, P., 'The Excluded Poems: Steps to *The Temple*', in E. Miller and R. DiYanni, eds., *Like Season'd Timber: New Essays on George Herbert* (New York: Peter Lang, 1987), 151–168.

Gieskes, E., *Representing the Professions: Administration, Law, and Theater in Early Modern England* (Newark: University of Delaware Press, 2006).

198 BIBLIOGRAPHY

Giner-Sorolla, R., and J. Sabo, 'Disgust in the Moral Realm: Do All Roads Lead to Character?', in R. Duschinsky, S. Schnall, and D. Weiss, eds., *Purity and Danger Now: New Perspectives* (London: Routledge, 2016), 87–102.

Glimp, D., 'Figuring Belief: George Herbert's Devotional Creatures', in J. H. Anderson and J. Pong Linton, eds., *Go Figure: Energies, Forms, and Institutions in the Early Modern World* (New York: Fordham University Press, 2011), 112–131.

Gordis, L., 'The Experience of Covenant Theology in George Herbert's *The Temple*', *Journal of Religion*, 76/3 (1996), 383–401.

Gowing, L., 'Girls on Forms: Apprenticing Young Women in Seventeenth-Century London', *Journal of British Studies*, 55/3 (2016), 447–473.

Green, I., *Print and Protestantism in Early Modern England* (Oxford: Oxford University Press, 2000).

Greenblatt, S., 'Filthy Rites', *Daedalus*, 111/3 (1982), 1–16.

Guibbory, A., *Ceremony and Community from Herbert to Milton: Literature, Religion, and Cultural Conflict in Seventeen-Century England* (Cambridge: Cambridge University Press, 1998).

Haigh, C., *The Plain Man's Pathways to Heaven: Kinds of Christianity in Post-Reformation England, 1570–1640* (Oxford: Oxford University Press, 2007).

Hailwood, M., 'Sociability, Work, and Labouring Identity in Seventeenth-Century England', *Cultural and Social History*, 8/1 (2011), 9–29.

Hamling, T., *Decorating the 'Godly' Household: Religious Art in Post-Reformation Britain* (New Haven: Yale University Press, 2010).

Hamling, T., 'Old Robert's Girdle: Visual and Material Props for Protestant Piety in Post-Reformation England', in J. Martin and A. Ryrie, eds., *Private and Domestic Devotion in Early Modern Britain* (Farnham: Ashgate, 2012), 135–164.

Hamling, T., and C. Richardson, *A Day at Home in Early Modern England. Material Culture and Domestic Life, 1500–1700* (New Haven: Yale University Press, 2017).

Hanley, S., 'Temples in *The Temple*: George Herbert's Study of the Church', *SEL 1500–1900*, 8/1 (1968), 121–135.

Harman, B., *Costly Monuments: Representations of the Self in George Herbert's Poetry* (Cambridge, MA: Harvard University Press, 1982).

Higbie, R., 'Images of Enclosure in George Herbert's *The Temple*', *Texas Studies in Literature and Language*, 15 (1974), 627–398.

Hill, T., *Pageantry and Power: A Cultural History of the Early Modern Lord Mayor's Show, 1585–1639* (Manchester: Manchester University Press, 2011).

Hillier, R. M., '"Th'action fine": The Good of Works in George Herbert's Poetry and Prose', *Renascence*, 68/1 (2016), 3–26.

Hochschild, A. R., *The Managed Heart: Commercialization of Human Feeling* (1983; Berkeley: University of California Press, 2012).

Hodgkins, C., *Authority, Church, and Society in George Herbert: Return to the Middle Way* (Columbia: University of Missouri Press, 1993).

Hodgkins, C., 'The Church Legible: George Herbert and the Externals of Worship', *Journal of Religion*, 71 (1991), 217–241.

Hole, C., *The English Housewife in the Seventeenth Century* (London: Chatto and Windus, 1953).

Hufton, O., *The Prospect Before Her: A History of Women in Western Europe ... 1500–1800* (London: Harper Collins, 1995).

Hunt, A., *The Art of Hearing: English Preachers and their Audiences, 1590–1640* (Cambridge: Cambridge University Press, 2010).

Huntley, F., 'George Herbert and the Image of Violent Containment', *GHJ*, 8/1 (1984), 17–27.

Hutchins, E., *Cognition in the Wild* (Cambridge, MA: M. I. T. Press, 1995).

Institute of Historical Research, *The Victoria History of the County of Huntingdon*, 3 vols. (London, 1926–1938).

Institute of Historical Research, *The Victoria History of the County of Wiltshire*, 18 vols. (London, 1953–2011).

BIBLIOGRAPHY 199

Jackson, S., 'The Visual Music of the Masque and George Herbert's *Temple*', *English Literary Renaissance*, 45 (2015), 377–399.

Jenner, M., 'Early Modern English Conceptions of "Cleanliness" and "Dirt" as Reflected in the Environmental Regulation of London, *c*.1530–1700', D.Phil Oxford (1992).

John, P., et al., *Nudge, Nudge, Think, Think. Experimenting with Ways to Change Civic Behaviour* (2011; London: Bloomsbury Academic, 2013).

Johnson, K., *Made Flesh: Sacrament and Poetics in Post-Reformation England* (Philadelphia: University of Pennsylvania Press, 2014).

Jones, M., *The Print in Early Modern England. An Historical Oversight* (New Haven: Yale University Press, 2010).

Kadue, K., *Domestic Georgic: Labors of Preservation from Rabelais to Milton* (Chicago: University of Chicago Press, 2020).

Kahneman, D., 'New Challenges to the Rationality Assumption', *Journal of Institutional and Theoretical Economics*, 150 (1994), 18–36.

Kahneman, D., *Thinking, Fast and Slow* (2011; London: Penguin, 2012).

Kahneman, D., J. L. Knetsch, and R. H. Thaler, 'Anomalies: The Endowment Effect, Loss Aversion, and Status Quo Bias', *Journal of Economic Perspectives*, 5 (1991), 193–206.

Kahneman, D., and A. Tversky, eds., *Choices, Values, and Frames* (Cambridge: Cambridge University Press, 2000).

Kaufman, P. I., *Prayer, Despair, and Drama: Elizabethan Introspection* (Urbana: University of Illinois Press, 1996).

Kelliher, H., 'Crashaw at Cambridge', in J. R. Roberts, ed., *New Perspectives on the Life and Art of Richard Crashaw* (Columbia: University of Missouri Press, 1990), 180–214.

Kendrick, M., *At Work in the Early Modern English Theater: Valuing Labour* (Madison: Fairleigh Dickinson University Press, 2015).

Kerridge, E., ed., *Surveys of the Manors of Philip, First Earl of Pembroke and Montgomery, 1631–32, Wiltshire Archaeological and Natural History Society: Records Branch*, 9 (1953).

Kerrigan, J., *Shakespeare's Binding Language* (Oxford: Oxford University Press, 2016).

Kilgore, R., 'From "Employment" 1 to "Grace": George Herbert's Restructuring of Work', *GHJ*, 35/1–2 (2011–2012), 72–81.

Knieger, B., 'The Purchase-Sale: Patterns of Business Imagery in the Poetry of George Herbert', *Studies in English Literature, 1500–1900*, 6/1 (1966), 111–124

Körner, A., and F. Strack, 'Conditions for the Clean Slate Effect after Success or Failure', *Journal of Social Psychology*, 159 (2019), 95–105.

Korpela, K. M., 'Place Identity as a Product of Environmental Self-Regulation', *Journal of Environmental Psychology*, 9/3 (1989), 241–256.

Kress, G., and T. van Leeuwen, *Reading Images: The Grammar of Visual Design* (London: Routledge, 1996).

Kronenfeld, J., 'Probing the Relation Between Poetry and Ideology', *John Donne Journal*, 2/1 (1983), 55–80.

Kuchar, G., *George Herbert and the Mystery of the Word: Poetry and Scripture in Seventeenth-century England* (Cham: Palgrave Macmillan, 2017).

Kuchar, G., 'Introduction: Distraction and the Ethics of Poetic Form in *The Temple*', *Christianity and Literature*, 66 (2016), 4–23.

Kyle, C. R., 'It will be a Scandal to show what we have done with such a number': House of Commons Committee Attendance Lists, 1606–1628', in C. R. Kyle, ed., *Parliament, Politics, and Elections 1604–1648*, Camden Fifth Series 17 (2001), 179–236.

Lake, P., 'The Laudian Style: Order, Uniformity, and the Pursuit of the Beauty of Holiness in the 1630s', in K. Fincham, ed., *The Early Stuart Church, 1603–1642* (Stanford: Stanford University Press, 1993), 161–185.

Ledin, P., and D. Machin, 'How Lists, Bullet Points, and Tables Recontextualize Social Practice: A Multimodal Study of Management Language in Swedish Universities', *Critical Discourse Studies*, 12 (2015), 463–481.

200 BIBLIOGRAPHY

Lee, S. W. S., and N. Schwarz, 'Clean-Moral Effects and Clean-Slate Effects: Physical Cleansing as an Embodied Procedure of Separation', in Robbie Duschinsky, Susan Schnall, and Daniel Weiss, eds., *Purity and Danger Now: New Perspectives* (London: Routledge, 2016), 148–173.

Leed, D., ' "Ye shall have it cleane": Textile Cleaning Techniques in Renaissance Europe', *Medieval Clothing and Textiles*, 2 (2006), 101–120.

Leverenz, D., *The Language of Puritan Feeling: An Exploration in Literature, Psychology, and Social History* (New Brunswick: Rutgers University Press, 1980).

Lievsay, J., *Stefano Guazzo and the English Renaissance, 1575–1675* (Chapel Hill: University of North Carolina Press, 1961).

Llewellyn, N., *Funeral Monuments in Post-Reformation England* (Cambridge: Cambridge University Press, 2000).

Llewellyn, N., with J. Schofield, 'Post-Medieval, 1530–1666', in J. Schofield, *St. Paul's Cathedral Before Wren* (Swindon: English Heritage, 2011), 184–215.

Low, A., *The Georgic Revolution* (Princeton: Princeton University Press, 1985).

Lyne, R., 'Reading for Evidence of Faith in Herbert's Poems', *Review of English Studies*, 71 (2020), 74–92.

Lull, J., *The Poem in Time: Reading George Herbert's Revisions of The Church* (Newark: University of Delaware Press, 1990).

Mack, P., 'The Dialogue in English Education of the Sixteenth Century', in M. T. Jones-Davies, ed., *Le Dialogue au Temps de la Renaissance* (Paris: Jean Touzot, 1984), 189–212.

Malcolmson, C., *Heart-Work: George Herbert and the Protestant Ethic* (Stanford: Stanford University Press, 1999).

Mason, J., 'Walt Whitman's Catalogues: Rhetorical Means for Two Journeys in "Song of Myself"', *American Literature*, 45 (1973), 34–49.

Maycock, A. L., *Nicholas Ferrar of Little Gidding* (1938; Grand Rapids: W. B. Eerdmans, 1980).

Mehta, R., and R. J. Zhu, 'Blue or Red? Exploring the Effect of Color on Cognitive Task Performance', *Science*, 323 (2009), 1226–1239.

Menary, R., 'Introduction: The Extended Mind in Focus', in R. Menary, ed., *The Extended Mind* (Cambridge, MA: M. I. T. Press, 2010), 1–26.

Merritt, J. F., 'Puritans, Laudians, and the Phenomenon of Church-Building in Jacobean London', *The Historical Journal*, 41/4 (1998), 935–960.

Mertes, K., *The English Noble Household, 1250–1600. Good Governance and Politic Rule* (Oxford: Basil Blackwell, 1988).

Miller, W. I., *The Anatomy of Disgust* (Cambridge, MA: Harvard University Press, 1997).

Milner, M., *The Senses and the English Reformation* (Farnham: Ashgate, 2011).

Moloney, M. F., 'A Note on Herbert's "Season'd timber"', *Notes and Queries*, 202 (Oct. 1957), 434–435.

Montgomeryshire Genealogical Society, *Montgomeryshire Records. Parish of Montgomery: St. Nicholas and Non-Conformist Churches. Memorial Inscriptions* (1996).

Morgan, E. S., *Visible Saints: the History of a Puritan Idea* (New York: New York University Press, 1963).

Morgan, O., *Turn-Taking in Shakespeare* (Oxford: Oxford University Press, 2019).

Morgan, V., with C. Brooke, *A History of the University of Cambridge. Vol. 2*: 1546–1750 (Cambridge: Cambridge University Press, 2004).

Moshenka, J., ' "A Sensible Touching, Feeling and Groping": Metaphor and Sensory Experience in the English Reformation', in B. Cummings and F. Sierhuis, eds., *Passions and Subjectivity in Early Modern Culture* (Farnham: Ashgate, 2013), 183–199.

Moss, A., *Printed Commonplace-Books and the Structuring of Renaissance Thought* (Oxford: Clarendon Press, 1996).

Mugglestone, L., ' "Next to Godliness?" Exploring Cleanliness in Peace and War', *History of European Ideas*, 45/3 (2019), 322–337.

Muir, L. R., and J. A. White, eds., *Materials for the Life of Nicholas Ferrar. A Reconstruction of John Ferrar's Account of his Brother's Life, Based on All the Surviving Copies* (Leeds: Leeds Philosophical and Literary Society, 1996).

BIBLIOGRAPHY 201

Murphy, K., '"No Things but in Thoughts": Traherne's Poetic Realism', in E. S. Dodd and C. Gorman, eds., *Thomas Traherne and Seventeenth-Century Thought* (Cambridge: Cambridge University Press, 2016), 48–68.

Myers, A., 'Restoring "The Church-porch": George Herbert's Architectural Style', *English Literary Renaissance*, 40/3 (2010), 427–457.

Narveson, K., *Bible Readers and Lay Writers in Early Modern England: Gender and Self-definition in an Emergent Writing Culture* (2012; London: Routledge, 2016).

Narveson, K., 'Flesh, Excrement, Humors, Nothing: The Body in Early Stuart Devotional Discourse', *Studies in Philology*, 96/3 (1999), 313–333.

Narveson, K., 'Herbert and Early Stuart Psalm Culture: Beyond Translation and Meditation', in C. Hodgkins, ed., *George Herbert's Pastoral: New Essays on the Poet and Priest of Bemerton* (Newark: University of Delaware Press, 2010), 211–234.

Neelands, W. D., 'Predestination', in W. J. T. Kirby, ed., *A Companion to Richard Hooker* (Leiden: Brill, 2008), 185–220.

Netzley, R., *Reading, Desire, and the Eucharist in Early Modern Religious Poetry* (Toronto: University of Toronto Press, 2011).

North, S., *Sweet and Clean? Bodies and Clothes in Early Modern England* (Oxford: Oxford University Press, 2020).

Northway, K., '"To kindle an industrious desire": The Poetry of Work in Lord Mayors' Shows', *Comparative Drama*, 41/2 (2007), 167–192.

Oakley, A., *The Sociology of Housework* (1974; Bristol: Policy Press, 2018).

Olson, J., 'Biblical Narratives and Herbert's Dialogue Poems', *GHJ*, 12/1 (1988), 17–28.

Ong, W. J., *Orality and Literacy: the Technologizing of the Word*, ed. J. Hartley (1982; London: Routledge, 2012).

Ong, W. J., *Ramus, Method, and the Decay of Dialogue: from the Art of Discourse to the Art of Reason* (1958; Cambridge, MA: Harvard University Press, 1983).

Orlin, L. Cowen, ed., *Elizabethan Households: An Anthology* (Washington, D.C.: Folger Shakespeare Library, 1995).

Osmond, R., 'Body and Soul Dialogues in the Seventeenth Century', *English Literary Renaissance*, 4/3 (1974), 364–403.

Oxford Dictionary of National Biography (https://www.oxforddnb.com/).

Patterson, M., *Domesticating the Reformation: Protestant Best Sellers, Private Devotion, and the Revolution of English Piety* (Cranbury: Fairleigh Dickinson Press, 2007).

Pevsner, N., *Bedfordshire and the County of Huntingdon and Peterborough* (Harmondsworth: Penguin, 1968).

Potkay, A., 'Spenser, Donne, and the Theology of Joy', *Studies in English Literature, 1500–1900*, 46/1 (2006), 43–66.

Powers-Beck, J., *Writing the Flesh: The Herbert Family Dialogue* (Pittsburgh: Duquesne University Press, 1998).

Preston, J. L., and R. S. Ritter, 'Cleanliness and Godliness: Mutual Association Between Two Kinds of Personal Purity', *Journal of Experimental Social Psychology*, 48/6 (2012), 1365–1368.

Proshansky, H. M., A. K. Fabian, and R. Kaminoff, 'Place-Identity: Physical World Socialisation of the Self', *Journal of Environmental Psychology*, 3 (1983), 57–83.

Puterbaugh, J., '"Truth hath the victory": Dialogue and Disputation in John Foxe's *Actes and Monuments*', in D. Heitsch and J-F. Vallée, eds., *Printed Voices: The Renaissance Culture of Dialogue* (Toronto: University of Toronto Press, 2004), 137–156.

Ransome, J., '"Courtesy" at Little Gidding', *The Seventeenth Century*, 30/4 (2015), 411–431.

Ransome, J., 'George Herbert, Nicholas Ferrar, and the "Pious Works" of Little Gidding', *GHJ*, 31/1–2 (2007), 1–19.

Ransome, J., *The Web of Friendship: Nicholas Ferrar and Little Gidding* (Cambridge: James Clarke and Co., 2011).

Ray, R. H., ed., 'The Herbert Allusion Book: Allusions to George Herbert in the Seventeenth Century', *Studies in Philology*, 83/4 (1986), 1–182.

202 BIBLIOGRAPHY

Rayner, K., E. R. Schotter, and R. Treiman, ' "So Much to Read, So Little Time": How Do We Read, and Can Speed Reading Help?', *Psychological Science in the Public Interest*, 17/1 (2016), 4–34.

Read, S., *Eucharist and the Poetic Imagination in Early Modern England* (Cambridge: Cambridge University Press, 2013).

Rechtien, J., 'Logic in Puritan Sermons in the Late Sixteenth Century and Plain Style', *Style*, 13/3 (1979), 237–258.

Rechtien, J., 'The Visual Memory of William Perkins and the End of Theological Dialogue', *Journal of the American Academy of Religion*, 45/1 (1977), 69–99.

Rhodes, N., and J. Sawday, eds., *The Renaissance Computer: Knowledge Technology in the First Age of Print* (London: Routledge, 2000).

Richards, J., *Rhetoric and Courtliness in Early Modern Literature* (Cambridge: Cambridge University Press, 2003).

Richardson, C., *Domestic Life and Domestic Tragedy in Early Modern England: The Material Life of the Household* (Manchester: Manchester University Press, 2006).

Rickey, M. E., *Utmost Art: Complexity in the Verse of George Herbert* (Lexington: University of Kentucky Press, 1966).

Rivlin, E., *The Aesthetics of Service in Early Modern England* (Evanston: Northwestern University Press, 2012)

Roberts, J., and E. Evenden, 'Bibliographical Aspects of the *Acts and Monuments*', *Acts and Monuments Online* (http://www.johnfoxe.org/index.php?realm=more&gototype=modern&type=essay&book=essay2).

Royal Commission on Historical Documents, *An Inventory of the Historical Monuments in Huntingdonshire* (London: H. M. S. O., 1926).

Royal Commission on Historical Monuments, *Ancient and Historical Monuments in the City of Salisbury: Vol. 1* (London: H.M.S.O., 1980).

Rutter, T., *Work and Play on the Shakespearean Stage* (Cambridge: Cambridge University Press, 2008).

Ryrie, A., *Being Protestant in Reformation Britain* (Oxford: Oxford University Press, 2013).

Sandberg, J., 'The Georgic Mode and "Poor Labours" of George Herbert', *Renaissance Studies*, 30/2 (2016), 218–235.

Schildt, J., ' "In my private reading of the scriptures": Protestant Bible-reading in England, c.1580–1720', in A. Ryrie and J. Martin, eds., *Private and Domestic Devotion in Early Modern Britain* (Aldershot: Ashgate, 2012), 189–209.

Schnall, S., 'Clean, Proper, and Tidy are More than the Absence of Dirty, Disgusting, and Wrong', *Emotion Review*, 3/3 (2011), 264–266.

Schoenfeldt, M. C., 'The Art of Disgust: Civility and the Social Body in *Hesperides*', *GHJ*, 14/1–2 (1990–1991), 127–154.

Schoenfeldt, M. C., *Bodies and Selves in Early Modern England: Physiology and Inwardness in Spenser, Shakespeare, Herbert, and Milton* (Cambridge: Cambridge University Press, 1999).

Schoenfeldt, M. C., 'George Herbert's Consuming Subject', *GHJ*, 18/1–2 (1994–1995), 105–132.

Schoenfeldt, M. C., 'George Herbert's Divine Comedy: Humor in *The Temple*', *GHJ*, 29/1–2 (2005–2006), 45–66.

Schoenfeldt, M. C., *Prayer and Power: George Herbert and Renaissance Courtship* (Chicago: University of Chicago Press, 1991).

Schreiner, S., *Are You Alone Wise? The Search for Certainty in the Early Modern Era* (Oxford: Oxford University Press, 2010).

Scott, J. C., *Domination and the Arts of Resistance: Hidden Transcripts* (New Haven: Yale University Press, 1990).

Scott, J. C., *Weapons of the Weak: Everyday Forms of Peasant Resistance* (New Haven: Yale University Press, 1985).

Seaver, P., *Wallington's World: A Puritan Artisan in Seventeenth-Century London* (London: Methuen, 1985).

BIBLIOGRAPHY 203

Shafer, R. G., 'Herbert's Poetic Adaptation of St. Paul's Image of the Glass', *Seventeenth-Century News*, 35 (1977), 10–11.

Shaw, R. B., *The Call of God: The Theme of Vocation in the Poetry of Donne and Herbert* (Cambridge, MA: Cowley Publications, 1981).

Shuger, D., 'Laudian Feminism: The Household Republic of Little Gidding', *Journal of Medieval and Early Modern Studies*, 44/1 (2014), 69–94.

Singleton, M. W., *God's Courtier: Configuring a Different Grace in George Herbert's Temple* (Cambridge: Cambridge University Press, 1987).

Skwise, S., 'George Herbert, Sin, and the Ague', *GHJ*, 28 (2004–2005), 1–27.

Slack, P., 'Religious Protest and Urban Authority: The Case of Henry Sherfield, Iconoclast, 1633', *Studies in Church History*, 9 (1972), 295–302.

Slights, C. Wells, *The Casuistical Tradition in Shakespeare, Donne, Herbert, and Milton* (Princeton: Princeton University Press, 1981).

Smyth, A., ' "Art Reflexive": The Poetry, Sermons, and Drama of William Strode (1601?–1645)', *Studies in Philology*, 103/4 (2006), 436–464.

Smyth, A., ' "Shreds of holinesse": George Herbert, Little Gidding, and Cutting Up Texts in Early Modern England', *English Literary Renaissance*, 42 (2012), 452–481.

Spence, R., *Lady Anne Clifford: Countess of Pembroke, Dorset, and Montgomery (1590–1676)* (Stroud: Sutton, 1997).

Spicer, A., 'Holiness and *The Temple*: Thomas Adams and the Definition of Sacred Space in Jacobean England', *The Seventeenth Century*, 27/1 (2012), 1–24.

Spring, R. O. C., *The Stained Glass of Salisbury Cathedral* (Salisbury: Friends of Salisbury Cathedral, 1979).

Stachniewski, J., *The Persecutory Imagination: English Puritanism and the Literature of Religious Despair* (Oxford: Clarendon Press, 1991).

Steinroetter, V., ' "Reading the List": Casuality Lists and Civil War Poetry', *ESQ: a Journal of the American Renaissance*, 59 (2013), 48–78.

Stevenson, J., *Performance, Cognitive Theory, and Devotional Culture: Sensual Piety in Late Medieval York* (New York: Palgrave Macmillan, 2010).

Stevenson, L. C., *Praise and Paradox: Merchants and Craftsmen in Elizabethan Popular Literature* (Cambridge: Cambridge University Press, 1984).

Stewart, W. H., *Chelsea Old Church*, rev. K. A. Esdaile and R. Blunt (Oxford, 1932).

Strier, R., 'George Herbert and the World', *Journal of Medieval and Renaissance Studies*, 11 (1981), 211–236.

Strier, R., 'Herbert and Tears', *English Literary History*, 46 (1979), 221–247.

Strier, R., *Love Known: Theology and Experience in George Herbert's Poetry* (Chicago: University of Chicago Press, 1983).

Strier, R., *Resistant Structures: Particularity, Radicalism, and Renaissance Texts* (Berkeley: University of California Press, 1995).

Strier, R., *The Unrepentant Renaissance: From Petrarch to Shakespeare to Milton* (Chicago: University of Chicago Press, 2011).

Sullivan, C., 'The Art of Listening in the Seventeenth Century', *Modern Philology*, 104 (2006), 34–71.

Sullivan, C., *Literature in the Public Service: Sublime Bureaucracy* (Basingstoke: Palgrave Macmillan, 2013).

Sullivan, C., *The Rhetoric of the Conscience in Donne, Herbert, and Vaughan* (Oxford: Oxford University Press, 2008).

Summers, J. H., *George Herbert: his Religion and Art* (London: Chatto and Windus, 1954).

Sutton, J., 'Material Agency, Skills and History: Distributed Cognition and the Archaeology of Memory', in C. Knappett and L. Malafouris, eds., *Material Agency: Towards a Non-Anthropocentric Approach* (Berlin: Springer, 2008), 37–55.

Swaim, K., 'The "Season'd Timber" of Herbert's "Vertue"', *GHJ*, 6/1 (1982), 21–25.

Swanner, S., 'The Beauty of Ho(me)liness: The Unhandsome Sacramentality of Almost-shape Poems in George Herbert's *The Temple*', *Studies in Philology*, 115 (2018), 544–579.

204   BIBLIOGRAPHY

Taylor, A., 'The Seventeenth-Century Church Towers of ... Leighton Bromswold (?c.1640)', *Architectural History*, 27 (1984), 281–296.

Taylor, A., '"Use alone": Usefulness and Revision in George Herbert's *The Temple*', *GHJ*, 34/1–2 (2010–2011), 78–101.

Tebeaux, E., *The Emergence of a Tradition: Technical Writing in the English Renaissance, 1475–1640* (Amityville: Baywood, 1997).

Tebeaux, E., 'Pillaging the Tombs of Noncanonical Texts: Technical Writing and the Evolution of English Style', *Journal of Business and Technical Communication*, 18 (2004), 165–197.

Tebeaux, E., 'Technical Writing and the Development of the English Paragraph, 1473–1700', *Journal of Technical Writing and Communication*, 41 (2011), 219–253.

Thaler, R., and C. R. Sunstein, *Nudge: Improving Decisions about Health, Wealth, and Happiness* (2008; New York: Penguin, 2009).

Thomas, K., 'Cleanliness and Godliness in Early Modern England', in A. Fletcher and P. Roberts, eds., *Religion, Culture and Society in Early Modern Britain: Essays in Honour of Patrick Collinson* (Cambridge: Cambridge University Press, 1994), 56–83.

Thorley, D., ' "In all a weak disabled thing": Herbert's Ill-health and its Poetic Treatments', *GHJ*, 34/1–2 (2010-11), 1–33.

Tilgher, A., *Work: What It Has Meant to Men Through the Ages*, trans. D. C. Fisher (London: George Harrap, 1931).

Tomlinson, R., 'Thinking with Lists in French Vernacular Writing, 1548–1596', D. Phil Oxford (2008).

Trettien, W., *Cut/Copy/Paste: Fragments from a History of Patchwork* (Minneapolis: University of Minnesota Press, 2022).

Tribble, E., *Margins and Marginality: the Printed Page in Early Modern England* (Charlottesville: University Press of Virginia, 1993).

Tversky, A., and D. Kahneman, 'Availability: A Heuristic for Judging Frequency and Probability', *Cognitive Psychology*, 5 (1973), 207–232.

Tversky, A., and D. Kahneman, 'The Framing of Decisions and the Psychology of Choice', *Science*, 211 (1981), 453–458.

Tversky, A., and D. Kahneman, 'Judgment Under Uncertainty: Heuristics and Biases', *Science*, 185 (1974), 1124–1131.

Tyrwhitt, H., and R. Tyrwhit, *Notices and Remains of the Family of Tyrwhitt ... 1067 to 1872* (1858; 1872).

Veblen, T., *The Theory of the Leisure Class: An Economic Study of Institutions* (1899), ed. M. Banta (Oxford: Oxford University Press, 2007).

Veith, G. B., ' "Brittle crazy glass": George Herbert, Vocation, and the Theology of Presence', in C. Hodgkins, ed., *George Herbert's Pastoral: New Essays on the Poet and Priest of Bemerton* (Newark: University of Delaware Press, 2010), 52–71.

Veldman, I. M., 'Representations of Labour in Late Sixteenth-Century Netherlandish Prints: the Secularization of the Work Ethic', in J. Ehmer and C. Lis, eds., *The Idea of Work in Europe from Antiquity to Modern Times* (London: Ashgate, 2009), 149–175.

Vendler, H., *The Poetry of George Herbert* (Cambridge: Harvard University Press, 1975).

Vigarello, G., *Concepts of Cleanliness: Changing Attitudes in France Since the Middle Ages*, trans. J. Birrell (1985; Cambridge: Cambridge University Press, 1988).

Vijgen, B., 'The Listicle: An Exploring Research on an Interesting Shareable New Media Phenomenon', *Studia Universitatis Babes-Bolyai-Ephemerides*, 59 (2014), 103–122.

Vine, A., *Miscellaneous Order: Manuscript Culture and the Early Modern Organization of Knowledge* (Oxford: Oxford University Press, 2019).

Voak, N., 'English Molinism in the Late 1590s: Richard Hooker on Free Will, Predestination, and Divine Foreknowledge', *Journal of Theological Studies*, 60/1 (2009), 130–177.

Walker, J. D., 'The Architectonics of George Herbert's *The Temple*', *ELH*, 29/3 (1962), 289–305.

Wall, J. N., *Transformations of the Word: Spenser, Herbert, Vaughan* (Athens: University of Georgia Press, 1988).

Wall, W., *Staging Domesticity: Household Work and English Identity in Early Modern Drama* (Cambridge: Cambridge University Press, 2002).

Weber, M., *The Protestant Ethic and the Spirit of Capitalism*, trans. T. Parsons (1930; London: Allen & Unwin, 1985).

Webster, T., 'Writing to Redundancy': Approaches to Spiritual Journals and Early Modern Spirituality', *The Historical Journal*, 39/1 (1996), 33–56.

Westminster Abbey, 'Edmund Spenser' (https://www.westminster-abbey.org/abbey-commemorations/commemorations/edmund-spenser).

Whalen, R., *The Poetry of Immanence: Sacrament in Donne and Herbert* (Toronto: University of Toronto Press, 2002).

Whittle, J., 'The House as a Place of Work in Early Modern Rural England', *Home Cultures*, 8/2 (2011), 133–150.

Williams, A., *The Common Expositor: An Account of the Commentaries on Genesis, 1527–1633* (Chapel Hill: University of North Carolina Press, 1948).

Wingren, G., *Luther on Vocation* (1957), trans. C. Rasmussen (Eugene, Oregon: Wipf and Stock, 2004).

Winston, C., *Memoirs Illustrative of the Art of Glass-Painting* (London: John Murray, 1865).

Winston, J., *Lawyers at Play: Literature, Law, and Politics at the Early Modern Inns of Court, 1558–1581* (Oxford: Oxford University Press, 2016).

Wolberg, K., 'All Possible Art': George Herbert's The Country Parson (Madison: Fairleigh Dickinson Press, 2008).

Wolberg, K., 'George Herbert's *The Country Parson* and Stefano Guazzo's *The Civile Conversation*', *GHJ*, 27/1–2 (2003–2004), 105–118.

Wolberg, K., 'Posture and Spiritual Formation: Sanctification in George Herbert's *The Country Parson* and *The Temple*', *Christianity and Literature*, 66/1 (2016), 57–72.

Wolkowitz, C., 'Linguistic Leakiness or Really Dirty? Dirt in Social Theory', in Ben Campkin and Rosie Cox, eds., *Dirt: New Geographies of Cleanliness and Contamination* (London: I. B. Taurus, 2007), 15–24.

Wood, C., 'George Herbert and the Widow Bagges: Poverty, Charity, and the Law', in C. Hodgkins, ed., *George Herbert's Pastoral: New Essays on the Poet and Priest of Bemerton* (Newark: University of Delaware Press, 2010), 173–180.

Yan, Y., 'George Herbert and Plague', *GHJ*, 36/1 (2012), 77–98.

Yates, N., *Buildings, Faith, and Worship: the Liturgical Arrangement of Anglian Churches, 1600–1900* (1991; Oxford: Clarendon Press, 2000).

Zhong, C-B., and K. Liljenquist, 'Washing Away Your Sins: Threatened Morality and Physical Cleansing', *Science*, 313/5792 (2006), 1451–1452.

Zlatar, A. Bevan, *Reformation Fictions: Polemical Protestant Dialogues in Elizabethan England* (Oxford: Oxford University Press, 2011).

Index

For the benefit of digital users, indexed terms that span two pages (e.g., 52–53) may, on occasion, appear on only one of those pages.

Albrecht, Roberta, 69–70
Ames, William, 138
Anderson, Miranda, 15
Andrewes, John, 141–142
Angier, John, 54–55
Aubrey, John, 82, 91–92

B., I., 116–118
B., R., 40
Bacon, Francis, 108, 176–177
Bagnall, Robert, 72–73, 163–165
Barrell, Robert, 72–73
Basse, William, 129–130
Bayly, Lewis, 55–56, 139, 145–146
Beale, Robert, 176–177
Behavioural Analysis Team, 3–4
Behavioural economics, *see* Prospect theory
Belknap, Robert, 134, 153, 159
Bemerton manor, *see* Estate surveys
Bemerton Rectory, 7, 79–80
Benet, Diana, 177–179
Bentley, Thomas, 51, 55–56, 84
Bergson, Henri, 160–161
Bernard, Richard, 47–48, 55, 144–145
Blair, Ann, 133–134
Blaise, Anne-Marie, 177–179
Blanking, *see* Ignoring
Blum, Beth, 32
Bolton, Robert, 137, 143
Bonoeil, John, 171–172
Booy, David, 150–151
Botero, Giovanni, 171–172
Bourne, Immanuel, 165–166
Bowker, Geoffrey C., 134–135, 157
Bozeman, Theodore D., 66, 136
Breton, Nicholas, 142–143
'Breviate Touching the Order ... of a Nobleman's House, A', 40
Brinsley, John, 112–113, 118–119
Brookes, Matthew, 72–73
Brown, Kathleen, 36
Brown, Matthew, 133–134, 151
Brown, Warren, 13

Browne, John, 170–171, 173
Browning, John, 67
Bryson, Anna, 107
Buildings, *see* Church buildings
Bullet points, *see* Lists
Burke, Peter, 107
Byfield, Nicholas, 147–151

C., I., 164–165
Cahn, Susan, 38
Calling, *see* Work (works)
Calvin, Jean, 147, 163–164, 166 n.21, 177–179
Cambers, Andrew, 11
Carpenter, John, 173–174
Casa, Giovanni della, 45–46, 62–63, 65, 109–111, 123–124, 129–130
Catalogues, *see* Lists
Catechising, 69–70, 72–73, 103–104, 106, 152–153, 155–156 n.76
Cecil, William, 164–165
Chalmers, David, 9, 15
Charles, Amy, 77–80
Checklists, 143–145
Cheerfulness (devotional), 6–7, 32, 34, 47, 113, 149–150, 168, 189
Chenovick, Clarissa, 16
Choice architecture, *see* Prospect theory
Chores, *see* Cleaning
Church buildings, 67–69
Church of England,
    Canons, 53, 73–75, 94
    Thirty-nine Articles, 162, 165–166
Churchyard, Thomas, 54
Cicero, M.T., 107
Civility, *see* Tact
Clark, Andy, 9, 13, 15
Clark, Sandra, 142
Clay, Thomas, 173–174
Cleaning, 36, 49–50
Cleaver, Robert, 51, 59–60, 114–115, 144
Cleland, James, 108
Clifford, Anne, 86–87
Clifton, Katherine, 77

INDEX   207

Clutterbuck, Charlotte, 141–142
Cognitive niches, *see* Distributed cognition
Cohen, Charles Lloyd, 16
Cohen, William, 62–63, 65
Collinson, Patrick, 102–103
Commonplaces, 133–134, 154
Contracts (devotional), 16, 29–32, 159
Contzen, Eva von, 161
Conversation, 100–107
Cooley, Ronald W., 124–125, 179
Cornwallis, William, 109
Cotta, John, 174
Cotton, Clement, 145–146
Courtesy, *see* Tact
Covenants, *see* Contracts (devotional)
Cox, Virginia, 118
Crashaw, William, 26–27

Darell, Walter, 52
Dawson, Brent, 14–15
Deakins, Roger, 118
Dekker, Thomas, 164–165
Deloney, Thomas, 176
Denison, Stephen, 144
Dent, Arthur, 117–118, 147
Despair (devotional), 5, 144–145, 177–179
Diagrams (branch), *see* Lists
Dialogue, *see* Conversation
Digges, Dudley, 138–139
Dirt, *see* Cleaning
Discussion, *see* Conversation
Disputation (academic), 119
Distributed cognition, 4, 9–10, 14–15, 83, 136
Dixon, Leif, P1.P12, 33
Dod, John, 144
Donne, John, 136–137, 165–166, 180
Doubt (devotional), 62–63, 65–66, 147–151, 159–161
Douglas, Mary, 36–37, 62–63, 65
Dowd, Michelle M., 50–51
Downame, John, 47–48
Dust, *see* Cleaning
Dyck, Paul, 69–70
Dyke, Daniel, 26–27

Eamon, William, 133–134
Eco, Umberto, 142, 154–155 n.72, 155
Ehrenreich, Barbara, 44
Environment (devotional), 5, 9–10–30, 14, 57, 67–69, 168
Epitaphs, *see* Monuments
Erasmus, Desiderius, 108, 108 n.19, 123–124
Estate surveys, 78–81
Extended mind, *see* Distributed cognition

F., A., 144–145
Face saving, *see* Tact
Faret, Nicholas, 108
Faunt, Nicholas, 176–177
Ferrar family, 7–9, 16–17, 41–44, 78, 85–86, 95–96, 102, 120–121
    Collett, Anna (the Patient), 17, 19, 121
    Collett, Ferrar, 20–21
    Collett, Hester (the Cheerful), 8, 78
    Collett, John (the Resolved), 22, 120–121
    Collett, Joyce (the Submisse), 20, 120–121
    Collett, Margaret (or Elizabeth; the Affectionate), 19, 43, 162, 170
    Collett, Mary (the Chief, then the Mother), 8, 17, 20, 162
    Collett, Susannah Ferrar (the Moderator), 18–21, 78, 120–121
    Ferrar, Bathsheba, 17
    Ferrar, John (the Guardian), 17–19, 43, 77–79, 85–86, 118–119, 134 n.11
    Ferrar, Mary (the Founder or the Mother), 21, 41–42, 43–44 n.28, 78, 81
    Ferrar, Nicholas (the Visitor), 7 n.16, 10–11, 16–18, 20, 33, 52–53, 52–53 n.54, 76–79, 82, 85–86, 95–96, 102, 120
    Mapletoft, Susanna, 21
    Woodnoth, Arthur, 7, 17, 33, 77–78, 181, 188
Ferrell, Lori Anne, 151
Fish, Stanley, 72–73, 89, 106, 123–124, 156–157
Fitzherbert, John, 38–39, 170–171, 175
Fleming, Giles, 67, 83
Fosset, Thomas, 129–130, 176
Foxe, John, 84, 120
Fugglestone manor, *see* Estate surveys
Furey, Constance, 124

Gaston, Paul, 56
Gifford, George, 117
Glass, *see* Windows
Glimp, David, 14–15
Gouge, William, 23, 26–27
Grace, *see* Predestination
Green, Ian, 136–137, 145–146
Greenham, Richard, 113, 144–145
Griffith, Matthew, 72–73
Guazzo, Stefano, 109 n.24
Guibbory, Achsah, 13–14

Habermann, Johann, 51
Haigh, Christopher, 120
Hall, Joseph, 50–51 n.49
Hamling, Tara, 10–11, 17, 46–47
Harman, Barbara, 89
Harmonies, Little Gidding, 134

208 INDEX

Harvey, Christopher, 31–32, 49, 63–64, 82
Herbert, George
  Poems, English
    'Affliction' 1, 57–58, 122, 129, 160, 181–183,
      187
    'Affliction' 3, 15, 122–123
    'Affliction' 4, 57–58, 129
    'Affliction' 5, 57–58
    'Altar, The', 70–71, 152–153
    'Anagram', 82, 152–153
    'Answer, The', 77–78, 182–184
    'Artillerie', 57, 124, 126–127
    'Assurance', 57, 124–125
    'Businesse', 183
    'Charms and Knots', 158
    'Church-floore, The', 59, 70–71, 82
    'Church-lock and key', 57, 82
    'Church-monuments', 82, 88–91
    'Church-musick, 82, 122–123, 128–129
    'Church-porch, The', 52–54, 59–61, 63–65,
      69–72, 112, 158, 182–185
    'Clasping of Hands', 15
    'Collar, The', 108, 122, 127–128
    'Coloss. 3.3', 91–93, 97, 152–153
    'Confession', 70–71, 182
    'Conscience', 122, 124–125
    'Constancie', 153–155
    'Content', 59–60, 124–125, 182–183
    'Crosse, The', 77–78, 185
    'Dawning, The', 59–60
    'Decay', 122
    'Deniall', 60–61, 128
    'Dialogue', 125–126
    'Dialogue-Antheme, A', 124–125
    'Discharge, The', 182–183
    'Dooms-day', 60–61
    'Dulnesse', 65, 183
    'Easter-wings', 152–153
    'Elixer, The', 58, 97, 184
    'Employment' 1, 181–182
    'Employment' 2, 57, 106, 181–183, 187
    'Ephes. 4.30', 122, 124–125
    'Even-song', 60–61, 63–64, 122–124, 186
    'Familie, The', 60–61, 122, 124–125
    'Flower, The', 54
    'Forerunners, The', 59–60, 128–129
    'Giddinesse', 182
    'Glimpse, The', 57, 70–71
    'Good Friday', 29–30, 65
    'Grace', 182–183, 186
    'Gratefulnesse', 61–62
    'H. Communion, The', 70–71
    'H. Scriptures I, The', 153–155
    'H. Scriptures II, The', 15

    'Holdfast, The', 70–71, 94–95, 122, 127,
      158–161
    'Invitation, The', 57–58
    'Jordan' 1, 70–71, 122–123
    'Jordan' 2, 57, 122, 129, 182–183
    'Judgement', 29–30
    'Justice' 2, 70–71, 96–97
    'L'Envoy', 63–64
    'Lent', 63–64
    'Longing', 128
    'Love' (Williams manuscript), 56
    'Love' 1, 57, 59–60
    'Love' 3, 122–124
    'Love Unknown', 49, 57–60, 81, 94–95,
      127–130, 158–161
    'Love-joy', 94–95, 97, 124
    'Man', 61, 71–72, 122, 129, 181–182
    'Mans Medley', 57
    'Marie Magdalen', 61–62
    'Method, The', 65, 159
    'Miserie', 59–60, 63–64, 122
    'Mortification', 61, 155–157
    'Nature', 29
    'Obedience', 30–31, 80–81
    'Odour, The', 128–129
    'Parodie, A', 122, 128
    'Peace', 122
    'Pearl, The', 57, 106, 155–157
    'Praise' 1, 181–182
    'Praise' 3, 57, 61, 70–71, 182, 185
    'Prayer' 1, 70–71, 80, 153–155, 158
    'Priesthood, The', 64, 70–71, 158
    'Providence', 14–15, 57, 153–155, 158,
      181–182, 185
    'Pulley, The', 69–71, 130
    'Quidditie, The', 153–155
    'Quip, The', 128, 155–157, 182
    'Redemption', 80–81, C4.46, 123–124
    'Reprisall, The', 128
    'Sacrifice, The', 130
    'Sepulchre', 29, 61
    'Sinne' 1, 155–157
    'Sinner, The', 70–71, 128
    'Sinnes Round', 72–73
    'Sion', 72–73
    'Starre, The', P6.P37, 186
    'Submission', 126, 188
    'Sunday', 61, 70–71, 163
    'Superliminare', 65
    'Thanksgiving, The', 70–71, 158–161,
      168–169, 182, 187
    'Time', 57–58, 122, 127–128, 182–183
    'To all Angels and Saints', 124
    'true Hymne, A', 122, 128–129, 160–161
    'Ungratefulnesse', 61, 70–71

'Unkindnesse', 63–64, 155–157
'Vanitie' 1, 122, 155–157, 182
'Vertue', 69–70
'Water-course, The', 70–71
'Whitsunday', 57–58
'Windows, The', 82, 93–94, 97–98, 177–179
'World, The', 70–71, 122
Poems, Latin
  'De labe maculisique', 63
  'In Catharum quendam', 63
  'Martha: Maria', 59–60
  'In S. Scripturas', 57
  Memoriae matris sacrum, 38–39
Prose
  Country Parson, The, 28, 49–50, 53–54,
    58–61, 64, 73–75, 104–106, 116–117,
    139–140, 176–180
  'Oration ... [at the] Return from Spain of ...
    Prince Charles', 34
  Outlandish Proverbs, 71–72, 106, 181
Herbert, Henry, 77, 106 n.12, 123 n.68
Herbert, Jane, 91–93, 105
Herbert, Magdalen, 38–39, 87–88, 103–104
Heresbach, Conrad, 176
Hieron, Samuel, 115–116
Higbie, Robert, 61
Hillier, Russell, 61–62, 177–179
Hodgkins, Christopher, 61–62, 89
Holbrooke, William, 165–166, 173, 180
Homilies, Book of, 163–164, 166
Hooker, Richard, 6, 9–10
Housework, *see* Cleaning
Hufton, Olwen, 38
Humour, 60–61, 100–102, 105, 127–128, 130,
  160–161, 184–185
Hunnis, William, 48
Hunt, Arnold, 140
Huntley, Frank, 61
Hutchins, Edwin, 9
Hutchinson, F.E., 58–59, 73–75, 77

Ignoring, 116, 120, 128, 159
Inscriptions, *see* Monuments
Instructions, *see* Requests
Irony, *see* Humour

Jackson, Abraham, 52, 112–114, 164–165
Jackson, Simon, 123
Johnson, Kimberley, 13–14
Jokes, *see* Humour
Jonson, Ben, 136–137

Kadue, Katie, 38
Kahneman, Daniel, *see* Nudges
Kaufman, Peter Iver, 5, 149–150

Kilgore, Robert, 177–179
Kuchar, Gary, 61–62

Lake, Peter, 67
Lambarde, William, 131–132
Laudian aesthetics, 67, 75–76, 97–98
Laundry, *see* Cleaning
Le Muet, Pierre, 73
Ledin, Per, 134–135
Leverenz, David, 5, 159–160
Levinson, Stephen, 100
Leybourn, William, 73
Light, *see* Windows
Listicles, 135–136
Lists, 23–24, 131–136
Little Academy, *see* Ferrar family
Little Gidding, *see* Ferrar family
Little Gidding manor, *see* Estate
  surveys
Llewellyn, Nigel, 85–86
Loe, William, 163–166, 180
London parish buildings, 75–76, 93–94
Lord Mayor's Shows, 172–173
Low, Anthony, 177–179
Lull, Janis, 58–59
Luther, Martin, 147, 168, 177–179, 185
Lyne, Raphael, 156–158

Machin, David, 134–135
Malcolmson, Cristina, 58–59, 177–179, 184
Malynes, Gerard, 173
Markham, Gervase, 40, 173, 175
Marks (of grace), *see* Lists
Marvell, Andrew, 90
Meditations, 141–143
Meres, Francis, 165–166
Merritt, J.F., 53, 75–76
Miller, William, 36, 62–63, 65
Milner, Matthew, 10–11
Mirrour of Complements, The, 111
Montaigne, Michel de, 118–119
Monuments, 83
Morgan, Oliver, 107, 128
Moshenka, Joe, 10–11
Myers, Anne, 69–70

Narveson, Kate, 32, 61–62, 151
Netzley, Ryan, 13–14
Norden, John, 163–166, 180
North, Susan, 49–50

Oakley, Ann, 38
Oaths, *see* Contracts (devotional)
Objects (devotional), *see* Environment
  (devotional)

210 INDEX

Oley, Barnabus, 82, 102–103, 124
Olson, John, 124–125
Ong, Walter J., 132

P., S., 73
Page, Samuel, 12
Patterson, Mary, 11
Peacham, Henry, 139–140
Penelope Brown, 100
Perkins, William, 16, 33, 47–48, 50–51, 58,
  58–59 n.76, 59–61, 72–73, 113–114, 116,
  128, 141, 144–145, 168–170, 180,
  182–184, 186
Petitions, *see* Requests
Playfere, Thomas, 6
Politeness, *see* Tact
Powell, Thomas, 170–171
Powers-Beck, Jeffrey, 58
Practical divinity, 4–6, 14, 33, 36, 50–51, 62–63,
  112–118, 136, 163–170, 189
Praise, *see* Meditation
Prayers, 12, 51, 55–56, 128, 164–165
Predestination, 5, 15, 33, 100, 158–162, 169
Preparationism, *see* Practical divinity
Preston, John, 16, 169–170, 182–183
Price, Daniel, 165–166
'Proclamation [on] ... decayes of Churches', 76
Prospect theory, 1–4, 33
  Heuristics
    Anchor and adjust, 2
    Availability, 2
    Confidence, 3, 18–19
    Consistency, 19, 26–27
    Group decisions, 3
    Hot/cold decision states, 3, 151–152
    Informational cascades, 19
    Loss aversion, 3
    Order preferences, 3
    Probability ranking, 3
    Representativeness, 2
    Unreasonable optimism, 3
  Nudges
    Anonymity, 3
    Cleanliness, 36–37, 46
    Colour, 96–97
    Commitment strategies, 3, 16
    Curated options, 3, 20–21, 149–150,
      149–150 n.54
    Default settings, 3
    Disgust, 45–46, 59–60, 62–64
    Face saving and attacking, 100–101
    Incentives, 3, 29, 67, 146, 147 n.48, 170–171
    Light, 68, 97–98
    Listing, 3, 131

Mental budgets, 3, 24–26, 52, 164–165
Numbering, 134–141, 143–145, 147–151
Peer pressure, 3, 18, 20, 20 n.70, 22, 26, 30,
  164–165
Priming devices, 67 n.2, 165–166 n.17,
  170–171, 173, 176
Saccade reading, 92–93
Saliency, 8, 24
Sludge, 135–136, 139–140
SMART targets, 24, 27–28
Proverbs, *see Outlandish Proverbs*
Puterbaugh, Joseph, 120

Quintilian, M.F., 118–119

R., S., 110–111
Ramus, Peter, 132, 137
Rank, 100–104, 110–111, 123, 125–126, 128–130
Ransome, Joyce, 18, 20, 33
Rathborne, Aaron, 175
Read, Sophie, 156–157
Rebuke, 104–105, 109, 114, 124–128
Rechtien, John, 137
Repairs, *see* Church buildings
Reproof, *see* Rebuke
Requests, 100–101
Reyner, Edward, 114–116, 128
Rhodes, Neil, 133–134
Richards, Jenny, 107
Richardson, Catherine, 46–47
Robarts, Fulke, 12
Roberts, Lewis, 131–132, 172–173
Rogers, Richard, 24–28, 39, 114, 116–117,
  116–117 n.49, 144–145, 150–151
Rudeness, *see* Rebuke
Ryrie, Alec, 6, 22–23, 151

Sacraments, 13–14, 144
Salem covenanters, 22–23
Sales, Francis de, 55, 55 n.69, 110, 112–113, 186
  n.85
Saltonstall, Wye, 175
Sandberg, Julianne, 177–179
Sawday, Jonathan, 133–134
Schoenfeldt, Michael, 59, 63–64, 123, 127–128,
  130
Schreiner, Susan, 147
Scott, James C., 101
Scott, William, 170–171, 180
Seaver, Paul, 150–151
Self-help, 30–32, 149
Shaw, Robert B., 177–179
Sherfield, Henry, 93–94
Shuger, Debora, 19

INDEX 211

Sibbes, Richard, 16
Signs (of grace), *see* Lists
Singleton, Marion, 177–179
Skinner, Robert, 68
Smells, *see* Cleaning
Smyth, Adam, 94–95 n.98, 134, 157–158
Sola fide, *see* Work (works)
Sorocold, Thomas, 51
Space (devotional), *see* Church buildings
Spenser, Edmund, 85–87, 89
Spice Garbellers of London, 175
St Andrew's, Bemerton, 69, 79–80
St Mary the Virgin, Leighton Bromswold, 69,
    76–80, 83–84, 86, 91–93
St Paul's Cathedral, 75–76, 85–86
St Peter's, Fugglestone, 69, 79–80, 83
Stachniewski, John, 5
Star, Susan Leigh, 134–135, 157
Steinroetter, Vanessa, 155
Stevenson, Jill, 10–11
Stockton, Owen, 25–26
Strawn, Brad, 13
Strier, Richard, 16, 29–30, 34, 61–62, 89, 112,
    123–124, 160–161
Sub-headings, *see* Lists
Summers, Joseph, 89
Sunstein, Cass, 3–5, 135–136
Supererogation, 162–163, 165–166
Sutton, Christopher, 11–12
Sutton, John, 4
Swaim, Kathleen, 69–70
Swan, John, 12–13

T., R., 68, 86, 97–98
Tact, 100–116, 123–127
Tasso, Torquato, 44–45
Taylor, Amanda, 182–183
Tebeaux, Elizabeth, 132
Temples, *see* Church buildings
Thaler, Richard, 3–5, 135–136
Thomas, Keith, 54
Tidying, *see* Cleaning

Tilgher, Adriano, 164
Tombs, *see* Monuments
Tomlinson, Rowan, 132, 152–153
Trettien, Whitney, 134
Turn-taking (in conversation), 106–111, 120
Tversky, Amos, *see* Nudges
Tyrwhit family, 83–86

Vaughan, Henry, 31–32, 90
Veblen, Thorstein, 171, 176
Veith, Gene, 177–179
Vendler, Helen, 61–62
Vigarello, Georges, 49–50
Vijen, Bram, 135–136
Voak, Nigel, 6
Vocation, *see* Work
Vows, *see* Contracts (devotional)

Wall, Wendy, 38
Wallington, Nehemiah, 11–12, 23–25, 88–89,
    150–151, 164
Walton, Izaak, 77, 79–80, 82, 103–104
Webbe, George, 116, 144–145
Weber, Max, 4–5
Webster, Tom, 151
Weever, John, 85, 89
Wesley, John, 54
Whalen, Robert, 13–14
Wilcox, Helen, 29–30, 54, 59, 90–91, 158
Windows, 68, 91
Wingren, Gustaf, 168
Wolberg, Kristine, 16, 53–54, 88–89
Wolkowitz, Carol, 38
Wood, Chauncey, 29
Woolley, Hannah, 40–41
Work (good works), 27–28, 50–51, 72–73, 115,
    162–177

Yates, Nigel, 73–75
Youths Behaviour, or Decency in Conversation,
    109

Zlatar, Antoinina Bevan, 118